D1389638

Aberdeenshire Library and Information Service
www.aberdeenshire.gov.uk/libraries
Renewals Hotline 01224 661511

- 4 JUN 2009

1 7 FEB 2011

- 6 MAR 2012

- 4 NOV 2013

- 3 OCT 2014

2 1 NOV 2015

2 0 FEB 2016

2 7 MAR 2016

3 0 DEC 2017

1 5 JAN 2018

1 4 FEB 2019

INGRAM, Christine

The rice & risotto
cookbook

A L I S

1704019

the rice & risotto cookbook

the rice & risotto cookbook

the complete guide to choosing, using and cooking the world's best-loved grain, with over 200 truly fabulous recipes

christine ingram

LORENZ BOOKS

This edition is published by Lorenz Books

Lorenz Books is an imprint of Anness Publishing Ltd

Hermes House, 88–89 Blackfriars Road, London SE1 8HA

tel. 020 7401 2077; fax 020 7633 9499

www.lorenzbooks.com; info@anness.com

© Anness Publishing Ltd 1999, 2005

UK agent: The Manning Partnership Ltd

tel. 01225 478444; fax 01225 478440; sales@manning-partnership.co.uk

UK distributor: Grantham Book Services Ltd

tel. 01476 541080; fax 01476 541061; orders@gbs.tbs-ltd.co.uk

North American agent/distributor: National Book Network

tel. 301 459 3366; fax 301 429 5746; www.nbnbooks.com

Australian agent/distributor: Pan Macmillan Australia

tel. 1300 135 113; fax 1300 135 103; customer.service@macmillan.com.au

New Zealand agent/distributor: David Bateman Ltd

tel. (09) 415 7664; fax (09) 415 8892

All rights reserved. No part of this publication may be reproduced, stored in a retrieval system,
or transmitted in any way or by any means, electronic, mechanical, photocopying, recording or
otherwise, without the prior written permission of the copyright holder.

A CIP catalogue record for this book is available from the British Library.

Publisher: Joanna Lorenz

Editor: Sarah Ainley

Copy Editor: Jenni Fleetwood

Designer: Penny Dawes

Indexer: Vicki Robinson

Photography: Dave King (recipes) and David Jordan (cutouts and techniques)

Food for Photography: Jennie Shapter (recipes) and Sara Lewis (cutouts and techniques)

Stylist: Jo Harris

Recipes: Carla Capalbo, Kit Chan, Roz Denny, Rafi Fernandez, Silvana Franco, Deh-Ta Hsiung,
Shezad Husain, Christine Ingram, Soheila Kimberley, Masaki Ko, Elizabeth Lambert Ortiz, Ruby Le
Bois and Sallie Morris

Previously published as *Rice & Risotto*

1 3 5 7 9 10 8 6 4 2

ABERDEENSHIRE LIBRARY AND INFORMATION SERVICE	
1704019	
CAW	366368
641.63	£14.99
AD	ROSP

NOTES

For all recipes, quantities are given in both metric and imperial measures and, where
appropriate, measures are also given in standard cups and spoons. Follow one set,
but not a mixture because they are not interchangeable.

Standard spoon and cup measures are level.

1 tsp = 5ml, 1 tbsp = 15ml, 1 cup = 250ml/8fl oz

Australian standard tablespoons are 20ml. Australian readers should use 3 tsp in place
of 1 tbsp for measuring small quantities of gelatine, cornflour, salt etc.

Medium eggs are used unless otherwise stated.

CONTENTS

INTRODUCTION

The rice grain is famous for its versatility, and has been a favourite ingredient with cooks worldwide for thousands of years. Rice cultivation has certainly played a part in man's development, and this fascinating book opens with a look at its history, and at the mystical reverence with which some cultures regard rice, even today. For reference, there is a photographic directory to the world's rices, plus information on the different ways of cooking rice. Each of the world's major cuisines has its own way of dealing with rice, and the recipes here include the very best of them, to help you explore and appreciate this highly important and endlessly versatile, staple food.

RICE IS A SUPREMELY important crop. It is a food that feeds half the population of the world, and is the grain that has sculpted the cultures of Asia, linking Heaven and Earth, mortal to gods. In Bangladesh, Thailand and China, a common greeting, instead of "How are you?", is "Have you eaten rice today?". And at New Year, the traditional saying is "May your rice never burn". To upset a bowl of rice is a sign of bad luck, while deliberately upending a fellow diner's rice bowl is a deadly insult.

Festivals and traditions all over South-east Asia celebrate the importance of rice. In Cambodia, for instance, where people believe the rice spirit, Yiey Tep, lives on in the rice fields, farmers show their devotion by praying and making offerings of sweet rice. The Balinese have numerous rice rituals, from laying pinches of rice along the edges of fields to keep away evil spirits, to fabulous celebrations in the island's many temples.

There are two distinct attitudes to rice and two distinct types of rice eater. For many of us in the West, rice is just another grain, albeit a valued one.

We view rice as a pleasant alternative to potatoes, pasta or bread; we make pilaffs and risottos, or use rice to serve as a salad or to accompany a curry.

But for the peoples of Indonesia, Thailand and other South-east Asian countries, rice is central to life itself. Many Asians eat rice three times a day and in some languages, such as Thai, the phrase for eating rice is the same as for eating food. For many Chinese or Malays, for instance, rice is the food that you eat; the rest is merely relish. On average, in the West, we each consume 1.8kg/4lb of rice a year, compared with the 150kg/330lb a year average annual consumption per person in Asia. In this book we suggest cooking 225g/8oz of rice – a generous cupful – to serve four people, yet that would scarcely satisfy a single hungry Indonesian or Chinese adult. The world produces about 350 million tonnes of rice each year and over half of this amount is consumed within 48km/ 30 miles of where it was grown.

Paddy fields are one of the most defining images of South-east Asia. The sight of the two-thousand-year-old

terraces of the Ifugao of Luzon in the northern Philippines is one of the wonders of the world. Rice that is growing in the field is called paddy, which comes from the word *padi*, meaning "rice growing in deep water". Rice is known as paddy until it has been threshed.

In Asia, most rice is still planted, tended and harvested by hand. By direct contrast, in the USA and Australia the process is highly mechanized and involves lasers, low-flying aircraft, combine harvesters and computers.

Yet the lack of technology in the Asian paddy fields belies the complex organization that is rice farming. Entire families are involved in the growing and harvesting of the rice they eat, and each member has a specific role to play in the process. Rice provides the family with a living, so long as the weather is predictable and the rains forthcoming, and rice cultivation shapes their way of life.

Below: Rice is farmed throughout France, including here in Provence, although the country is not a major exporter.

Left: Chinese workers harvesting rice in a paddy field in the 19th century.

The myths of these rich cultures tell us a great deal about the history of rice, and highlight its central role in people's lives. How and when it was first grown is more difficult to discover. What is certain is that it is native to South-east Asia and has been cultivated there for perhaps 8000 years. Evidence from a cave in northern Thailand proves that rice was being cultivated from around 6000 BC.

Rice, which is a member of the grass family, grew extensively in Thailand. It is likely that early man first grew wild rice, and only later began cultivating local species. Some scholars believe that this first rice would have been dry and that wet rice was a later development. Others say that people grew whatever rice was best suited to their particular environment. Certainly rice is adaptable, and will accommodate itself to the habitat; some varieties tolerate floods and cold nights, while others survive hot temperatures and relatively little water.

Gradually, people realised the value of this sustaining crop, and rice began to travel. From north-east India and Thailand, rice spread first through South-east Asia, and then further afield.

THE STORY OF RICE

Study the history of rice and you will discover that it is bound up with many strange and fascinating myths. Rice has fed more people than any other crop, and the story of its cultivation must rank as one of the most important developments in history. Almost every culture in the East has its own rice legend, and in many Asian countries these stories are still celebrated today.

In Bali and other parts of Indonesia, puppets act out a creation myth, which tells of how Lord Vishnu caused the Earth to give birth to rice, and the god Indra taught the people how it should be grown. From China comes the story of a devastating flood, which left all the crops destroyed. Facing certain starvation, the people of the town one day saw a dog with strange yellow seeds hanging from its tail. Rice grew when the seeds were planted in the waterlogged soil.

In the many myths from around Indonesia, Thailand and Japan, the rice spirit is always feminine. She is young and tender – a beautiful maiden, dusted with rice powder to emphasize her perfect white skin. In almost all of the many Asian cultures, the femininity of rice is reflected in the way it is grown. Men prepare the land, build the dykes and attend to irrigation, but it is the women who plant the rice, tend it in the fields, cut it and, finally, cook it.

There are numerous signs all over South-east Asia that rice is still highly revered today. A family will traditionally store its rice in a rice barn. These beautiful and elaborate buildings are where the rice spirit is said to reside until the time of the next planting, and there are often strict rules about who may enter these barns. Usually, only the women are allowed inside, and even then only once a day.

Above: Famine in the streets of Bombay in 1900. Rice is given to the starving.

Rice cultivation is believed to have begun in China in the Yangtze River delta around 4000 BC, although the rice may at first have been considered nothing more than a weed, as taro root was cultivated in parts of this region around this time. Rice isn't thought to have become an important part of the Chinese diet until around 800 BC.

By the 9th century AD, rice was widely eaten in southern China, but in the north, where it could not be grown, it was food only for the wealthy. Remarkably, rice was not cultivated in Japan until the second century BC and even then, millet remained the principal cereal for most Japanese. Twelve hundred years later, in spite of famine, rice was still mainly a food for the rich and was not to be consumed in any large quantity for another 800 years.

THE REST OF THE WORLD

It is difficult to chart exactly how and when the cultivation of rice spread beyond Asia. In the Middle East and the Mediterranean, wheat was initially the main crop, while in America, maize was by far the most important cereal. Rice was not known here until the Spanish introduced it in the late 16th century.

Rice is enjoyed in many Middle Eastern countries, and basmati rice, in particular, has a special place in people's affections. Today, the Middle Eastern repertoire of rice dishes is wide-ranging,

but it clearly wasn't always so. Rice was probably introduced via northern India and Afghanistan through conquest, expansion and trading. However, even in the 13th century, rice was still regarded as a luxury item in Baghdad.

Rice came to Europe by various routes. Its popularity was determined not so much by its versatility, but by whether or not the crop could be cultivated. Unless rice could be produced locally, the cost of transporting it made the price high, and limited supply and demand. By the middle of this century, the cost of transporting foodstuffs became relatively cheap and foods such as rice, once thought of as exotic, became affordable to the majority and not just the élite.

In Spain, rice was introduced by the Moors, who ruled that country for about 300 years, from the beginning of the 8th century. It was the Moors who built the irrigation canals around Valencia and in the hills around Murcia, which are still used today for rice growing.

The Arabs introduced a dry or upland rice to Sicily, and shortly afterwards there is evidence of paddy fields in northern Italy, around Piedmont and on the Lombardy plains. Here, a wet short grain rice was cultivated, which most scholars believe was introduced not via the south of the country, but from Spain, where another short grain variety of rice had long been

Above: Rice irrigation in China, during the Yuan Dynasty, 13–14th century.

grown. Either way, from around the 14th century onwards, rulers around Pisa and Milan became aware that rice was a good alternative to wheat as a staple food. After a series of devastating famines, they began in earnest to encourage the cultivation of rice. In the 18th century, Piedmont rice was of such high quality that Thomas Jefferson, then US Minister in France, smuggled some out of Italy and sent it to friends in Charleston with instructions for its cultivation. (This was the same Thomas Jefferson who had written the Declaration of Independence and who was later to become the third president of the United States.)

In parts of Europe where cultivation was not an option, rice was often regarded with suspicion, and there appears to have been some resistance to eating it. In Britain at least, it has taken many years, notwithstanding the ubiquitous rice pudding, for rice to become truly accepted. However, rice was not totally unknown in England; in the 13th century, knights returning from the Crusades brought back rice along with other Arabian products such as sugar and lemons.

For a long time in Britain, rice was regarded in the same way as the newly arrived spices. Expensive to buy, it was used by chefs to the aristocracy to make delicate sweets and desserts,

Left: Men and women harvesting rice in China during the 13–14th century: threshing, winnowing and sorting rice.

Above: A flooded rice field in Queensland, Australia. The water will be drained from the field before the rice is harvested.

but was not considered a food for working people. Apart from rice pudding, its most famous appearance was in the savoury breakfast dish, kedgeree, developed in India during 19th-century colonial rule. Based on the Indian dish *kitchiri*, kedgeree is a creamy mixture of smoked haddock, eggs and basmati rice, flavoured with nutmeg and often lightly curried. It gained great popularity in Victorian England and is now an established national favourite.

Rice was introduced to the Americas by the conquering Spanish and Portuguese, and it has flourished ever since. Nowadays, rice is a hugely important crop in many South American countries, most notably Brazil, which grows as much rice as Japan yet still

cannot meet its own needs. Brazil is second only to Europe as the world's largest importer of rice.

Some scholars believe rice came to North America with the slaves, who brought the seeds with them from West Africa. It was said that only they had the knowledge of how to grow rice. Another story talks of a ship from Madagascar that was blown off course and put into harbour in Charleston, South Carolina. As a gift of thanks, the captain presented the town with some "seeds of gold", which is a type of rice named for its colour. The reality is probably a combination of these legendary stories.

The first Spanish colonists in Florida brought rice with them from the Old World, along with wheat and bread. While Florida proved a congenial environment for growing rice, it was South Carolina which became the main

focus for rice cultivation. Attempts to grow upland rice in North Carolina had failed but Carolina Gold, grown in the freshwater island swamps of South Carolina, proved successful. By the late 17th century Carolina Gold was being produced in large quantities.

South Carolina's rice fields were worked entirely by slaves, and it was this situation that contributed directly to the collapse of the rice industry in the Carolinas. When the slaves were freed after the American Civil War in the 1860s, the rice fields were left empty. The war put an end to large scale rice cultivation in the Carolinas and Georgia, but it did continue along the Mississippi River, in Louisiana, Arkansas and Texas. In the early 20th century rice cultivation spread to California, where rice is still a major crop today. The United States is now the world's second major rice exporter.

THE RICE FIELD

Just before harvest time, the paddy fields of Asia are a spectacular sight. On the mountain sides and in the valleys, the land is a sea of soft, luminescent shades of green, and from a distance seems to sway as if in perpetual motion. View it from the air, and you'll notice that some fields are flooded, but many are dry. These are the fields ready for harvest, where the farmer has drained the paddy while the grain continues to ripen, so that the ground is easy to walk upon. It is a mistake to think that the rice plant spends its entire life under water. Water is used to flood the fields, and the plant will remain under water for some weeks or months, but the careful farmer will always regulate this flooding.

Classification

There are numerous varieties of rice although all stem from a single species. In simple terms, each of these varieties can be classified as one of three main types of grain: indica, japonica and javonica. Indica, as the name suggests, is the rice of India. The grains are long and tend to remain separate after cooking. Japonica, which is grown in other parts of Asia, has short grains that are sticky or glutinous when cooked. The third group, javonica, is long-grained but has sticky properties.

Cultivation

Rice is the only important cereal to grow in water. The water brings nutrients to the plant, insulates it against extreme heat and cold and, some believe, helps to keep down weeds, although weeding is still required.

In America the rice checks (rice fields) are flooded through a system of canals, which introduce fresh water from a nearby river wherever it is needed. In much of South-east Asia, water for the paddy fields flows constantly, but relying on Nature for the supply can be problematic. Either there is too much or too little, or the water flows too quickly or not at all. The plant will survive wet or dry periods, and can grow in still water, but ideally the paddy should be flooded after the plant has flowered, and drained dry before harvest.

Rice today is grown throughout the world, but the principal growing regions are the southern United States, Brazil, Egypt, Spain and Italy. The biggest rice-producing area is South-east Asia, from Pakistan in the east to Japan and the Philippines in the west.

In the West, as you would expect, mechanization has taken over the jobs that in Asia are still carried out by manual labour. The rice fields of Texas and Louisiana look very different from those of Bali or Thailand. It is only in Asia where you will find the traditional images associated with rice growing: water buffalo harrowing the paddy fields, men hoeing the flooded fields before planting, and women in conical hats, planting rice seeds.

In many parts of Asia, farmers aim to achieve two crops a year, and the first job is to prepare the land. A hoe is used to break up the soil, which is then flooded prior to planting. In mountainous areas, rice is planted in the highest fields first, and the water is allowed to flow downhill to the lower terraces once the first fields are soaked. Oxen or water buffalo may be used for harrowing the flooded field, which is then planted, often by women. It can take several days to plant one paddy field, and during the growing season all members of the family are needed to help with the ongoing work of adding fertilizers and pesticides, and weeding.

Harvesting

In many Asian countries, come harvest, the women once again move back into the fields to cut the rice stalks, using a small, sharp knife. Rice is so central to people's lives here that people continue to honour the old traditions; women will conceal the cutting knife in order to protect the rice spirit from the knowledge that she must die.

Once they have been cut, the rice stalks are stacked in bundles and threshed – beaten over hard ground with flails or drawn over spikes to release the rice grains. Mechanization is creeping in, predominantly in the developed world, but you may still see hand threshing in parts of Java and Bali. Here, the grain is manually husked and winnowed to dispel the straw and chaff before being stored in the traditional family rice barn, the highly elaborate shrine to the rice spirit.

Below: Modern rice production in Spain. The milled grains are laid out to dry under the hot summer sun (bottom) before being bagged and weighed (top).

Milling

Unless it has been threshed and husked manually, paddy, once cut, is taken to the mill where the bran and husk is removed to give fully milled or "polished" white rice. Unmilled rice that has had only the husk removed is known as cargo rice. It is in this form that rice is imported into Europe from both Asia and America, so that the milling process can be completed at one of the modern mills that exist in Europe, most notably in the Netherlands.

In Europe, milling is a mechanized procedure, although the basic principle is much the same as in the small, noisy mills of Asia. The brown rice passes between rubber rollers that rub away the brown outer skin, leaving the white grain. Once fully milled this is known as "polished" rice, and while once this did imply that the grain had been treated with glycerine or talc to make the grains glossy, this operation is now fairly rare.

Marketing

Until recently, all the rice grown on a typical Asian plot would have been for the family's own consumption, and even today less than 4 per cent is traded between countries. Demand for rice is growing worldwide, however, and as agriculture and jobs diversify, a greater proportion of the rice farmer's annual crop will be sold either for the local market or for export.

Europe is the biggest importer of rice, followed by Brazil and the Middle East. Many rice-growing countries import rice to supplement their own crop, as in the case of Brazil, or so that the home-grown rice can be exported. In order to earn foreign currency, China exports the greater part of its high grade rice and imports a low grade rice for its own population. In parts of the Punjab where basmati rice is grown, almost the entire crop is exported. The price that basmati can fetch means that there is a huge incentive to sell this quality rice. Paradoxically, within the region, bread is more commonly eaten than rice.

NUTRITION

Rice is a non-allergenic food, rich in complex carbohydrates and low in salts and fats. Because brown rice retains the bran, it has twice the nutritional content of white rice and is therefore considered the healthy choice. This shouldn't deter you from eating white rice, however, as all rice is known to be good for you.

Starch/Carbohydrate Rice contains two main starches. It is these starches that determine how sticky or glutinous a rice is. Rice is an excellent carbohydrate food, supplying energy without increasing fat intake.

Protein Brown and white rice contain a small amount of easily digestible protein.

Minerals Rice contains small amounts of phosphorous, magnesium, potassium and zinc. Since these minerals are contained in the bran, they are mostly found in brown rice and, to a lesser extent, in par-boiled rice, the production of which involves a process that "glues" nutrients into the grain.

Fibre The rice bran in brown rice provides some fibre. Little fibre remains in white rice after the bran has been taken out.

Vitamins Rice contains small amounts of Vitamin E, B vitamins, Thiamine, Riboflavin, Niacin, Vitamin B6 and folic acid, although since most of the vitamins are contained in the bran, brown rice is a richer source. Par-boiled rice also contains a higher proportion of vitamins than white rice.

TYPES OF RICE

There are thousands of varieties of rice. In the world's major rice-growing areas, it is not unknown for each paddy field to yield its own particular strain. This does not mean, however, that people who live in these areas are faced with a bewildering choice; on the contrary, most only eat the rice that is grown locally. It is said that, with just one or two exceptions worldwide, 65 per cent of rice is eaten within 500 metres of where it is grown.

There are several possible ways of classifying rice: by region; by colour; by cooking properties; even by price. Visit an ethnic store and you are likely to find rice grouped in one of these ways, but the most common classification, and the one most supermarkets favour, is by the length of the grain, which can be long, medium or short. As a general rule long and medium grain rices are used for savoury dishes, while short grain is used for desserts, although there are exceptions: risotto is only ever made with special short grain rices, for example. In America the terms Patna, rose and pearl are used by millers to describe long, medium and short grain rice respectively.

Left: From left, white and brown long grain rices.

Below: Organic rice is grown entirely free of chemicals.

Organic Rice

This is rice that has been grown without the use of pesticides or fertilizers. It can be long, medium or short grain.

Long Grain Rices

Long grain rice is three or four times as long as it is wide. When cooked, the individual grains separate. Long grain rice can be used in a variety of recipes.
White Long Grain Rice This is the most commonly available white rice and may come from any of a number of countries. America is the most significant producer of long grain rice sold in Europe. China, India, Malaysia and Thailand, among others, produce far greater amounts of this rice than does America, but their production is principally used for the home market and is not exported.

In China long grain rice is called simply *xian* or *indica* (*oryza indica* is the generic name for all long grain rice). In the rice eating areas of China it is the cheapest and most widely available rice for everyday consumption.

The white variety of long grain rice has been fully milled, and all of the bran and outer coating has been removed. The grains are white and slightly shiny, a feature often described by the expression "polished", although strictly speaking, this would mean that glycerine or talc has been used to polish the grains, giving them a smooth and glossy appearance. This practice is relatively rare these days, although the term "polished rice" still persists in some quarters. While white rice hasn't the flavour of basmati or Thai fragrant rice, it is still a firm favourite and is a good choice for a large number of Western-style and oriental dishes.

Below: From left, white and brown basmati rices, admired for their fragrance and for the slender grains, which provide such a unique texture.

Brown Long Grain Rice Sometimes called wholegrain rice, this is the whole of the grain complete with bran – the rice equivalent of wholemeal bread. In countries where rice is a staple food and thus eaten in large quantities, brown rice is generally disliked and is seldom eaten. Most brown rice is consumed in the West, where it is considered a healthier alternative to white rice, and is enjoyed for its pleasant texture and nutty flavour. Almost all brown rice is long or medium grain. Short grain rice, perhaps because it is generally used for sweet puddings and desserts, is almost always milled first to remove the bran, although it is possible to buy brown short grain rice from health food shops.

Right: American long grain rice

Basmati Rice

This rice is grown in northern India, in the Punjab, in parts of Pakistan adjacent to West Punjab and in the foothills of the Himalayas. The particular soil and climate of this region is thought to account for basmati's unique taste and texture. The word "basmati" means "the fragrant one" in Hindi, and it is rightly considered by most rice lovers around the world to be the prince of rice. Basmati has a fine aromatic flavour. The grains are long and slender and become even longer during cooking, which partly accounts for its wonderful texture. There are various grades of basmati, but it is impossible for the shopper to differentiate between them except by trying the brands to discover the variety with the best fragrance and flavour. Basmati is excellent in almost any savoury rice dish and is perfect for pilaffs or for serving with curries. It is also an essential ingredient in biryani.
Brown Basmati Like all types of brown rice, brown basmati comes with the bran. It has all the flavour of white basmati with the texture typical of brown rice. It would not be used in Indian dishes but is superb in any number of Western-style meals.

*Above: Thai
fragrant rice*

Patna Rice

At one time, most of the long grain rice sold in Europe came from Patna in India, and the term was used loosely to mean any long grain rice. The custom persists in parts of America, but elsewhere Patna is used to describe a specific variety of long grain rice from the Bihar region of India.

Dehra Dun

A long grain, non-sticky Indian rice. It is not generally available outside India, except from specialist stores.

Domsiah Rice

A fine grained, Persian rice, available from Middle Eastern stores.

Thai Fragrant Rice or Jasmine Rice

This fragrant long grain rice is cultivated in Thailand and is widely used in Southeast Asian and oriental cooking. The rice has a faintly scented, almost milky aroma that is a perfect match for the exotic flavours of oriental cuisine. Once cooked, the grains are slightly sticky. Thai fragrant rice is excellent both for savoury dishes and for sweet ones. To fully appreciate its fragrance, it is best cooked by the absorption method.

American Aromatic Rice

America grows several familiar aromatic rices, including Jasmine, and has developed several of its own.

Texmati, an American version of basmati, is not sold outside the United States, although it can often be found in specialist American stores.

Medium Grain Rices

Medium grain rice is about twice as long as it is wide. After cooking, the grains are moist and tender, and tend to cling together more than long grain. Medium grain rice is sold in both brown and white varieties. In Spain, white medium grain rice is often used for making paella.

Short Grain Rices

Mention short grain rice and most people will either think of risotto or creamy, slow-cooked puddings. Both these dishes owe their success to the ability of short grain rice to absorb liquid, becoming soft and sticky in the process. Short grain rice is almost as broad as it is long and is sometimes described as round grain. The grains stick together when cooked.

Pudding Rice

This is a catch-all name for any short grain rice. Virtually all pudding rice is white, with short, plump grains. Carolina rice was the original name for American short grain rice, taking its name from the state where it was first grown. The name is seldom used today, although you may occasionally find cookbooks calling for Carolina rice.

Italian Rice

Italy produces more rice, and in greater variety, than any other country in Europe. Most is grown in the north of the country, in the Po Valley around Piedmont. Italian rice is classified by size, ranging from the shortest grain, *ordinario*, to *semi-fino*, *fino* and *superfino*. Most of the varieties of risotto rice are either *fino* or *superfino*.

*Right: Short grain
pudding rice*

Left: Italian risotto rices. Clockwise from top, Arborio, Carnaroli and Vialone Nano.

rice grown is a medium short grain variety, which has a slightly sticky consistency when cooked. It is particularly popular for making paella. A longer grain rice is also grown and is generally added to soups.

Within Spain, rice is graded by the amount of whole grains included in the weight: *Categoria Extra* (red label) is the finest rice, with 95 per cent whole grains, *Categoria Uno* (green label) has 87 per cent whole grains, while *Categoria Dos* (yellow label) has 80 per cent whole grains. *Calasperra* is a top quality short grain rice that is quite easy to locate outside Spain, unlike most Spanish rices, which must be bought from specialist stores.

Grano Largo or Variedad Americana A long grain white rice. The brown equivalent is called *arroz integral*.

Bahia A medium grain rice used for making paella.

Bomba Another paella rice. Like an Italian risotto rice, the plump grain absorbs a lot of liquid.

Oriental Rices

In Japan, two basic types of rice are eaten: glutinous rice (see separate entry) and a plump short grained rice, called *uruchimai* and often sold simply as Japanese rice. Although not a glutinous rice, even the ordinary rice has sticky properties – a non-sticky rice would be difficult to eat with chopsticks.

Sushi Rice In the West, a packet labelled sushi rice will almost inevitably contain a short grain rice that will need to be cooked before you can use it to make sushi. Typical examples are Japanese Rose, Kokuho Rose and Calrose. Ask for sushi rice in Japan, however, and you are likely to be offered rice that has been cooked with vinegar, sugar and salt, and is thus ready for making sushi.

Shinmai This is a highly esteemed Japanese rice that is sold in Japan in late summer. It is the first rice of the season. Because of its high moisture content, it needs less water for cooking.

Arborio This is one of the best known varieties of Italian risotto rice, and takes its name from a town in the Vercelli region of north-west Italy. Unlike the finer risotto rices such as Carnaroli, Arborio has a comparatively large plump grain with a high proportion of amylopectin. This is the starch that dissolves during cooking to give *risotti* their creamy texture. However, because of the length of the grain and because it contains less amylose (the firm inner starch) it is easy to overcook Arborio rice. Recipes often recommend turning off the heat when the risotto is almost cooked and "resting" it for a few minutes. The rice will continue to cook, due to its own heat, without becoming pappy.

Vialone Nano This is another popular risotto rice. It has a plump grain. Vialone Nano contains less amylopectin than Arborio and has a higher proportion of amylose, so retains a firm "bite" at the centre of the grain when the rest of the rice has cooked to a creamy consistency. Risottos made using this rice tend to be of a rippling consistency, which is described in Italian as *all' onda*. Vialone Nano is especially popular for making Venetian- and Verona-style risottos.

Carnaroli This is considered the premium risotto rice. It was developed by a Milanese rice grower who crossed Vialone Nano with a Japanese rice. The outer part of the grain is made up of a soft starch that dissolves during cooking to leave the inner grain, which has a satisfying, firm "bite".

Spanish Rices

Rice is grown extensively in Spain, particularly in the swampy regions outside Valencia. The most common

Glutinous Rice

There are several types of glutinous rice. The name is misleading – the grains contain no gluten – but they are renowned for the way they stick together after cooking. Often known as sticky or sweet rice, glutinous rice is not usually eaten with savoury dishes, but is sweetened and served, hot or cold, with fruit as a dessert.

Japanese Glutinous Rice This short-grained rice is sticky when cooked, a characteristic that makes it perfect for shaping. It has a slightly sweet taste.

Chinese Glutinous Rice In China, glutinous rice is called *geng* rice. It is also known by the generic name for short grain rice (*oryza japonica*). There are white and black varieties, and also a pinkish red rice that grows along the Yangtze river. Glutinous rice is used for puddings and dim sum.

Above: Short-grained white Chinese glutinous rice.

Thai Glutinous Rice Also available in white and black grains, Thai glutinous rice is very popular in puddings and desserts. The cooked black rice grain is really a deep blue-purple colour.

Red Rice

Red rice is not unheard of in rice growing areas, but its presence is not always welcome as it means the rice is reverting to a wild strain, and is likely to be brittle, shatter easily and prove difficult to harvest. In the Camargue region of France, however, a red rice has been developed that is the result of cross pollination between the local white rice and an indigenous wild red rice. The uncooked grain is a reddish brown, and as it cooks the colour intensifies and the water turns a distinct shade of red. Like most wholegrain rice, red rice needs to be cooked for longer than white rice. It has a nutty flavour and a good firm texture. Use in place of brown rice or long grain white rice.

Above: The semi-wild hybrid, red rice.

Left: Sushi rices. Clockwise from top, a sweetened variety, Kokuho and sushi rice.

Wild Rice

This is not a true rice at all, but a grass that grows in the marshy areas around the American Great Lakes. Wild rice was once a favourite food of the Native American Indians, and today much of America's wild rice is harvested by Native Americans, who have treaty agreements to harvest this rice.

Wild rice needs to be soaked for several hours before cooking, and must be cooked for about 40 minutes until the inner grain breaks through the husk. Wild rice has acquired a fashionable status throughout the West, but its greatest popularity is still in the United States. It is used at Thanksgiving for stuffing the turkey, a symbol of the fact that wild rice was an important staple food for the early settlers when the wheat and barley they had brought with them failed to thrive in the New World.

Below: Canadian wild rice

Giant Canadian Wild Rice

Canadian wild rice is similar to the variety from the United States, but the grains are longer and the Canadian rice is considered to have a superior flavour. The rice is grown on lakes in the north and on the west coast of Canada, where it is harvested by local Indians, who traditionally beat the overhanging grass stems with canoe paddles. The grain that falls into their canoes is theirs to keep, while the remainder, which settles in the shallow water, is for next year's harvest. Like all wild rice, this giant version should be soaked in water for several hours and rinsed, before being cooked for at least 40 minutes, until the tough outer husk has burst open.

Wild Rice and Basmati

This is simply a mixture of two popular and well flavoured grains. Because wild rice normally takes much longer to cook than plain basmati, the makers of this product balance the equation by using a par-boiled basmati, which has a longer cooking time, matching it with a strain of wild rice that requires less cooking than usual. Check the packet for exact cooking times.

Par-boiled or Easy-cook Rice

In spite of its name, par-boiled rice (sometimes labelled "easy-cook") is not a quick cooking rice; indeed, it takes almost half as long again to cook as most long grain rices. Par-boiling is an ancient technique that was developed in India. The whole grain rice is soaked in water and then steamed, which has the effect of locking in the nutrients that are in the bran layer. For white rice, the bran is then removed.

In parts of India and the Middle East, par-boiled rice is very popular. In the West it is mainly – and mistakenly – perceived to be an easy-to-cook rice, although a better description might be "difficult to ruin" as it can stand up to quite a bit of abuse during cooking.

The par-boiled rice grains are more yellow than those of normal rice, although this coloration disappears during cooking; when fully cooked, par-boiled white rice is a brilliant white. Par-boiled rice does take longer to cook than normal rice, but the advantage, for those who enjoy this rice, is that the rice grains stay noticeably separate and slightly chewy. Some people, however, dislike the over-assertive texture and complain that the flavour is bland.

If you're not sure, try both types and compare the results. There are par-boiled versions of white and brown basmati and white and brown long grain rice.

Right: Nowadays, there is a wide choice of convenience rices on the market. Some are ready-mixed with flavourings or vegetables for an instant side dish.

Below: Wild and basmati rices

Quick-cook Rices

Boil-in-the-bag Rice This is a called a convenience rice, although it takes just as long to cook as regular rice; the main convenience is that the pan doesn't have to be washed afterwards. Most boil-in-the-bag rices are prepared with par-boiled (easy-cook) rice.

Pre-cooked and Quick-cook Rice

Not to be confused with par-boiled, pre-cooked rice is just that – rice that has been fully cooked in advance and only needs to be rehydrated and heated in order to be ready to serve. There are a number of different brands available, each with different rehydrating and reheating instructions, so it is important to check the packet carefully before cooking.

Frozen Rice Also a pre-cooked rice, this needs only to be thawed and reheated, which can often be done in the microwave; check the instructions on the packet.

Canned Rice This type of rice really couldn't be simpler to use; just open the can, tip into a bowl and reheat in the microwave or in a conventional oven. For single people with little time for cooking, canned rice may be a handy standby, but it is a hugely expensive way to eat rice, and the flavour is severely diminished.

RICE PRODUCTS

Flaked Rice

Flaked rice is commonly used in Chinese, Thai and Vietnamese cooking for stuffings and desserts. The par-boiled rice is flattened with heavy rollers, so the rice cooks quickly and evenly. In the West, flaked rice is used by the food trade for breakfast cereals and snacks but it is seldom used in recipes. Flaked rice is available from oriental stores.

Ground Rice

More granulate than rice flour, this is used for milk puddings, and was once particularly popular in England. Ground rice is also widely used for biscuits and baking and is a good substitute for wheat flour, especially for people who cannot tolerate gluten.

Rice Flour

Finer than ground rice, this is also used in both oriental and Western cooking for cakes, biscuits and desserts.

Glutinous Rice Flour

This is made from glutinous rice and is normally labelled rice powder. It is used for sweet puddings.

Shiratamo-Ko

A Japanese version of glutinous rice flour.

White Rice Vinegar

Made from glutinous rice, Japanese rice wine vinegar has a subtle, delicate flavour. It is excellent not only in oriental cooking but for any dressing where you need a mild, unassuming flavour. Chinese rice wine vinegar is not as delicate but it makes a good alternative to wine vinegar.

Black Rice Vinegar

Though dark in colour, black rice vinegar has a surprisingly mild taste. It can be used for oriental soups and for dipping sauces.

Red Rice Vinegar

Much spicier than other rice vinegars, Chinese red rice vinegar is used mainly in hot dipping sauces to be served with seafood.

Shaoxing

This Chinese rice wine, which is made from glutinous rice, yeast and water, has a rich, mellow flavour. It is popular throughout China for cooking and drinking, and is available in Chinese groceries and some wine stores. Although both are rice wines, do not confuse Shaoxing with sake, which has a completely different taste.

From left: Flaked rice and ground rice. Both cook quickly and evenly, which makes them good for puddings, desserts and baking.

Left: Glutinous rice flours. The top product is made from cooked glutinous rice, while the bottom product is made from uncooked rice. The difference between the two will affect recipe cooking times and flavours.

Above: From left, Japanese seasoned rice vinegar, Chinese red rice vinegar and Japanese sweetened vinegar. The mild Japanese vinegars are used for a variety of cooking purposes; the spicy Chinese vinegar is generally only used for sharper-flavoured dishes and dipping sauces.

Sake

This Japanese rice wine is quite sweet with a mild flavour that belies its potency. It is served in small cups – about the size of egg cups – and can be chilled but is more often served warm. Nowadays, sake is often drunk with a meal, which is a shift in emphasis; traditionally, sake was the central attraction, and the small portions of food that accompanied it were there to enhance the flavour of this celebrated drink.

Mirin

A sweet cooking sake with a light delicate flavour, mirin is normally stirred into Japanese dishes during the final stages of cooking. It adds a mild sweetness to sauces or dips. Combined with soy sauce, it is the basis of teriyaki sauce, which is popular for basting grilled foods. Mirin is available from any Japanese food store and from many of the larger supermarkets.

Rice-stick Noodles

These flat noodles vary in thickness; each is roughly the same length as a chopstick. To cook rice-stick noodles, soak them in warm water or stock for 20 minutes to soften before draining.

The noodles are used to thicken soups and casseroles, and for stir-fries.

Rice Vermicelli Noodles

These hair-like noodles are very popular in Thai, Vietnamese and Indonesian cooking. Don't confuse them with bean thread noodles (which look similar and are confusingly called vermicelli noodles) as these are made from ground mung beans. Soak rice vermicelli noodles in warm water for 5–10 minutes to soften, then use according to the recipe.

Japanese Harusame Noodles

Similar to rice vermicelli noodles, these are also made from ground rice and are sold in fragile-looking loops. Prepare the noodles in the same way as rice vermicelli noodles.

Below: Round and triangular rice papers. Clockwise from top, Thai, Chinese and Vietnamese varieties.

Above: Chinese and Thai rice-stick and rice vermicelli noodles.

Rice Paper

Sometimes called rice wrappers, these wafer thin papers are made from rice flour, salt and water. They are sold dried in oriental stores and supermarkets, and can be round or triangular in shape. Before use, dip the rice papers into hot water for a few seconds to soften them. They are used in Vietnamese cooking to make spring rolls, and are popular in some Chinese dishes. Don't confuse them with spring roll wrappers, which are made from wheat flour and water, nor with the edible rice paper used for lining baking sheets.

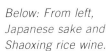

Below: From left, Japanese sake and Shaoxing rice wine.

COOKING PERFECT RICE

BOILED RICE

Choosing the Rice

Which rice you choose will depend largely on the meal you intend to cook. Basmati, with its wonderful fragrance and flavour, is for many the only rice to serve with an Indian meal. For a Chinese, Thai or Indonesian meal, Thai fragrant rice, with its pleasant aroma and slightly sticky texture (important if you intend to use chopsticks) is excellent, while the versatile American long grain rice is great for stir-fries, pilaffs, jambalayas and gumbos.

There are a few instances where only a specific type of rice will do – risottos, for example, can only be made successfully with risotto rice – but in general, providing you know a little about the qualities of the rice, there are no hard and fast rules. Although tradition demands rice puddings be made with a short grain rice, there's no reason why you shouldn't use long grain. Thai fragrant rice and basmati make delicious puddings too.

Quantities

There are no absolute rules. In the West, 450g/1lb/2⅓ cups of uncooked rice is the quantity recommended for eight people as an accompaniment, but would barely be enough for two Javanese workmen. The following quantities of uncooked rice apply to basmati rice, Thai fragrant rice and brown and white long grain rices.
• For side dishes allow 50–75g/2–3oz rice per person or 225–350g/8–12oz rice to serve four.
• For pilaffs allow 50g/2oz rice per person or 225g/8oz to serve four,
• For salads allow 25–40g/1–1½oz per person or 115–175g/4–6oz to serve four.
• For short grain rice puddings allow 15–20g/½–¾oz per person or 50–75g/2–3oz to serve four.
The weight of rice doubles in weight after cooking, although this depends on the type of rice, the amount of liquid and the cooking time. As a basic rule, when a recipe calls for cooked rice, use just under half the weight in uncooked rice.

Preparing Rice

Some types of rice benefit from being rinsed in cold water, while others should be left to soak before use. Precisely which procedure to follow will be outlined in individual recipes.

Rinsing

• Suitable for: basmati, brown basmati, Thai fragrant rice, brown and white long grain, sushi, glutinous and short grain rice.

Rinsing rice before it is cooked is not essential but it does help to remove excess starch and any dust that may have accumulated in storage. Most types of rice benefit from being rinsed. Do not rinse if using rice in a risotto. If you rinse rice which is to be used in a paella or any other dish where it is fried at the beginning of the recipe, be sure to drain it thoroughly first.

1 Cover the rice with cold water and swirl the grains between your fingers. The water will become slightly cloudy.

2 Allow the rice to settle, then tip the bowl so that the water drains away. Cover the rice once more with cold water, then rinse. Repeat several times until the water runs clear.

COOK'S TIP

In Japan, it is common practice for rice to be rinsed and then left to drain for 30 minutes or longer.

Soaking

• Suitable for: basmati, brown basmati, glutinous rice and sometimes American long grain, brown long grain rice, short grain rice and Thai fragrant rice.

Soaking is seldom essential but it does increase the moisture content of the grains, which means the rice will cook more quickly and will be less sticky. Soaking is particularly beneficial for basmati rice; less so for Thai fragrant rice, where a slight stickiness is an advantage. Risotto rice must not be soaked. Occasionally, rice that has been soaked will be fried; if this is the case, drain it very thoroughly first.

1 To soak rice, simply place it in a large bowl and cover with double the volume of cold water.

2 Leave the rice in the bowl for about 30 minutes or for the time suggested in the recipe, then drain it thoroughly in a sieve or colander.

Making Perfect Boiled Rice

Pan-of-water method

• Suitable for: most types of rice, but particularly for basmati, brown basmati, American long grain, red Camargue and brown rice. Not recommended for Thai fragrant rice.

In Asia, cooks often add a few drops of vegetable oil as well as salt when cooking rice by this method.

1 Put the rice in a large saucepan. Pour in a large amount of boiling water or stock (about 1.2 litres/2 pints/5 cups for every 200g/7oz/1 cup rice) and add a pinch of salt. Bring back to the boil, then lower the heat and simmer, uncovered, for the time indicated on the packet, until just tender.

2 Strain the cooked rice in a sieve or colander and rinse thoroughly with plenty of hot water.

3 Either return the rice to the pan or set the sieve over the pan. Cover with the pan lid or a dish towel and leave the rice to stand for 5 minutes. Fork through before serving, adding butter or oil if you like.

Adding flavourings Stock can be used instead of water, and flavourings such as bay leaves, curry leaves or whole spices can be added if you like, especially if the rice is to be used for a salad, a fried rice dish or a stuffing.

Absorption method

• Suitable for: basmati, Thai fragrant rice, short grain rice and glutinous rice. Sometimes used for brown basmati and American long grain rice.

This is also known as the covered pan method. The rice is cooked in a measured amount of water in a pan with a tightly fitting lid until the water has been absorbed. The proportion of rice to water, and the cooking time, will depend on the type of rice used. Use this method if you need cooked rice for stir-frying, or for a rice salad. It is also used when making some rice puddings.

1 Put the rice into a pan and pour in the measured liquid. Bring back to the boil, then reduce the heat to the lowest possible setting.

2 Cover and cook until the liquid has been absorbed. This can take up to 25 minutes, depending on the type of rice.

3 Remove the pan from the heat and leave to stand, covered with the lid or with foil or a dish towel, for 5 minutes. Steam holes will have appeared on the surface of the rice. If the grains are not completely tender, replace the cover tightly and leave the rice to stand for 5 minutes more.

Adding flavourings If you want to flavour the rice, the absorption method provides the perfect opportunity. Lemon grass, curry leaves and whole spices can be added with the liquid, which can be water, stock, coconut milk or a mixture. This method of cooking rice is the basis of several pilaff-style dishes, where onions, garlic and other ingredients, such as spices, are fried before the rice and liquid are added.

COOK'S TIP

It is vital that the pan is covered tightly and that the rice is cooked at as low a heat as possible. If the lid of the pan is loose, cover the pan with foil or a dish towel before fitting the lid, making sure that any excess fabric is kept well away from the heat source. White rice will cook however low the heat. If, after bringing the liquid back to the boil, the pan is removed entirely from the heat, the rice would continue to cook but would just take longer.

The absorption method is the best way to cook Thai fragrant rice, and basmati rice will retain its excellent flavour when cooked by this method.

Microwave method

• Suitable for: basmati, brown basmati, Thai fragrant and white and brown long grain rice.

Although no faster than conventional cooking, using the microwave is very convenient. It frees a burner on the hob, and the rice can be served in the dish in which it is cooked.

1 Using the same quantities of rice and liquid as for the absorption method, put the rice in a deep glass bowl or microwave container and stir in the boiling water or stock.

2 Cover the bowl with a lid or with microwave-proof clear film and cook on 100% Full Power. Check your microwave instruction book for timings. Leave the rice to stand for 10 minutes before using.

Adding flavourings Cooking in the microwave is essentially the same as when following the absorption method and simple flavourings can be added. If using a large number of additional ingredients, consult your microwave instruction book as the cooking times may differ.

Oven method

• Suitable for: basmati, brown basmati, American long grain, brown long grain, and red Camargue rice.

This is a combination of two methods: the rice is partially cooked first in a pan on the hob, before being finished in the oven. It produces a slightly dry rice, with separate grains.

1 Cook the rice by the pan-of-water method or the absorption method for three-quarters of the normal cooking time. Drain, if necessary, then spoon the rice into a baking dish.

2 Dot with butter or ghee, then cover tightly and cook in a moderate oven for 10–20 minutes. The oven temperature can be between 160°C/325°F/Gas 3 and 190°C/375°F/Gas 5 but the cooking time will need to be adjusted accordingly.

Adding flavourings Flavourings can be added to the rice during the first stage of cooking, or part of the cooked rice can be coloured and flavoured with a saffron or spice, if you like. Fried onions, garlic or cardamoms can be dotted over the partly cooked rice before it is placed in the oven.

Steaming

• Suitable for: white basmati, American long grain and Thai fragrant rice.

This method is also combined. The rice is partially cooked first in a pan of simmering liquid, before being steamed. This method of cooking is used for plain boiled rice and some glutinous rice dishes.

1 Cook the rice by the pan-of-water method or the absorption method for about three-quarters of the normal cooking time. Tip the part-cooked rice into a sieve or colander.

2 Transfer the cooked rice to a muslin bag set inside a pan of simmering water. Cover and steam for 5–10 minutes for white rice; 15 minutes for brown rice. If the grains of rice still feel hard, steam for a little longer.

Adding flavourings The rice can be flavoured during the first stage of cooking, in the same way as for the pan-of-water or absorption methods. Replace the cooking water with stock, coconut milk or a mixture, if you like, and add bay leaves, curry leaves, lemon grass or whole spices with the liquid.

Electric rice cooker

• Suitable for: all types of rice.

1 Put the rice into the cooker and add the required amount of water as indicated in your instruction booklet. Do not add salt. Cover the cooker with the lid and switch it on. The cooker will switch itself off automatically when the rice is ready, and will keep the rice hot until you are ready to serve.

Quick-cook method

Rice can be soaked in boiling water and then quickly cooked at the last minute. This works particularly well with basmati rice that is to be cooked by the pan-of-water method. It is a useful cooking method if you are entertaining and want the rice to cook quickly, and with as little fuss as possible.

1 Put the measured rice into a large bowl and pour over boiling water to cover. Leave to stand, uncovered, for at least 30 minutes or up to 1 hour.

2 Bring a saucepan of lightly salted stock or water to the boil. Drain the rice, add it to the pan and cook for 3–4 minutes until tender.

Adding flavourings Flavourings can be added in the same way as for boiled rice.

Cooking Brown Rice

Brown rice takes longer to cook than white rice, but how much longer will depend on the type of rice; always check the packet instructions. Soaking brown rice in a bowl of water first will soften the grains but it will not shorten the cooking time.

Cooking Glutinous Rice

Glutinous rice should be soaked before cooking, for at least 1 hour and up to 4 hours. After being drained, the rice can then be simmered with coconut milk and sugar if it is to be served as a dessert. For a savoury accompaniment, steam the drained rice for about 10–15 minutes, until it is tender.

Cooking Wild Rice

Although this is not strictly a rice, wild rice can be treated in the same way. It takes a lot of cooking, and for best results, should be soaked in water for 1 hour before being boiled in lightly salted water for 45–60 minutes. Check the instructions on the packet as cooking times differ according to the size of the grains. Wild rice is cooked when the inner white grain bursts out of the black husk.

Cooking Par-boiled or Easy-cook Rice

This takes longer to cook than regular rice. Check the packet for instructions. Easy-cook rice can be cooked by the pan-of-water or the absorption method. It can also be cooked in the microwave or in a rice cooker. This type of rice is fine for accompanying a meal, but is not as good for fried rice dishes.

Cooking/Heating Frozen or Canned Rice

Follow the instructions on the packet or can. Most can be reheated or cooked on the hob or in the microwave.

Storing Rice

Raw (uncooked) rice can be kept in a cool, dark place for up to three years in the unopened packet or in an airtight container. It should be kept perfectly dry; if the moisture content creeps up, the rice will turn mouldy. If the rice is very old, it may need more water or longer cooking. Check the packet for "best before" dates.

Cooked rice can be stored for up to 24 hours if cooled, covered and kept in the fridge. You can also freeze the cooled rice; reheat it in a covered casserole in the oven or thaw it and use for fried rice or in a salad. Reheated rice should be piping hot all the way through.

RICE COOKING TIPS

• Always leave cooked rice to stand for 5 minutes after draining and before serving to "rest" it and complete the cooking process.
• Remember that rice absorbs water as it cooks. If you use too much water with the absorption method, or cook the rice for too long, it will become soggy.
• If rice is still a little undercooked after cooking (by whatever method), cover it tightly and set aside for 5–10 minutes. It will continue to cook in the residual heat.
• If cooking rice for a rice salad, use the pan-of-water method and rinse the drained, cooked rice under cold water. Drain it thoroughly before mixing with the other ingredients.
• If cooked rice is required for a fried rice dish, cook it either by the absorption method (Thai fragrant rice) or the pan-of-water method (basmati rice). Avoid over-cooking. The rice should be dry and fluffy.
• Be sure to use a pan with a tight fitting lid if you are cooking rice by the absorption method.

Above: Cooked, cooled rice freezes well.

RISOTTO

This simple Italian dish is very much a peasant food and it says a great deal about the changing attitudes towards food and healthy eating that in the last decade or so, this dish, like much *cucina povera*, has come to be so widely appreciated. Nowadays you will see risotto on the menu at some of the classiest restaurants in town, enjoyed for the same reasons it has always been valued, because it is healthy, satisfying and extremely good to eat. Yet what could be simpler than a risotto? Although there are complicated and elaborate versions, some of the best risottos are made using little more than rice, a good stock and a few fresh herbs or cheeses. These simple risottos, like *Risi e Bisi* (Rice and Peas) or *Risotto alla Parmigiana* (Rice with Cheese) are probably the most traditional of all, and are no less tasty for their plain ingredients.

Since the first risottos were the food of poorer people, there is no long line of recipes that chart the popularity of this dish. Recipe books written in Italy during risotto's infancy tended to concern themselves with costly meats or spices and were written for the wealthy who could afford these expensive ingredients. Peasants and poor farmers had neither the time, the ability nor the inclination to read what they knew already: that rice was a cheap and sustaining food that was also delicious when cooked with care.

Short grain rice, which is the central ingredient in risotto, has been grown in Italy for several hundred years. The Arabs introduced rice into Italy during the Middle Ages, but this early rice was a longer grained variety and was grown in Sicily and the south of the country.

At some point though, rice was introduced to Lombardy in northern Italy, and by the 15th century, rice cultivation had become an established part of the Italian way of life. It was around this time that the custom of cultivating rice in fields flooded with water was adopted in Italy; this method of growing rice followed the process used in Asia, as opposed to the method of dry cultivation favoured by the Arabs.

Today, Italy shares with Spain the honour of being Europe's leading rice producer. Risotto rices are still grown in the north of the country, where the rice fields are irrigated with water running down from the Alps. The varieties of rice grown today have been improved and refined since earlier times, yet the characteristic starchy short grain has remained the same.

The method of cooking rice in stock may have been influenced by cooking styles in France and Spain but, whether by accident or design, it is difficult to imagine a better way of doing justice to fine rice than to serve it as a risotto.

Risotto is traditionally eaten as a separate course before the meat and vegetables. Only rice and stock are the essential ingredients, but you should choose these carefully. The stock must be home-made (or the very best you can afford) and the rice must be one of those recommended for the purpose. Have the stock simmering in a pan adjacent to the risotto pan, and add it slowly and lovingly. Observe the standing time at the end, as this allows the rice to rest and reach perfection. Do all this – and it is not difficult – and you'll find risotto one of the most simple and rewarding rice dishes you can make.

Types of Risotto Rice

It is essential to use a risotto rice, but precisely which one is up to you. Named risotto rices are becoming more widely available, but you will often find packages labelled simply Italian risotto rice. Of the named varieties, Arborio is the most widely available, with Carnaroli and Vialone Nano becoming increasingly easy to find in Italian delicatessens and good supermarkets. Other specific types of risotto rice include Baldo, Vialone Nano Gigante and Roma. Each has its own particular qualities, which will be familiar to those who specialize in cooking *risotti*. Some recipes call for a named risotto rice, but most are non-specific and any risotto rice will give a good result.

INSTANT RISOTTOS

There are several instant risottos on the market, available from supermarkets and delicatessens. They are easy to make, all you need to do is add water, heat and stir. Packets give simple instructions and recommend simmering for about 10 minutes – roughly half the time required for making a classic risotto. Instant risottos come in several flavours, including four cheeses, spinach, saffron, tomato and black cuttlefish. They are handy for a quick meal, and the colours supplied by the flavourings make them pretty to serve. More importantly, these risottos taste surprisingly good.

Left: Clockwise from top, instant risottos flavoured with cuttlefish, tomatoes, saffron and spinach.

Making Perfect Risotto

1 In a large, deep saucepan, fry the onion, garlic and any other vegetable(s) in extra virgin olive oil over a medium heat for a few minutes, stirring all the time. Unless the recipe specifies otherwise, the onion and other vegetables should be softened but not browned.

2 If using any uncooked meat or poultry, add these ingredients to the onions in the pan, unless the recipe specifies otherwise. Turn up the heat to high and cook, stirring frequently, until browned on all sides.

3 Tip the risotto rice into the pan, and stir, so that every grain is coated in the oil. Fry the rice over a high heat for 3–4 minutes, stirring all the time. You will notice that the grains of rice become transparent as they are stirred into the hot oil, except for the very centre of the grain, which remains opaque.

4 Add a little wine, if this is what is called for in the recipe, or a ladleful of hot stock. Stir the rice until all the liquid has been absorbed.

5 Lower the heat to moderate, then add another ladleful of hot stock and stir it into the rice. Keep the pan over a moderate heat so that the liquid bubbles but the rice is in no danger of burning. Stir the rice frequently.

6 Add the remaining stock a ladleful at at a time, making sure that each ladleful is used up before adding the next. This process will take about 20 minutes. As the risotto cooks, the grains of rice will begin to soften and merge together.

7 When the risotto begins to look creamy, grate in the cheese or add extra butter. The rice should be virtually tender, but still a little hard in the centre. At this point remove the pan from the heat, cover with a dish towel and leave to rest for about 5 minutes. The risotto will cook to perfection in the residual heat.

RISOTTO TIPS
• To begin, fry the rice in hot oil, stirring all the time, until the grains are coated and begin to turn translucent.
• Add any wine or sherry to the risotto before adding the stock. The alcohol will evaporate, but the flavour will remain.
• Use a good quality, home-made stock for your risotto. Alternatively, buy cartons of fresh stock, which are available from delicatessens and large supermarkets.
• The stock added to a risotto must always be hot. Have it simmering in a separate pan adjacent to the pan in which you are cooking the risotto.
• Add the hot stock slowly, ladleful by ladleful. Make sure all the liquid has been absorbed before adding the next ladleful.
• Avoid overcooking the risotto. Remove the pan from the heat while the rice is still slightly undercooked.
• For best results, season the risotto after cooking but before leaving it to rest. Stock, salted butter and Parmesan cheese will all contribute some saltiness, as may other ingredients, so always taste the risotto before adding any extra salt.
• Don't use ready-grated Parmesan. For the best flavour, buy good quality Parmesan in one piece and grate it yourself.

Equipment

There are only three essential pieces of equipment needed for cooking a risotto, and with luck you'll have them already.
• A heavy-based pan. Ideally, this should be a wide, straight-sided pot, deep enough to contain the cooked risotto. A deep frying pan can be used for smaller quantities.
• A wooden spoon.
• A saucepan for the simmering stock.

Adding Risotto Ingredients

Recipes will tell you when to stir in any additional ingredients needed for the risotto, but this guide may be helpful when devising your own risotto recipes.

Vegetables Onions and garlic are fried until soft at the beginning, before the rice is added. Most other vegetables, such as aubergines, carrots, courgettes and pepper, are sautéed with the onions. Vegetables that require little cooking, such as spinach and asparagus, should be stirred in towards the end of cooking. Mushrooms are usually fried at the same time or just after the onions, before adding the rice.

Above: Onions and garlic are essential ingredients in a good risotto. Use red onions or shallots for variations in flavour.

Above: Fresh green vegetables, such as courgettes, spinach and asparagus, add texture to the risotto. They retain their shape and colour during cooking, and always look impressive.

Fish and shellfish These are generally cooked before being added to the risotto. It is usual for fillets of fish, such as salmon, plaice or sea bass to be poached, then flaked. Scallops should be lightly cooked, then sliced. Stir fish or shellfish into the risotto about three-quarters of the way through cooking.

Above: Almost any fresh fish and seafood can be used in a risotto, including salmon fillets, haddock, plaice and tiger prawns.

Meat and poultry These are usually added at an early stage, at the same time as the onions; the rice is added later, so that both ingredients cook together. The exception is cooked meats, such as sausage or ham, which tend to be stirred into the risotto towards the end of cooking.

Above: Chicken fillets and gammon are both very successful ingredients for risottos, but the choice really is endless. Cut the meat into small pieces and brown with the onions before stirring in the rice.

Herbs Robust herbs are sometimes cooked with the onions, but more delicate herbs, such as parsley or coriander, are usually added at the end of cooking, at the same time as the Parmesan cheese or butter.

Above: Delicate-flavoured herbs, such as thyme, sage, coriander and tarragon, can all be stirred into the cooked rice for a simple risotto.

Cheese Where cheese is the dominant flavouring, as in a four-cheese risotto, it can be added halfway through cooking, but it is more usual for grated Parmesan to be added just before the risotto is left to rest.

Above: Most cheeses can be used in risottos but the one essential cheese is Parmesan. Use it either on its own as a simple flavouring or to complement other ingredients in the recipe. Fresh shavings of Parmesan can be used to garnish the risotto, or supply a bowl of Parmesan, grated fresh from the block, to be passed separately when serving.

MAKING STOCKS

Chicken Stock

MAKES ABOUT 1.5 LITRES/2½ PINTS/6¼ CUPS

INGREDIENTS
1 onion, quartered
2 celery sticks, chopped
1 carrot, roughly chopped
about 675g/1½lb fresh chicken,
  either ½ whole chicken or 2–3
  chicken quarters
1 fresh thyme or marjoram sprig
2 fresh parsley sprigs
8 whole peppercorns
salt

1 Put the prepared vegetables in a large, heavy-based saucepan and lay the chicken on top. Pour over cold water to cover the chicken (about 1.5 litres/2½ pints/6¼ cups).

2 Bring to the boil slowly. Do not cover the pan. When bubbling, skim off any fat that has risen to the surface.

3 Add the herbs, peppercorns and a pinch of salt. Lower the heat, cover the pan and simmer the stock gently for 2–2½ hours, until the chicken is tender.

4 Using a slotted spoon, transfer the chicken or chicken pieces to a plate. Remove any skin or bones; the chicken can be used in another recipe. Strain the stock into a clean bowl, leave it to cool, then chill in the fridge.

5 A layer of fat will form on the surface of the chilled stock. Remove this just before use. The stock can be kept in the fridge for up to 3 days or frozen for up to 6 months.

Fish Stock

MAKES ABOUT 2.5 LITRES/4 PINTS/10 CUPS

INGREDIENTS
900g/2lb white fish bones and
  trimmings, but not gills
2.5 litres/4 pints/10 cups water
1 onion, roughly chopped
1 celery stick, chopped
1 carrot, chopped
1 bay leaf
3 fresh parsley sprigs
6 peppercorns
5cm/2in piece of pared lemon rind
75ml/5 tbsp/⅓ cup dry white wine

1 Put the fish bones and fish heads in a large, heavy-based saucepan. Pour in the water.

2 Bring the liquid to the boil, using a spoon to skim off any scum that rises to the surface. Add the onion, celery, carrot, bay leaf, parsley, peppercorns, lemon rind and white wine.

3 Lower the heat, and cover the pan with the lid. Simmer the stock gently for 20–30 minutes, then leave to cool.

4 Strain the cooled stock through a muslin bag into a clean bowl. Keep the stock in the fridge for up to 2 days or freeze it for up to 3 months.

COOK'S TIP
Do not allow the fish stock to boil for a prolonged period or the bones will begin to disintegrate and the stock will acquire an unpleasant, bitter flavour.

Vegetable Stock

MAKES ABOUT 1.2 LITRES/2 PINTS/5 CUPS

INGREDIENTS
3–4 shallots, halved
2 celery sticks or 75g/3oz celeriac,
  chopped
2 carrots, roughly chopped
3 tomatoes, halved
3 fresh parsley stalks
1 fresh tarragon sprig
1 fresh marjoram or thyme sprig
2.5cm/1in piece of pared orange rind
6 peppercorns
2 allspice berries
1.5 litres/2½ pints/6¼ cups water

1 Put all the vegetables into a heavy-based saucepan. Add the fresh herbs, orange rind and spices. Pour in the water.

2 Bring the liquid to the boil, then lower the heat and simmer the stock gently for 30 minutes. Leave it to cool completely.

3 Strain the stock through a sieve into a large bowl, pressing out all the liquid from the vegetables using the back of a spoon. Store the cold stock in the fridge for up to 3 days or in the freezer for up to 6 months.

PAELLA

In Spain, paella is not just a meal, it is an occasion. Come fiestas and holidays (and there are many of these in Spain), it is not unknown for someone to say, "how about a paella", and, the weather being good, and the company convivial, ingredients, utensils and plenty of red wine will then be gathered up and the party will head outdoors, to the beach or into the mountains. The ingredients can be many and various. Rice – the short grain variety – is an obvious essential, but saffron, garlic and olive oil will inevitably be included, too. Everyone will help to gather wood and light a fire, after which one of the men will prepare and cook the paella. Other men will doubtless make their contribution. There will be advice for the chef on when to add the rice, how much stock to use and whether to add herbs early or late, but the principle is that men do the cooking.

Traditionally, a paella should always be cooked out of doors, over a wood fire by a man. The indoor version, cooked more conventionally over a stove, and by a woman, is strictly speaking not a paella at all but an *arroz* – a rice.

There are other conventions concerning paella, some more imperative than others. Short grain rice and saffron are essential ingredients. Purists believe that an authentic paella should contain only eels, snails and beans, the ingredients used in the original Valencian paella, but most Spanish people today are fairly relaxed about using other ingredients. Fish, shellfish, meat and poultry are routinely used, sometimes together.

More important in Spain is the manner in which the paella is eaten. For the Spanish, paella is the epitome of convivial eating: it is always served with generous amounts of wine and is inevitably made for a large party of people. The paella dish – the *paellera* – is placed on the table as a spectacular centrepiece, and everyone helps themselves to the food, while the conversation, lubricated by the wine, is, in true Spanish fashion, animated and lively.

For all these reasons, paella has become one of the world's best loved rice dishes. There are hundreds of variations, with restaurants up and down the country producing their own speciality. Although tradition dictates that paella should be cooked out of doors, superb paellas can be made in conventional kitchens, albeit on a more modest scale. A paella can be simple or elaborate and you can vary the combination of meat, poultry, fish and shellfish to suit your taste, your pocket and the occasion.

Making Perfect Paella

1 Cut the meat or joint the poultry into large pieces; season if the recipe requires. Fry the meat or poultry in olive oil in the paella pan or in a large frying pan until it turns an even, deep golden brown. Transfer the cooked meat or poultry to a plate. Slice the sausage.

2 Prepare any fish and shellfish that is to be included according to type: steam mussels (discarding any that fail to open), prepare squid and peel prawns. Fry the fish and shellfish briefly, if required by the recipe, and transfer to a plate.

3 In a paella pan, fry the onions in olive oil until golden. Add the garlic, tomatoes and any firm vegetables. Stir in cooked dried beans, if using. Stir briefly, then add water or stock and any seasonings. Bring to the boil.

4 Tip in the rice, stirring so that it is evenly distributed, then add the meat or poultry, and any sausage. Cook, uncovered, over a medium heat (so that the liquid simmers nicely) for 15 minutes.

5 Lower the heat, and add any softer vegetables, fish or shellfish. Add saffron to give the paella its distinctive colour. Cook over a low heat for 10 minutes until the liquid has been absorbed, then cover and rest for 5–10 minutes.

To Stir or Not to Stir

Read any guide to making paella, and you'll be told that the paella mustn't be stirred or disturbed in any way. This is fine advice for a true paella – cooked over an open fire so that the heat is distributed evenly over the base of the pan. But if you're using a gas or electric flame, the uneven heat distribution will mean that the centre will cook more quickly than the outside. To get around this problem, you can either break the rules and stir occasionally, or cook the paella in the oven. That way it will cook evenly, although technically, in Spain, it would be a "rice" (*arroz*) and not a paella.

A GUIDE TO PAELLA QUANTITIES

Individual paella recipes will usually specify quantities of rice, liquid and other ingredients, although the following can be used as a rough guide.

Amount of rice	Amount of liquid	Servings
200g/7oz/1 cup	550ml/18fl oz/2¼ cups	2–3
350g/12oz/1¾ cups	900ml/1½ pints/3¾ cups	4–6
450g/1lb/2⅓ cups	1.2 litres/2 pints/5 cups	6
500g/1¼lb/3 cups	1.3 litres/2¼ pints/5½ cups	8

Allow between 65–75g/2½–3oz/⅓–½ cup rice per person

PAELLA TIPS

• Use the right type of rice. The Spanish will occasionally use a medium grain rice, although the traditional choice is a short grain rice that absorbs liquid well. The round grained and stubby Spanish rice Calasperra would be ideal, or use Italian Arborio risotto rice.
• It is important to use a large pan. The rice needs to be cooked in a shallow layer so there should be plenty of room to spread it out. If at all possible use a paella pan (called a *paellera*), which is a wide flat metal pan. If you don't have a paella pan, you can use a frying pan – the largest you have – but this will probably only be large enough for a paella for three or four people.
• Always use fresh ingredients, especially the fish and seafood. Paella is not a dish for leftovers.
• Cook other ingredients carefully before you start to cook the paella. Meats should be cooked until golden brown, as should onions, as this will add flavour to the dish. Fish should be seared lightly, and added to the rice towards the end of cooking, to avoid overcooking it.

Below: The width and shallow depth of the paella pan allow an even distribution of heat when the rice is cooking.

• Less tender cuts of meat or larger pieces of poultry may require longer cooking. Always check instructions in the recipe for timings.
• Use a well-flavoured stock – preferably home-made chicken, meat, fish or vegetable.
• Bring the stock or other liquid in the pan to a fierce boil before tipping in the rice. (This is the opposite of the technique used when making a risotto, where the stock is added slowly to the rice.)
• Use saffron strands rather than turmeric or any other colouring.
• Once the liquid has been absorbed by the rice, cover the paella with a dampened dish towel and allow it to rest for a few minutes before serving, to complete the cooking.

SUSHI

Sushi is wonderful food. Sushi bars, or *sushiya*, are to be found everywhere in Tokyo and are now a familiar sight in London, New York, Sydney and other large cities. The little snacks are a superb treat – clean tasting yet surprisingly filling. They are not difficult to prepare at home and make an attractive and impressive snack or starter.

A Japanese short grain rice should be used for sushi. Some supermarkets and delicatessens sell a rice labelled sushi rice, which takes the guesswork out of the process. Japanese short grain rice is slightly sticky, which makes it easy to pick up with chopsticks and ideal for sushi, as the grains of rice cling together. Glutinous rice is not suitable for making sushi, as it is too sticky.

The rice should be rinsed and left to drain for 30 minutes before being cooked by the absorption method. You can use an electric rice cooker but don't be tempted to use the pan-of-water method as the results will be disastrous.

Nori This dried seaweed is sold in paper-thin sheets. It is dark green to black in colour and almost transparent in places. Some nori comes ready-toasted (yaki-nori), often seasoned with soy sauce and sesame oil. Alternatively, toast the nori under a hot grill before use.

Gari Pale pink ginger pickles, which are excellent for serving with sushi.

Shoyu This Japanese soy sauce is milder than Chinese soy sauce. Serve with sushi.

Wasabi A hot green horseradish to serve with fish. It is sold as a paste or as a powder, to which water is added.

Above: Clockwise from top, bamboo rolling mat, gari, wasabi paste, shoyu and nori sheet.

Making Perfect Sushi

1 Rinse the rice and drain for 30–60 minutes, then put in a heavy pan and add a piece of dried kelp (kombu). Add water (see Quantities below), and bring to the boil. Remove the kelp, cover the pan and cook gently over a low heat for about 15 minutes. Increase to high for 10 seconds, then remove from the heat and let stand for 10 minutes. Lift the lid. Steam holes will have appeared in the rice and it will be tender.

2 Prepare the sushi vinegar. For every 450g/1lb/2⅓ cups rice, mix together 60ml/4 tbsp rice vinegar, 15ml/1 tbsp granulated sugar and 2.5ml/½ tsp salt.

3 Stir the sushi vinegar into the rice, cover with a damp cloth and leave to cool. Do not put the rice in the fridge as this will make it go hard.

Quantities

Use between 600ml/1 pint/2½ cups and 750ml/1¼ pints/3 cups water for every 450g/1lb/2⅓ cups sushi rice, depending on the type of rice; always check the instructions on the packet. If you prefer, you could use sake instead of 30ml/2 tbsp of the water.

Rolled Sushi with Smoked Salmon

MAKES 24 SLICES

1 Line a bamboo mat with clear film. Arrange the smoked salmon across the mat, overlapping if necessary, so that there are no gaps or holes. Spread a generous layer of the dressed rice over the salmon.

2 Roll the mat away from you so that the salmon rolls up around the rice. Do not roll up the clear film with the fish. Make more rolls in the same way.

3 Chill the rolls in the fridge for about 10 minutes, then unwrap and cut each roll into six slices, using a wet knife. Cover with a damp cloth and keep cool.

Rolled Sushi with Nori and Filling

MAKES 24 SLICES

To make this sushi you will need sheets of yaki-nori (toasted seaweed). Two sheets will make four long rolls.

1 Cut the yaki-nori in half lengthways and place a half-sheet, shiny side down, on the bamboo mat.

2 Spread a layer of the dressed rice over the yaki-nori, leaving a 1cm/½in clear edge at the top and bottom.

3 Arrange a line of filling horizontally across the middle of the rice. The filling could be raw salmon or raw tuna, cut into 1cm/½in square long sticks, sliced raw scallops, Japanese omelette, roasted pepper, spring onions, cucumber or a selection of two or three of these.

4 Using the rolling mat as a guide, and working from the nearest edge of yaki-nori, roll up the yaki-nori and rice into a cigar (do not include the mat in the roll). Roll the mat in the palms of your hands so that the edges stick together.

5 Wrap the rolls in clear film and chill in the fridge for 10 minutes, then unwrap the rolls. Use a wet knife to cut each roll into six slices, rinsing the knife occasionally.

Shaped Sushi

1 Wet your hands. Take about 15–20g/ ½–¾oz/2–3 tbsp dressed sushi rice at a time and shape it into a rectangle, measuring about 2 x 5cm/¾ x 2in and 1cm/½in high.

2 Repeat this process until all the rice is used up. Gently spread a little wasabi paste in the middle of each of the rectangles of rice, then add your chosen topping.

Sushi Toppings

Make plain rolled sushi and top them with any one of these suggestions.

Raw sushi-grade salmon, raw sushi-grade tuna, salmon roe or other fish roe Cut the salmon and tuna into pieces that are roughly the same size as the rice portions.

Peeled raw prawn tails Cook the prawns for about 1 minute in a pan of simmering water, then drain. Slit each prawn along the belly and remove the dark vein, then carefully open out each prawn like a book. Mix together 15ml/ 1 tbsp rice vinegar and 5ml/1 tsp granulated sugar in a small bowl. Add the prawns, turn to coat, and leave to marinate in a cool place for about 10 minutes.

Blanched squid and boiled octopus Slice the squid and octopus into strips that are roughly the same size as the rice portions.

Rolled omelette slices Beat together 1 egg, 15ml/1 tbsp sake, 15ml/1 tbsp granulated sugar, 15ml/1 tbsp water and a pinch of salt. Heat a little groundnut oil in a small frying pan, then pour in the egg mixture. Fry over a medium to high heat until the egg is just set but not browned. Roll up the omelette and slice.

Garnishes

Fish sushi can be garnished with fresh chives, fresh coriander or toasted sesame seeds. Omelette sushi can be decorated by wrapping strips of yaki-nori around the moulded rice.

COOK'S TIP
Sushi rice should be cooked either by the absorption method or in an electric rice cooker. The pan-of-water method should not be used.

Sushi rice is very sticky when cooked. If you find it becomes unmanageable, rinse your hands in a bowl of water to which 5ml/1 tsp oil has been added. Pat your hands dry; they will be slightly oily and the rice will no longer stick to them.

BIRYANI

This is one of India's most famous rice dishes. Perfect for parties and other festivities, biryani is served with other vegetables and meats, but essentially takes centre stage itself. It is basically an all-in-one dish. The rice is piled on top of a meat or vegetable curry, with saffron milk dribbled over the top to give the rice a splash of golden colour.

Although biryani takes a little time to prepare, it is straightforward and simple. The only rule is to use basmati rice, which should be soaked for 3 hours, preferably in lightly salted water, a technique which the Persians, who are credited with inventing this dish, believed made the rice a brilliant white.

Lamb, chicken and beef are commonly used in biryanis, but duck and game work well, and vegetarian biryanis are popular, too. Biryanis should never be very hot, but are traditionally flavoured with fragrant spices. They can be made using coconut milk, but natural yogurt is more common. The sauce should be sweet and fragrant, with a creamy consistency.

Making Perfect Chicken Biryani

1 First make the saffron milk. Crumble a generous pinch (about 5ml/1 tsp) of saffron strands into 30ml/2 tbsp of warm milk in a small bowl. Stir, then leave to soak for about 3 hours.

2 Meanwhile, wash 275g/10oz/1½ cups basmati rice in cold water. Drain the rice thoroughly, then tip it into a large bowl and cover with more cold water. Stir in 10ml/2 tsp salt and leave to soak for 3 hours.

3 Prepare a chicken curry. Heat 45ml/ 3 tbsp oil in a frying pan and add 3 sliced onions. Cook until soft. Add 175g/6oz cubed chicken breasts, along with any spices you are using. Stir to coat the chicken in the spices, then add 2.5ml/½ tsp salt, 2–3 chopped garlic cloves and lemon juice to taste. Stir-fry for 5 minutes more, until the chicken is browned. Drain the rice and cook it in boiling salted water for 4–5 minutes until three-quarters cooked.

4 Spoon a little drained rice into a flameproof dish, just enough to cover the bottom, then add the curry. Spoon 150ml/¼ pint/⅔ cup natural yogurt evenly over the curry. Preheat the oven to 150°C/300°F/Gas 2.

5 Pile the remaining rice in a hillock on top of the curry, then, using the handle of a wooden spoon, make a 2.5cm/1in hole down from the peak to the bottom.

6 Dribble the saffron milk and 50ml/ ¼ pint/⅔ cup hot chicken stock over the rice, and dot with butter or ghee. Scatter over fried onions, sultanas and toasted almonds. Cover the dish tightly with a double piece of foil held in place by the lid. Cook in the oven for 40 minutes.

Spices for Chicken Biryani

For 175g/6oz chicken use 10 whole green cardamom pods; 1.5ml/¼ tsp ground cloves; 2–3 whole cloves; 5cm/2in cinnamon stick; 5ml/1 tsp ground cumin; 2.5ml/½ tsp ground black pepper; 5ml/1 tsp ground coriander; 5ml/1 tsp finely chopped fresh root ginger; 1.5ml/¼ tsp chilli powder.

LONTONG (COMPRESSED RICE)

This is a speciality of Indonesia and Malaysia. The rice is cooked in a confined space for longer than normal to form a compact solid mass, which when cooled, can be cut into squares. Lontong is eaten cold, usually with salads and satay, when it absorbs the spicy dressings and sauces.

Lontong is traditionally cooked in a banana leaf, although a muslin bag is generally easier to use.

Thai fragrant rice, basmati or any other long grain rice can be used for lontong. Do not be tempted to use par-boiled (easy-cook) rice, as it will not form a solid mass.

Making Perfect Lontong

1 You will need several muslin bags, each about 15cm/6in square. Leave the top of each bag open. Spoon in enough long grain rice to fill each bag one-third full (about 115g/4oz/generous ½ cup), then sew the opening closed.

2 Bring a pan of salted water to the boil, lower in the bags of rice and allow to simmer gently, uncovered, for about 75 minutes, making sure the pan doesn't boil dry and adding more water if necessary.

3 Remove the bags from the water and drain them thoroughly. Each bag should feel like a rather hard and solid lump.

4 When the lontong is completely cold, open the muslin bags, remove the blocks of compressed rice and cut each block into squares or oblongs, using a wet, sharp knife.

FRIED RICE TIPS
• Rice must be cooked and completely cold before frying. Warm rice will become soggy and oily if fried. If you are cooking rice especially for frying, spread it out on a baking sheet as soon as it has been cooked so that it cools rapidly. Leave it for at least 2–3 hours.
• Use long grain white or brown rice for frying.
• Other ingredients should be cooked before the rice is added.
• Always cook the rice over a low heat. It is important to heat the rice through completely, but take care not to overcook it.

FRIED RICE

Wherever rice is a staple food, every region, even every family, has its own fried rice recipe. When rice is served at almost every meal, there are inevitably leftovers, and it's a simple matter to fry these with other ingredients for breakfast, for a lunchtime snack or for a more elaborate evening meal.

There are several classic fried rice dishes – Nasi Goreng, one of the most famous, comes from Indonesia, but is more commonly associated with the Dutch *Rijstafel* (rice table). There are also several well known Chinese fried rices, Egg Fried Rice and Special Fried Rice being two of the most popular. Recipes for any of these dishes are extremely flexible. Provided you follow a few simple rules, the best way with any fried rice dish is to make up your own favourite mixture.

The choice of ingredients is up to the individual cook, but here are some suggestions.
Aromatics Sliced spring onions or shallots; red or yellow onions, sliced or cut into wedges; sliced or crushed garlic. Stir-fry in oil for 3–4 minutes, then add the meat, fish, vegetables and/or eggs. If choosing two or more different ingredients, stir-fry them individually before stirring together.
Meat Any tender cut of poultry or meat, such as chicken, duck, beef, lamb or pork fillet can be used. Slice meat thinly so that it cooks quickly. Meats can be marinated for 30 minutes before cooking (see individual recipes for marinade ingredients). Stir-fry with onions until cooked. Cooked meats only require heating through.
Fish Raw fish and shellfish work well and should be stir-fried after any meat. Cooked fish or prawns can be stirred in at the end.
Vegetables Choose colourful vegetables such as carrots, peppers, courgettes and mushrooms. Cut them into julienne strips so that they cook quickly and evenly. Stir-fry until just tender.
Eggs Beat together and scramble with the onions. Or use the eggs to make an omelette; roll it up, cut into slices and use to garnish the rice.

Making Perfect Fried Rice

1 Stir-fry any uncooked meat in oil in a wok or large, deep frying pan, then add onions. Transfer the meat to a plate.

2 Add beaten egg to the frying pan and scramble with sliced spring onions.

3 Add spices and flavourings such as soy sauce, rice wine, fresh chillies, tomato purée or spices.

4 Tip the cold rice into the frying pan and mix with the scrambled egg. Return any cooked meats, cooked fish or cooked vegetables to the pan at this stage, or add chopped herbs. Cook over a low heat, stirring occasionally, to warm the rice through completely.

RICE PUDDING

In one form or another, rice pudding is enjoyed all over the world. It is England's best known rice dish, and most other European countries have at least one favourite rice pudding to call their own.

Perhaps the popularity of rice pudding in the past arose from the fact that it is difficult to overcook it. In the eighteenth century, food was often badly cooked, and overcooked, stodgy savoury rice dishes were probably despised then as they are now. Rice pudding was one of the few foods that could stand up to such abuse. With its meltingly tender grains slowly cooked in creamy milk, flavoured with vanilla or nutmeg and sweetened with sugar, rice pudding quickly became a firm favourite in Britain and beyond.

English rice pudding is made with short grain rice but this is not essential. Thai fragrant rice and basmati rice can be used equally successfully. In Asia, glutinous rice, which is stickier than our short grain, is the favoured rice for making puddings.

Making Perfect English Rice Pudding

Oven method

1 Preheat the oven to 150°C/300°F/Gas 2. Following your chosen recipe, put the rice and sugar in a shallow baking dish and pour in cold milk. Stir well to mix and then dot the surface with a little butter.

2 Bake in the preheated oven for about 45 minutes, by which time a thick skin will have formed on top of the pudding.

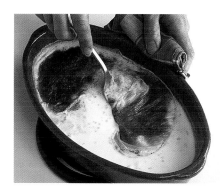

3 Stir the skin into the pudding and bake the pudding for about 1¼ hours more, stirring once or twice.

Pan method

1 Place the rice in a large saucepan. Add the quantity of milk and sugar as specified in the recipe and stir to mix.

2 Bring to the boil, then lower the heat, cover the pan and simmer very gently for 1¼ hours, stirring frequently.

3 Remove the lid and simmer for 15–20 minutes more until the rice mixture is thick and creamy.

Combination method

1 Partially cook the rice using the absorption method. Put the rice in a pan and add a third of the measured liquid. Simmer gently over a low heat.

2 When the liquid has been absorbed, stir in half the remaining liquid and simmer for about 6 minutes more.

3 Stir in the sugar, any flavourings and the remaining milk, then pour the mixture into a buttered baking dish.

4 Dot with butter and bake for 1–1½ hours at a temperature between 150°C/300°F/Gas 2 and 180°C/350°F/Gas 4. The lower temperature cooks slower but will give the pudding a creamier taste.

Making Perfect Glutinous Rice Pudding

1 Place the rice in a large bowl, add cold water to cover and leave to soak for 3–4 hours.

2 Drain the rice, put it in a saucepan and pour in coconut milk or cow's milk. Bring to the boil, then lower the heat, cover the saucepan and simmer gently for 25–30 minutes, stirring frequently.

3 Add sugar, creamed coconut and any flavourings, and cook for 5–10 minutes more, uncovered, until the rice reaches the consistency you like. Serve with slices of exotic fruits such as mango, papaya and pineapple, if you like.

Making Perfect Thai Rice Pudding

This is quick, easy and quite delicious. Cook Thai fragrant rice in boiling water using the absorption method. Leave it to stand for a few minutes, then stir in milk and sugar to taste, and creamed coconut, if you like. Serve the pudding hot, with fresh fruit.

Quantities

• For short grain rice pudding, use 600ml/1 pint/2½ cups milk for every 50g/2oz/generous ¼ cup rice. Stir in 45ml/3 tbsp granulated sugar. This should be sufficient to serve four.
• For glutinous rice pudding, use 300ml/½ pint/1¼ cups liquid for every 75g/3oz/scant ½ cup rice to serve four.
• For Thai rice pudding, use 475ml/ 16 fl oz/2 cups water, 120ml/4 fl oz/ ½ cup milk and 60ml/4 tbsp creamed coconut for every 50g/2oz/generous ¼ cup rice to serve four.

COOK'S TIPS

To give an English rice pudding a richer flavour, try any one of the following suggestions.
• Replace half the liquid with evaporated milk and add demerara sugar.
• If using the pan method, stir in a little cream just before serving.
• Beaten eggs can be stirred into the hot, cooked rice, or added to the part-cooked rice (see combination method).

Flavourings

Vanilla Give the milk a delicate vanilla flavour by heating it with a vanilla pod until the milk is hot but not boiling. Remove from the heat and leave to infuse for 1–2 hours. Strain the flavoured milk over the rice.
Nutmeg This is another very popular addition. Either grate it over the surface of a rice pudding that is to be baked, or stir grated nutmeg into the mixture in the pan. Ground cinnamon could be used instead.

Above: Aromatic nutmeg will add sweetness and warmth to the pudding.

Raisins or sultanas Stir into the rice or scatter at the bottom of the dish.
Spices Add lemon grass, cardamom pods, or pared orange, lemon or lime rind to the rice as it is cooking.
Nuts Chopped pistachios or almonds can be added during cooking to a rice pudding which is being cooked by the combination or pan method.

Above: Pistachios stirred into the pudding with shreds of fresh mint will provide texture and a slightly sweet flavour.

EQUIPMENT

Electric Rice Cooker

In Japan and other more affluent rice-eating countries, electric rice cookers have now replaced more conventional means of cooking rice. In the West they are also becoming increasingly popular, and cooks who use them often swear by them. The cookers cook rice perfectly and have the added advantage of keeping it warm throughout the meal, without it drying or becoming soggy. Another bonus of the rice cooker is that it frees hob space.

Saucepans

Even if you have invested in a rice cooker, you will always need saucepans. For plain boiled rice and for risottos, a heavy-based pan is the best choice – the actual size will depend on the quantities you are likely to be making but in general, bigger is better; small amounts of rice can be cooked in a large pan but you'll run into difficulties if you try cooking lots of rice in a pan that is too small. For risottos, some

Left: Electric rice cooker

Right: Colander and sieve

Below: Saucepans

cooks prefer to use a deep frying pan. A small frying pan or crêpe pan will be useful for frying the omelettes often used to garnish oriental rice dishes.

Colanders and Sieves

A colander or sieve is essential for draining boiled rice. Buy a good quality colander with a long handle, so that you can stand well back to pour the steaming rice out of the saucepan.

Measuring Jugs and Scales

It is important to measure rice accurately, and to add the correct quantity of water or other liquid, as specified in the recipe or on the packet, especially when cooking by the absorption method. In most recipes the rice is measured by weight, although it can also be measured by volume. Use a measuring jug when adding stocks and other liquids.

Flameproof Casserole

Several rice dishes are started off on the hob, then finished in the oven. A flameproof casserole is perfect for this, and will also prove useful for dishes that are entirely oven-baked. Casseroles should have well-fitting lids; if lids are at all loose, cover the casserole with foil before fitting the lid in place.

Earthenware Casserole

These cannot be used on the hob, but are very useful for oven-cooked pilaffs. It is essential for the casserole to have a well-fitting lid.

Parmesan Grater

Freshly grated Parmesan cheese is an essential ingredient in risottos. Although many supermarkets now stock freshly grated Parmesan, it is fairly expensive, and buying Parmesan as one whole piece and grating it yourself is a much better option. Small metal Parmesan graters are available, but the graters where you pop the cheese in the top and turn the handle allow you to grate only the amount you need.

Left: Earthenware and flameproof casseroles

Left: Bamboo steamer

Above: Chopsticks and
chopstick stands

Left: Japanese bamboo rolling
mats

Mortar and Pestle

Spices are not necessary for cooking rice, but for interesting meals, particularly those with an oriental flavour, they are essential.
The advantage of grinding your own spices is that you can be sure they are absolutely fresh; you'll notice the difference at once compared with ready ground spices. A mortar and pestle is the traditional piece of equipment for grinding spices, and has the advantage that you can grind very small quantities. The mortar is the container, while the pestle is used to pulverize spices, seeds, garlic or herbs. Mortar and pestle sets can be made of stone, wood or marble.

Spice Mill

A spice mill can be used instead of a mortar and pestle. It will grind spices very finely with very little effort.

Cooking Knives

Not specifically required for cooking rice, but good quality kitchen knives in a range of sizes and weights are essential for preparing other ingredients.

Paella Pan

If you are likely to make paella on a regular basis – or fancy bringing back a useful souvenir of your Spanish holiday – do invest in a paella pan. Bigger pans obviously make bigger paellas, but very large pans will probably turn out to be bigger than the ring on your cooker, which will mean the food will cook unevenly.

Wok

You will need a wok for any stir-fried rice dish and will also find one useful for making a wide variety of sauces and stir-fries to accompany rice dishes. Buy the appropriate wok for your cooker. Round-bottomed woks can only be used on gas hobs; a flat-bottomed wok should be used on an electric hob.

Steamers

You can use a rice steamer to cook rice and for "finishing" rice if you do not have an electric rice cooker.

Japanese Bamboo Rolling Mat

Essential for rolling rice when making sushi, this simple but very useful piece of equipment is flexible in one direction but rigid in the other.

Muslin Bag

This is not essential, but is useful for making your own lontong (compressed rice). If you don't have a bamboo steamer, the bag containing the rice can be set inside a pan of boiling water. You can make your own muslin bag by cutting two 25cm/10in squares of muslin and sewing them together around three sides, leaving one edge open.

Chopsticks and Chopstick Stands

Oriental cooks use long chopsticks for manipulating foods when stir-frying. You may like to have good quality chopsticks to use when serving a Chinese or Thai meal, as they add authenticity. Chopstick stands are used for chopsticks at the table; less elaborate ones can be used when cooking.

Rice Bowls

Not essential pieces of equipment, but very attractive accessories: Chinese or Japanese rice bowls will make a huge difference to the look of an oriental meal. Buy genuine sets from oriental markets, or when travelling, for use on special occasions.

Right: Rice
bowls

RICE
AND
RISOTTO
RECIPES

INDIA

We have India to thank for a large
number of our favourite rice dishes.
Whether side dishes or main meals,
there are countless rice recipes from
India. Some, like Chicken Biryani,
are known and loved across the
world. Others, like Saffron Rice
with Cardamoms, made with
fragrant basmati rice, are the
essential accompaniment to curries.

CHICKEN BIRYANI

EASY TO MAKE AND VERY TASTY, THIS IS THE IDEAL DISH FOR A FAMILY SUPPER.

SERVES FOUR

INGREDIENTS

10 whole green cardamom pods
275g/10oz/1½ cups basmati rice,
  soaked and drained
2.5ml/½ tsp salt
2–3 whole cloves
5cm/2in cinnamon stick
45ml/3 tbsp vegetable oil
3 onions, sliced
4 chicken breasts, each about
  175g/6oz, cubed
1.5ml/¼ tsp ground cloves
1.5ml/¼ tsp hot chilli powder
5ml/1 tsp ground cumin
5ml/1 tsp ground coriander
2.5ml/½ tsp ground black pepper
3 garlic cloves, chopped
5ml/1 tsp finely chopped fresh
  root ginger
juice of 1 lemon
4 tomatoes, sliced
30ml/2 tbsp chopped fresh coriander
150ml/¼ pint/⅔ cup natural yogurt
4–5 saffron strands, soaked in
  10ml/2 tsp hot milk
150ml/¼ pint/⅔ cup water
toasted flaked almonds and fresh
  coriander sprigs, to garnish
natural yogurt, to serve

1 Preheat the oven to 190°C/375°F/ Gas 5. Remove the seeds from half the cardamom pods and grind them finely, using a pestle and mortar. Set them aside. Bring a pan of water to the boil and add the rice, salt, whole cardamom pods, cloves and cinnamon stick. Boil for 2 minutes, then drain, leaving the whole spices in the rice.

2 Heat the oil in a frying pan and fry the onions for 8 minutes, until softened and browned. Add the chicken and the ground spices, including the ground cardamom seeds. Mix well, then add the garlic, ginger and lemon juice. Stir-fry for 5 minutes.

3 Transfer the chicken mixture to a casserole and arrange the tomatoes on top. Sprinkle on the fresh coriander, spoon the yogurt evenly on top and cover with the drained rice.

4 Drizzle the saffron milk over the rice and pour over the water. Cover tightly and bake for 1 hour. Transfer to a warmed serving platter and remove the whole spices from the rice. Garnish with toasted almonds and fresh coriander sprigs and serve with the natural yogurt.

BASMATI AND NUT PILAFF

VEGETARIANS WILL LOVE THIS SIMPLE PILAFF. ADD WILD OR CULTIVATED MUSHROOMS, IF YOU LIKE.

SERVES FOUR

INGREDIENTS
  15–30ml/1–2 tbsp sunflower oil
  1 onion, chopped
  1 garlic clove, crushed
  1 large carrot, coarsely grated
  225g/8oz/generous 1 cup basmati
   rice, soaked
  5ml/1 tsp cumin seeds
  10ml/2 tsp ground coriander
  10ml/2 tsp black mustard seeds
   (optional)
  4 green cardamom pods
  450ml/¾ pint/scant 2 cups vegetable
   stock or water
  1 bay leaf
  75g/3oz/¾ cup unsalted walnuts and
   cashew nuts
salt and freshly ground black pepper
fresh parsley or coriander sprigs,
  to garnish

1 Heat the oil in a large, shallow frying pan and gently fry the onion, garlic and carrot for 3–4 minutes. Drain the rice and then add to the pan with the spices. Cook for 1–2 minutes more, stirring to coat the grains in oil.

2 Pour in the stock or water, add the bay leaf and season well. Bring to the boil, lower the heat, cover and simmer very gently for 10–12 minutes.

3 Remove the pan from the heat without lifting the lid. Leave to stand for about 5 minutes, then check the rice. If it is cooked, there will be small steam holes on the surface of the rice. Remove and discard the bay leaf and the cardamom pods.

4 Stir in the nuts and check the seasoning. Spoon on to a platter, garnish with the parsley or coriander and serve.

COOK'S TIP
Use whichever nuts you prefer in this dish – even unsalted peanuts taste good, although almonds, cashew nuts or pistachios are more exotic.

SAVOURY RICE WITH MADRAS CURRY

BITE-SIZE CUBES OF STEWING BEEF SIMMER GENTLY WITH SPICES UNTIL THEY ARE TENDER ENOUGH TO MELT IN THE MOUTH. THEY ARE SERVED WITH BASMATI RICE, COOKED UNTIL LIGHT AND FLUFFY.

SERVES FOUR

INGREDIENTS
  225g/8oz/generous 1 cup basmati
    rice
  15ml/1 tbsp sunflower oil
  30ml/2 tbsp ghee or butter
  1 onion, finely chopped
  1 garlic clove, crushed
  5ml/1 tsp ground cumin
  2.5ml/½ tsp ground coriander
  4 green cardamom pods
  1 cinnamon stick
  1 small red pepper, seeded and diced
  1 small green pepper, seeded and diced
  300ml/½ pint/1¼ cups chicken stock
  salt and freshly ground black pepper
For the curry
  30ml/2 tbsp vegetable oil
  30ml/2 tbsp ghee or butter
  675g/1½lb stewing beef, cut into
    bite-size cubes
  1 onion, chopped
  3 green cardamom pods
  2 fresh green chillies, seeded and
    finely chopped
  2.5cm/1in piece of fresh root ginger,
    grated
  2 garlic cloves, crushed
  15ml/1 tbsp Madras curry paste
  5ml/1 tsp ground cumin
  5ml/1 tsp ground coriander
  150ml/¼ pint/⅔ cup beef stock

1 Start by making the curry. Heat half the oil and ghee or butter in a frying pan and fry the meat, in batches if necessary, until browned on all sides. Transfer to a plate and set aside.

2 Heat the remaining oil and ghee or butter and fry the onion for about 3–4 minutes until softened. Add the cardamom pods and fry for 1 minute, then add the chillies, ginger and garlic and fry for 2 minutes more.

3 Stir in the curry paste, ground cumin and coriander, then add the meat and stock. Season with salt, bring to the boil, then lower the heat and simmer very gently for 1–1½ hours, until the meat is tender.

4 When the curry is almost ready, prepare the rice. Put it in a bowl and pour over boiling water to cover. Set aside for 10 minutes, then drain, rinse under cold water and drain again. The rice will still be uncooked but should have lost its brittleness.

5 Heat the oil and ghee or butter in a flameproof casserole and fry the onion and garlic gently for 3–4 minutes until softened and lightly browned.

6 Stir in the cumin and ground coriander, cardamom pods and cinnamon stick. Fry for 1 minute, then add the diced peppers.

7 Add the rice, stirring to coat the grains in the spice mixture, and pour in the stock. Bring to the boil, then lower the heat, cover the pan tightly and simmer for about 8–10 minutes, or until the rice is tender and the stock has been absorbed. Spoon into a bowl and serve with the curry. Offer a little mango chutney, if you like.

COOK'S TIP
The curry should be fairly dry, but take care that it does not catch on the bottom of the pan. If you want to leave it unattended, cook it in a heavy-based pan or flameproof casserole, either on the hob or in an oven preheated to 180°C/350°F/Gas 4.

LAMB PARSI

This is similar to biryani, but here the lamb is marinated with the yogurt, a technique which is a Parsi speciality. Serve with a dhal or with spiced mushrooms.

SERVES SIX

INGREDIENTS

   900g/2lb lamb fillet, cut into
     2.5cm/1in cubes
   60ml/4 tbsp ghee or butter
   2 onions, sliced
   450g/1lb potatoes, cut into large
     chunks
   chicken stock or water (see method)
   450g/1lb/2⅓ cups basmati rice,
     soaked
   generous pinch of saffron strands,
     dissolved in 30ml/2 tbsp warm milk
   fresh coriander sprigs, to garnish
For the marinade
   475ml/16fl oz/2 cups natural yogurt
   3–4 garlic cloves, crushed
   10ml/2 tsp cayenne pepper
   20ml/4 tsp garam masala
   10ml/2 tsp ground cumin
   5ml/1 tsp ground coriander

1 Make the marinade by mixing all the ingredients in a large bowl. Add the meat, stir to coat, then cover and leave to marinate for 3–4 hours in a cool place or overnight in the fridge.

2 Melt 30ml/2 tbsp of the ghee or butter in a large saucepan and fry the onions for 6–8 minutes until lightly golden. Transfer to a plate.

3 Melt a further 25ml/1½ tbsp of the ghee or butter in the pan. Fry the marinated lamb cubes in batches until evenly brown, transferring each batch in turn to a plate. When all the lamb has been browned, return it to the pan and scrape in the remaining marinade.

4 Stir in the potatoes and add about three-quarters of the fried onions. Pour in just enough chicken stock or water to cover the mixture. Bring to the boil, then cover and simmer over a very low heat for 40–50 minutes until the lamb is tender and the potatoes are cooked. Preheat the oven to 160°C/325°F/Gas 3.

5 Drain the rice. Cook it in a pan of boiling stock or water for 5 minutes. Meanwhile, spoon the lamb mixture into a casserole. Drain the rice and mound it on top of the lamb, then, using the handle of a wooden spoon, make a hole down the centre. Top with the remaining fried onions, pour the saffron milk over the top and dot with the remaining ghee or butter.

6 Cover the pan with a double layer of foil and a lid. Cook in the oven for 30–35 minutes or until the rice is completely tender. Garnish with fresh coriander sprigs and serve.

COOK'S TIP
Take care not to overcook the rice when parboiling it. The grains should still be quite hard, but should have a slightly powdery consistency.

GOAN PRAWN CURRY WITH SOUTHERN-STYLE RICE

MAKE THIS CURRY AS MILD OR AS FIERY AS YOU WISH. GOANS TRADITIONALLY LIKE THEIR SEAFOOD DISHES FAIRLY HOT, BUT A MILDER CURRY IS JUST AS DELICIOUS, FLAVOURED WITH HERBS AND SPICES.

SERVES FOUR

INGREDIENTS
  15g/½oz/1 tbsp ghee or butter
  2 garlic cloves, crushed
  450g/1lb small raw prawns, peeled
    and deveined
  4 cardamom pods
  4 cloves
  1 cinnamon stick
  15ml/1 tbsp mustard seeds
  about 15ml/1 tbsp groundnut oil
  1 large onion, chopped
  ½–1 fresh red chilli, seeded and
    finely sliced
  4 tomatoes, peeled, seeded and
    chopped
  175ml/6fl oz/¾ cup fish stock or
    water
  350ml/12fl oz/1½ cups coconut milk
  45ml/3 tbsp fragrant spice mix (see
    Cook's Tip)
  10–20ml/2–4 tsp cayenne pepper
  salt
For the rice
  350g/12oz/1¾ cups basmati rice,
    soaked and drained
  5ml/1 tsp coriander seeds
  5ml/1 tsp cumin seeds
  30ml/2 tbsp urad dhal, rinsed
    (optional)
  2.5ml/½ tsp ground turmeric
  5ml/1 tsp brown mustard seeds
  115g/4oz/1 cup unroasted cashew
    nuts
  15ml/1 tbsp groundnut oil
  15ml/1 tbsp ghee or butter

COOK'S TIP
To make a fragrant spice mix, dry-fry 25ml/1½ tbsp coriander seeds, 15ml/ 1 tbsp mixed peppercorns, 5ml/1 tsp cumin seeds, 1.5ml/¼ tsp fenugreek seeds and 1.5ml/¼ tsp fennel seeds until aromatic, then grind finely in a spice mill. Alternatively, use ready-ground spices, in which case 15ml/ 1 tbsp ground coriander will be required.

1 Melt the ghee or butter in a flameproof casserole, add the garlic and stir over a low heat for a few seconds. Add the prawns and stir-fry briefly to coat. Transfer to a plate.

2 Dry-fry the cardamom pods, cloves and cinnamon stick for 2 minutes. Add the mustard seeds and fry for 1 minute. Heat the oil and fry the onion and chilli for 3–4 minutes. Add the remaining curry ingredients. Set aside.

3 Preheat the oven to 180°C/350°F/ Gas 4. Cook the rice for 5 minutes. Drain well. Meanwhile, dry-fry the coriander and cumin seeds with the urad dhal, if using, for a few minutes. Add the turmeric and grind the mixture finely in a spice mill.

4 Fry the mustard seeds and cashews in oil for a few minutes and stir into the rice with the ground spice mix.

5 Spoon the rice mixture into a large casserole and dot with ghee or butter. Cover tightly with foil or a muslin cloth before fitting the lid securely. Cook in the oven for 20 minutes.

6 About 10 minutes before the rice is ready, reheat the curry sauce and add the prawns. Simmer gently for 5–8 minutes until the prawns are cooked through. Spoon into a dish and serve with the rice.

CHICKEN KORMA WITH SAFFRON RICE

MILD AND FRAGRANT, THIS DISH IS — QUITE UNDERSTANDABLY — AN OLD FAVOURITE.

SERVES FOUR

INGREDIENTS

    75g/3oz/¾ cup flaked almonds
    15ml/1 tbsp ghee or butter
    about 15ml/1 tbsp sunflower oil
    675g/1½lb skinless, boneless
      chicken breasts, cut into bite-size
      pieces
    1 onion, chopped
    4 green cardamom pods
    2 garlic cloves, crushed
    10ml/2 tsp ground cumin
    5ml/1 tsp ground coriander
    1 cinnamon stick
    good pinch of chilli powder
    300ml/½ pint/1¼ cups canned
      coconut milk
    175ml/6fl oz/¾ cup chicken stock
    5ml/1 tsp tomato purée (optional)
    75ml/5 tbsp single cream
    15–30ml/1–2 tbsp fresh lime or
      lemon juice
    10ml/2 tsp grated lime or lemon rind
    5ml/1 tsp garam masala
    salt and freshly ground black pepper
    fresh coriander sprigs, to garnish
      (optional)
    poppadums, to serve (optional)
For the saffron rice
    275g/10oz/1½ cups basmati rice,
      soaked
    750ml/1¼ pints/3 cups chicken stock
    generous pinch of saffron strands,
      crushed, then soaked in hot water
      (see Cook's Tip)

1 Dry-fry the flaked almonds in a small frying pan until pale golden. Transfer about two-thirds of the almonds to a plate and continue to dry-fry the remainder until they are slightly deeper in colour. Transfer the darker almonds to a separate plate and set them aside for the garnish. Let the paler almonds cool, then grind them in a spice grinder or coffee mill.

2 Heat the ghee or butter and oil in a large frying pan or wok and fry the chicken pieces, in batches if necessary, until evenly brown. Transfer the chicken to a plate.

3 Add a little more oil if necessary and fry the onion for 2 minutes, then stir in the cardamom pods and garlic and fry for 3–4 minutes more, until the onion is lightly flecked with brown.

4 Stir in the ground flaked almonds, cumin, coriander, cinnamon stick and chilli powder and fry for 1 minute. Stir in the coconut milk, chicken stock and tomato purée, if using.

5 Bring to simmering point, then add the chicken and season. Cover and cook over a gentle heat for 10 minutes until the chicken is tender. Set aside, covered, while cooking the rice.

6 Drain the rice and put it in a saucepan. Add the seasoned stock and the saffron. Bring to the boil over a medium heat, then cover tightly and cook over a low heat for 10 minutes or according to the instructions on the packet.

7 Just before the rice is ready, reheat the korma until it is simmering gently. Stir in the cream, the citrus juice and rind and the garam masala. Taste and season as necessary. Pile the rice into a warmed serving dish and spoon the korma into a separate dish. Garnish with the reserved browned almonds and fresh coriander sprigs, and serve with poppadums, if you like.

COOK'S TIP
Saffron should always be soaked before use. Soak the strands for about an hour in either warm water or milk, according to the recipe.

BEEF BIRYANI

THE MOGULS INTRODUCED THIS DRY, SPICY RICE DISH TO CENTRAL INDIA. IT IS A MEAL IN ITSELF.

SERVES FOUR

INGREDIENTS

2 large onions
2 garlic cloves, chopped
2.5cm/1in piece of fresh root ginger, peeled and roughly chopped
½–1 fresh green chilli, seeded and roughly chopped
small bunch of fresh coriander
60ml/4 tbsp flaked almonds
30–45ml/2–3 tbsp water
15ml/1 tbsp ghee or butter, plus 25g/1oz/2 tbsp butter, for the rice
45ml/3 tbsp sunflower oil
30ml/2 tbsp sultanas
500g/1¼lb braising or stewing steak, cubed
5ml/1 tsp ground coriander
15ml/1 tbsp ground cumin
2.5ml/½ tsp ground turmeric
2.5ml/½ tsp ground fenugreek
good pinch of ground cinnamon
175ml/6fl oz/¾ cup natural yogurt
275g/10oz/1½ cups basmati rice
about 1.2 litres/2 pints/5 cups hot chicken stock or water
salt and freshly ground black pepper
2 hard-boiled eggs, quartered, to garnish

1 Roughly chop 1 onion and place it in a food processor or blender. Add the garlic, ginger, chilli, fresh coriander and half the flaked almonds. Pour in the water and process to a smooth paste.

2 Finely slice the remaining onion into rings or half rings. Heat half the ghee or butter with half the oil in a heavy-based, flameproof casserole and fry the onion rings over a medium heat for 10–15 minutes until they are a deep golden brown. Transfer to a plate with a slotted spoon. Fry the remaining flaked almonds briefly until golden and set aside with the onion rings, then quickly fry the sultanas until they swell. Transfer to the plate.

3 Heat the remaining ghee or butter in the casserole with a further 15ml/1 tbsp of the oil. Fry the meat, in batches, until evenly brown. Transfer to a plate and set aside.

4 Wipe the casserole clean with kitchen paper, heat the remaining oil and pour in the onion and ginger paste. Cook over a medium heat for 2–3 minutes, stirring all the time, until the mixture begins to brown lightly. Stir in all the spices, season with salt and pepper and cook for 1 minute more.

5 Lower the heat, then stir in the yogurt, a little at a time. When all of it has been incorporated into the spice mixture, return the meat to the casserole. Stir to coat, cover tightly and simmer over a gentle heat for 40–45 minutes until the meat is tender. Soak the rice in a bowl of cold water for 15–20 minutes.

6 Preheat the oven to 160°C/325°F/ Gas 3. Drain the rice, place in a saucepan and add the hot chicken stock or water, together with a little salt. Bring back to the boil, cover and cook for 5–6 minutes.

7 Drain the rice, and pile it in a mound on top of the meat in the casserole. Using the handle of a spoon, make a hole through the rice and meat mixture, to the bottom of the pan. Scatter the fried onions, almonds and sultanas over the top and dot with butter. Cover the casserole tightly with a double layer of foil and secure with a lid.

8 Cook the biryani in the oven for 30–40 minutes. To serve, spoon the mixture on to a warmed serving plate and garnish with the quartered hard-boiled eggs. Serve with parathas, naan bread or chapatis, if liked.

SPICY LAMB AND APRICOTS WITH PEA RICE

THE SLIGHTLY DRY FLAVOUR OF THE SPLIT PEAS AND BASMATI CONTRASTS WELL WITH THE SWEETNESS OF THE LAMB.

SERVES FOUR

INGREDIENTS
675g/1½lb lamb leg fillet
15ml/1 tbsp ghee or butter
1 onion, finely chopped
5ml/1 tsp ground coriander
10ml/2 tsp ground cumin
5ml/1 tsp fenugreek
2.5ml/½ tsp turmeric
pinch of cayenne pepper
1 cinnamon stick
120ml/4fl oz/½ cup chicken stock
175g/6oz ready-to-eat apricots,
   halved or quartered
salt and freshly ground black pepper
fresh coriander, to garnish
For the marinade
120ml/4fl oz/½ cup natural yogurt
15ml/1 tbsp sunflower oil
juice of half a lemon
2.5cm/1in pieces fresh root ginger,
   grated
For the rice
175g/6oz/½ cup chana dhal or yellow
   split peas, soaked for 1–2 hours
225g/8oz/generous 1 cup basmati
   rice, soaked and drained
15ml/1 tbsp sunflower oil
1 large onion, finely sliced
1 garlic clove, crushed
10ml/2 tsp finely grated fresh root
   ginger
60ml/4 tbsp natural yogurt
15ml/1 tbsp chopped fresh coriander
15ml/1 tbsp ghee or butter
salt

1 Trim the meat and cut into bite-size pieces. Make the marinade by blending together the yogurt, oil, lemon juice and ginger. Add the meat, stir to coat, then cover with clear film and leave in a cool place for 2–4 hours to marinate.

2 Put the chana dhal or yellow split peas in a large saucepan, cover with boiling water and boil for 20–30 minutes until tender. Drain and set aside. Cook the drained rice in boiling salted water until it is three-quarters cooked and almost tender. Drain and set aside.

3 Heat the oil in a frying pan and fry the onion rings until golden. Transfer to a plate. Stir in the garlic and ginger and fry for a few seconds, then add the yogurt and cook for a few minutes, stirring. Add the dhal, coriander and salt. Stir well, then remove from the heat and set aside. Preheat the oven to 180°C/350°F/Gas 4.

4 Drain the meat, reserving the marinade. Melt the ghee or butter in a flameproof casserole and fry the onion for 3–4 minutes until soft. Add the coriander, cumin, fenugreek, turmeric, cayenne pepper and cinnamon stick, and fry over a medium heat until the spices are sizzling.

5 Fry the meat until browned, then spoon in the remaining marinade, add the chicken stock and apricots, and season well. Slowly bring to the boil, then cover and cook in the oven for 45–55 minutes until the meat is tender.

6 Meanwhile, finish cooking the rice. Spoon the dhal mixture into a casserole and stir in the rice. Dot the top with ghee or butter and sprinkle with the onion rings. Cover with a double layer of foil, secured with the lid. Place in the oven 30 minutes before the lamb is ready. The rice and dhal should be tender but the grains should be separate. Serve the rice and spiced lamb together, garnished with fresh coriander.

INDIAN RICE <u>WITH</u> TOMATOES <u>AND</u> SPINACH

THIS TASTY RICE DISH CAN BE SERVED WITH A MEAT CURRY OR AS PART OF A VEGETARIAN MEAL.

SERVES FOUR

INGREDIENTS
    30ml/2 tbsp sunflower oil
    15ml/1 tbsp ghee or butter
    1 onion, chopped
    2 garlic cloves, crushed
    3 tomatoes, peeled, seeded and
      chopped
    225g/8oz/generous 1 cup brown
      basmati rice, soaked
    10ml/2 tsp dhana jeera powder or
      5ml/1 tsp ground coriander and
      5ml/1 tsp ground cumin
    2 carrots, coarsely grated
    900ml/1½ pints/3¾ cups vegetable
      stock
    275g/10oz baby spinach leaves,
      washed
    50g/2oz/½ cup unsalted cashew nuts,
      toasted
    salt and freshly ground black pepper

1 Heat the oil and ghee or butter in a flameproof casserole and gently fry the onion and garlic for 4–5 minutes until soft. Add the chopped tomatoes and cook for 3–4 minutes, stirring, until slightly thickened.

2 Drain the rice, add it to the casserole and cook gently for 1–2 minutes, stirring, until the rice is coated with the tomato and onion mixture.

COOK'S TIP
If you can't get baby spinach leaves, use larger fresh spinach leaves. Remove any tough stalks and chop the leaves roughly.

3 Stir in the dhana jeera powder or coriander and cumin, then add the carrots and season with salt and pepper. Pour in the stock and stir well to mix.

4 Bring to the boil, then cover tightly and simmer over a very gentle heat for 20–25 minutes until the rice is tender. Lay the spinach on the surface of the rice, cover again and cook for 2–3 minutes until the spinach has wilted. Fold the spinach into the rest of the rice and check the seasoning. Sprinkle with cashews and serve.

SWEET RICE WITH HOT SOUR CHICK-PEAS

MUCH MORE THAN US IN THE WEST, INDIANS ENJOY DISHES THAT COMBINE SWEET FLAVOURS WITH HOT OR SOUR ONES. HERE, THE RICE IS DISTINCTLY SWEET BUT GOES WELL WITH THE HOT SOUR TASTE OF THE CHICK-PEAS.

SERVES SIX

INGREDIENTS

350g/12oz/1⅔ cups dried chick-peas, soaked overnight
60ml/4 tbsp vegetable oil
1 large onion, very finely chopped
225g/8oz tomatoes, peeled and finely chopped
15ml/1 tbsp ground coriander
15ml/1 tbsp ground cumin
5ml/1 tsp ground fenugreek
5ml/1 tsp ground cinnamon
1–2 fresh hot green chillies, seeded and finely sliced
2.5cm/1in piece of fresh root ginger, grated
60ml/4 tbsp lemon juice
15ml/1 tbsp chopped fresh coriander
salt and freshly ground black pepper

For the rice
40g/1½oz/3 tbsp ghee or butter
4 green cardamom pods
4 cloves
650ml/22fl oz/2¾ cups boiling water
350g/12oz/1¾ cups basmati rice, soaked and drained
5–10ml/1–2 tsp granulated sugar
5–6 saffron strands, soaked in warm water

1 Drain the chick-peas well and place them in a large saucepan. Pour in water to cover, bring to the boil, then simmer, covered, for 1–1¼ hours until tender, topping up the liquid from time to time. Drain the chick-peas, reserving the cooking liquid.

2 Heat the oil in a saucepan. Reserve about 30ml/2 tbsp of the chopped onion and add the remainder to the pan. Fry over a medium heat for 4–5 minutes, stirring frequently.

3 Add the tomatoes. Cook over a moderately low heat for 5–6 minutes, until they are very soft, stirring and mashing them frequently.

4 Stir in the coriander, cumin, fenugreek and cinnamon. Cook for 30 seconds, then add the chick-peas and 350ml/12fl oz/1½ cups of the reserved cooking liquid. Season with salt, then cover and simmer very gently for 15–20 minutes, stirring occasionally and adding more liquid if the chick-peas begin to dry out.

5 While the chick-peas are cooking, melt the ghee or butter in a saucepan and fry the cardamom pods and cloves for a few minutes. Remove the pan from the heat, and when the fat has cooled a little, pour in the boiling water and stir in the basmati rice. Cover tightly and cook by the absorption method for 10 minutes.

6 When the rice is cooked, add the sugar and saffron liquid and stir thoroughly. Cover again. The rice will keep warm while you finish cooking the chick-peas.

7 Mix the reserved onion with the sliced chillies, ginger and lemon juice, and stir the mixture into the chick-peas. Add the chopped coriander, adjust the seasoning and serve with the rice.

SAFFRON RICE <u>WITH</u> CARDAMOMS

THE ADDITION OF AROMATIC GREEN CARDAMOM PODS, CLOVES, MILK AND SAFFRON GIVES THIS DISH BOTH A DELICATE FLAVOUR AND COLOUR.

2 Add the cardamoms, cloves and salt. Stir, then bring to the boil. Lower the heat, cover the pan tightly and simmer for about 5 minutes.

3 Meanwhile, place the milk in a small saucepan. Add the saffron strands and heat gently.

4 Add the saffron milk to the rice and stir. Cover again and continue cooking over a low heat for 5–6 minutes. Remove from the heat without lifting the lid. Leave the rice to stand for 5 minutes before serving.

SERVES SIX

INGREDIENTS
   450g/1lb/2⅓ cups basmati rice, soaked
   750ml/1¼ pints/3 cups water
   3 green cardamom pods
   2 cloves
   5ml/1 tsp salt
   45ml/3 tbsp semi-skimmed milk
   2.5ml/½ tsp saffron strands, crushed

1 Drain the rice and place it in a saucepan. Pour in the water.

COOK'S TIP
The saffron milk can be heated in the microwave. Mix the milk and saffron strands in a suitable jug or bowl and warm them for 1 minute on Low.

PILAU RICE <u>WITH</u> WHOLE SPICES

THIS FRAGRANT RICE DISH MAKES A PERFECT ACCOMPANIMENT TO ANY INDIAN MEAL.

<u>SERVES FOUR</u>

INGREDIENTS
  generous pinch of saffron
    strands
  600ml/1 pint/2½ cups hot
    chicken stock
  50g/2oz/¼ cup butter
  1 onion, chopped
  1 garlic clove, crushed
  ½ cinnamon stick
  6 green cardamom pods
  1 bay leaf
  250g/9oz/1⅓ cups basmati rice
  50g/2oz/⅓ cup sultanas
  15ml/1 tbsp sunflower oil
  50g/2oz/½ cup cashew nuts
  naan bread and tomato and onion
    salad, to serve (optional)

1 Stir the saffron strands into a jug of hot stock and set aside.

2 Heat the butter in a saucepan and fry the onion and garlic for 5 minutes. Stir in the cinnamon stick, cardamoms and bay leaf and cook for 2 minutes.

3 Add the rice and cook, stirring, for 2 minutes more. Pour in the saffron-flavoured stock and add the sultanas. Bring to the boil, stir, then lower the heat, cover and cook gently for about 10 minutes or until the rice is tender and the liquid has all been absorbed.

4 Meanwhile, heat the oil in a frying pan and fry the cashew nuts until browned. Drain on kitchen paper. Scatter the cashew nuts over the rice. Serve with naan bread and a tomato and onion salad, if you like.

COOK'S TIP
Don't be tempted to use black cardamoms in this dish. They are coarser and more strongly flavoured than green cardamoms and are only used in highly spiced dishes that are cooked for a long time.

MUSHROOM PILAU

THIS DISH IS SIMPLICITY ITSELF. SERVE WITH ANY INDIAN DISH OR WITH ROAST LAMB OR CHICKEN.

SERVES FOUR

INGREDIENTS
  30ml/2 tbsp vegetable oil
  2 shallots, finely chopped
  1 garlic clove, crushed
  3 green cardamom pods
  25g/1oz/2 tbsp ghee or butter
  175g/6oz/2½ cups button
    mushrooms, sliced
  225g/8oz/generous 1 cup basmati
    rice, soaked
  5ml/1 tsp grated fresh root ginger
  good pinch of garam masala
  450ml/¾ pint/scant 2 cups water
  15ml/1 tbsp chopped fresh coriander
  salt

1 Heat the oil in a flameproof casserole and fry the shallots, garlic and cardamom pods over a medium heat for 3–4 minutes until the shallots have softened and are beginning to brown.

2 Add the ghee or butter. When it has melted, add the mushrooms and fry for 2–3 minutes more.

3 Add the rice, ginger and garam masala. Stir-fry over a low heat for 2–3 minutes, then stir in the water and a little salt. Bring to the boil, then cover tightly and simmer over a very low heat for 10 minutes.

4 Remove the casserole from the heat. Leave to stand, covered, for 5 minutes. Add the chopped coriander and fork it through the rice. Spoon into a serving bowl and serve at once.

ASIA

Rice is by far the most important cereal of South-east Asia, yet each country has its own favourite style of cooking rice, and each its own distinguishing rice-based cuisine. Fried Rice from China, Nasi Goreng from Indonesia or Sushi from Japan are just some of the classic Asian rice dishes now enjoyed all over the world.

SUSHI

ONCE BARELY KNOWN OUTSIDE JAPAN, THESE TASTY ROLLS OF FLAVOURED RICE AND PAPER-THIN
SEAWEED HAVE BECOME VERY POPULAR, PARTLY DUE TO THE PROLIFERATION OF SUSHI BARS THAT HAVE
SPRUNG UP IN MANY MAJOR CITIES.

SERVES FOUR TO SIX

INGREDIENTS
For the tuna sushi
  2–3 baby carrots, blanched
  3 sheets nori (paper-thin seaweed),
   cut in half
  115g/4oz fresh tuna fillet, cut into
   fingers
  5ml/1 tsp thin wasabi paste
   (Japanese horseradish mustard)
For the salmon sushi
  2 eggs
  10ml/2 tsp granulated sugar
  2.5ml/½ tsp salt
  10ml/2 tsp butter
  3 sheets nori
  150g/5oz fresh salmon fillet, cut into
   fingers
  ½ small cucumber, cut into strips
  5ml/1 tsp thin wasabi paste
For the sushi rice
  450g/1lb/4 cups sushi rice, rinsed
  about 650ml/22fl oz/2¾ cups water
For the sushi dressing
  60ml/4 tbsp rice vinegar
  15ml/1 tbsp sugar
  2.5ml/½ tsp salt
To serve
  sliced pickled ginger, cut in strips
  wasabi paste, thinned with water
  Japanese sushi soy sauce

1 Place the rice in a heavy pan and add 650ml/22fl oz/2¾ cups water or according to the instructions on the packet. Bring to the boil, cover tightly and cook over a very low heat for 15 minutes. Increase the heat to high for 10 seconds, then remove from the heat and let stand for 10 minutes. Meanwhile, blend together the rice vinegar, sugar and salt.

2 Stir the sushi dressing into the rice, then cover with a damp cloth and cool. Do not put in the fridge as this will make the rice go hard.

3 To make the tuna sushi, cut the carrots into thin strips. Cut one nori sheet in half and lay one half, shiny side down, on a bamboo rolling mat. Lay strips of tuna across the length of the nori and spread with a little wasabi. Place a line of carrots next to the tuna and, using the mat as a guide, roll up tightly. Repeat with the other half of nori. Set aside any extra tuna or carrot.

4 Place a square of greaseproof paper on the bamboo mat and spread with a little of the cooled sushi rice, leaving a 1cm/½in edge at the top and bottom.

5 Place the tuna-filled nori roll on top, about 2.5cm/1in from the edge of the rice, and roll up, using the paper as a guide (and making sure it doesn't get rolled up with the rice). Wrap the roll in greaseproof paper and chill for about 10 minutes. Make another sushi roll using the other tuna-filled nori roll.

6 To make the salmon sushi, beat together the eggs with 30ml/2 tbsp water and the sugar and salt. Melt about one-third of the butter in a small frying pan and add one-third of the egg mixture to make an omelette. Repeat until you have three small omelettes.

7 Place a nori sheet, shiny side down, on a bamboo rolling mat, cover with an omelette and spread with sushi rice, leaving a 1cm/½in edge at the top and bottom. Lay strips of salmon across the width and lay cucumber strips next to the salmon. Spread a little wasabi paste over the salmon. Roll the nori around the filling. Wrap in clear film and chill for 10 minutes. Repeat to make three rolls.

8 When the rolls are cool, remove the greaseproof paper and clear film. Using a wet knife, cut the rolls into six slices. Serve with pickled ginger, wasabi and Japanese sushi soy sauce.

RICE OMELETTE

RICE OMELETTES MAKE A GREAT SUPPER DISH. IN JAPAN, THEY ARE A FAVOURITE WITH CHILDREN, WHO USUALLY TOP THEM WITH A LIBERAL HELPING OF TOMATO KETCHUP.

SERVES FOUR

INGREDIENTS

1 skinless, boneless chicken thigh, about 115g/4oz, cubed
40ml/8 tsp butter
1 small onion, chopped
½ carrot, diced
2 shiitake mushrooms, stems removed and chopped
15ml/1 tbsp finely chopped fresh parsley
225g/8oz/2 cups cooked long grain white rice
30ml/2 tbsp tomato ketchup
6 eggs, lightly beaten
60ml/4 tbsp milk
5ml/1 tsp salt, plus extra to season
freshly ground black pepper
tomato ketchup, to serve

1 Season the chicken with salt and pepper. Melt 10ml/2 tsp butter in a frying pan. Fry the onion for 1 minute, then add the chicken and fry until the cubes are white and cooked. Add the carrot and mushrooms, stir-fry over a medium heat until soft, then add the parsley. Set this mixture aside. Wipe the frying pan with kitchen paper.

2 Melt a further 10ml/2 tsp butter in the frying pan, add the rice and stir well. Mix in the fried ingredients, ketchup and pepper. Stir well, adding salt to taste, if necessary. Keep the mixture warm. Beat the eggs with the milk in a bowl. Stir in the measured salt and add pepper to taste.

3 Melt 5ml/1 tsp of the remaining butter in an omelette pan. Pour in a quarter of the egg mixture and stir it briefly with a fork, then allow it to set for 1 minute. Top with a quarter of the rice mixture.

4 Fold the omelette over the rice and slide it to the edge of the pan to shape it into a curve. Slide it on to a warmed plate, cover with kitchen paper and press neatly into a rectangular shape. Keep hot while cooking three more omelettes from the remaining ingredients. Serve immediately, with tomato ketchup.

CHICKEN AND MUSHROOM DONBURI

"Donburi" means a one-dish meal that is eaten from a bowl, and takes its name from the eponymous Japanese porcelain food bowl. As in most Japanese dishes, the rice here is completely plain but is nevertheless an integral part of the dish.

SERVES FOUR

INGREDIENTS

  10ml/2 tsp groundnut oil
  50g/2oz/4 tbsp butter
  2 garlic cloves, crushed
  2.5cm/1in piece of fresh root ginger,
    grated
  5 spring onions, diagonally sliced
  1 green fresh chilli, seeded and
    finely sliced
  3 skinless, boneless chicken breasts,
    cut into thin strips
  150g/5oz tofu, cut into small cubes
  115g/4oz/1¾ shiitake mushrooms,
    stalks discarded and cups sliced
  15ml/1 tbsp Japanese rice wine
  30ml/2 tbsp light soy sauce
  10ml/2 tsp granulated sugar
  400ml/14fl oz/1⅔ cups chicken stock
For the rice
  225–275g/8–10oz/generous
    1–1½ cups Japanese rice or Thai
    fragrant rice

1 Cook the rice by the absorption method or by following the instructions on the packet.

2 While the rice is cooking, heat the oil and half the butter in a large frying pan. Stir-fry the garlic, ginger, spring onions and chilli for 1–2 minutes until slightly softened. Add the strips of chicken and fry, in batches if necessary, until all the pieces are evenly browned.

3 Transfer the chicken mixture to a plate and add the tofu to the pan. Stir-fry for a few minutes, then add the mushrooms. Stir-fry for 2–3 minutes over a medium heat until the mushrooms are tender.

4 Stir in the rice wine, soy sauce and sugar and cook briskly for 1–2 minutes, stirring all the time. Return the chicken to the pan, toss over the heat for about 2 minutes, then pour in the stock. Stir well and cook over a gentle heat for 5–6 minutes until bubbling.

5 Spoon the rice into individual serving bowls and pile the chicken mixture on top, making sure that each portion gets a generous amount of chicken sauce.

COOK'S TIP
Once the rice is cooked, leave it covered until ready to serve. It will stay warm for about 30 minutes. Fork through lightly just before serving.

CHINESE FRIED RICE

THIS DISH, A VARIATION ON SPECIAL FRIED RICE, IS MORE ELABORATE THAN THE MORE FAMILIAR EGG FRIED RICE, AND IS ALMOST A MEAL IN ITSELF.

SERVES FOUR

INGREDIENTS
50g/2oz cooked ham
50g/2oz cooked prawns, peeled
3 eggs
5ml/1 tsp salt
2 spring onions, finely chopped
60ml/4 tbsp vegetable oil
115g/4oz/1 cup green peas, thawed
    if frozen
15ml/1 tbsp light soy sauce
15ml/1 tbsp Chinese rice wine or dry
    sherry
450g/1lb/4 cups cooked white long
    grain rice

1 Dice the cooked ham finely. Pat the cooked prawns dry on kitchen paper.

2 In a bowl, beat the eggs with a pinch of salt and a few spring onion pieces.

VARIATIONS
This is a versatile recipe and is ideal for using up leftovers. Use cooked chicken or turkey instead of the ham, doubling the quantity if you omit the prawns.

3 Heat about half the oil in a wok, stir-fry the peas, prawns and ham for 1 minute, then add the soy sauce and rice wine or sherry. Transfer to a bowl and keep hot.

4 Heat the remaining oil in the wok and scramble the eggs lightly. Add the rice and stir to make sure that the grains are separate. Add the remaining salt, the remaining spring onions and the prawn mixture. Toss over the heat to mix. Serve hot or cold.

STIR-FRIED RICE AND VEGETABLES

THE GINGER GIVES THIS ORIENTAL DISH A WONDERFUL FLAVOUR. SERVE IT AS A VEGETARIAN MAIN COURSE OR AS AN UNUSUAL VEGETABLE ACCOMPANIMENT.

SERVES FOUR AS AN ACCOMPANIMENT

INGREDIENTS
 115g/4oz/generous ½ cup brown
   basmati rice, rinsed and drained
 350ml/12fl oz/1½ cups vegetable stock
 2.5cm/1in piece of fresh root ginger,
   finely sliced
 1 garlic clove, halved
 5cm/2in piece of pared lemon rind
 115g/4oz/1½ cups shiitake mushrooms
 15ml/1 tbsp groundnut oil
 15ml/1 tbsp ghee or butter
 175g/6oz baby carrots, trimmed
 225g/8oz baby courgettes, halved
 175–225g/6–8oz/about 1½ cups
   broccoli, broken into florets
 6 spring onions, diagonally sliced
 15ml/1 tbsp light soy sauce
 10ml/2 tsp toasted sesame oil

1 Put the rice in a saucepan and pour in the stock. Add the ginger, garlic and lemon rind. Slowly bring to the boil, then cover and cook very gently for 20–25 minutes until the rice is tender. Discard the flavourings and keep the pan covered so that the rice stays warm.

2 Slice the mushrooms, discarding the stems. Heat the oil and ghee or butter in a wok and stir-fry the carrots for 4–5 minutes until partially tender. Add the mushrooms and courgettes, stir-fry for 2–3 minutes, then add the broccoli and spring onions and cook for 3 minutes more, by which time all the vegetables should be tender but should still retain a bit of "bite".

3 Add the cooked rice to the vegetables, and toss briefly over the heat to mix and heat through. Toss with the soy sauce and sesame oil. Spoon into a bowl and serve immediately.

CRACKLING RICE PAPER FISH ROLLS

THE RICE IN THIS DISH IS IN THE RICE PAPER WRAPPERS, WHICH MANAGE TO HOLD THEIR SHAPE DURING COOKING, YET ALMOST MAGICALLY DISSOLVE IN YOUR MOUTH WHEN IT COMES TO EATING.

MAKES TWELVE

INGREDIENTS
 12 Vietnamese rice paper sheets
   (bahn trang), each about 20 x
   10cm/8 x 4in
 45ml/3 tbsp plain flour mixed to
   a paste with 45ml/3 tbsp water
 vegetable oil, for deep-frying
 fresh herbs, to garnish
For the filling
 24 young asparagus spears, trimmed
 225g/8oz raw prawns, peeled and
   deveined
 25ml/1½ tbsp olive oil
 6 spring onions, finely chopped
 1 garlic clove, crushed
 2cm/¾in piece of fresh root ginger,
   grated
 30ml/2 tbsp chopped fresh coriander
 5ml/1 tsp five-spice powder
 5ml/1 tsp finely grated lime or lemon
   rind
 salt and freshly ground black pepper

1 Make the filling. Bring a saucepan of lightly salted water to the boil and cook the asparagus for 3–4 minutes until tender. Drain, refresh under cold water and drain again. Cut the prawns into 2cm/¾in pieces.

2 Heat half of the oil in a small frying pan or wok and stir-fry the spring onions and garlic over a low heat for 2–3 minutes until soft. Using a slotted spoon, transfer the vegetables to a bowl and set aside.

3 Heat the remaining oil in the pan and stir-fry the prawns over a brisk heat for just a few seconds until they start to go pink. Add to the spring onion mixture with the ginger, coriander, five-spice powder, lime or lemon rind and a little pepper. Stir to mix.

4 To make each roll, brush a sheet of rice paper liberally with water and lay it on a clean surface. Place two asparagus spears and a spoonful of the prawn mixture just off centre. Fold in the sides and roll up to make a fat cigar. Seal the ends with a little of the flour paste.

5 Heat the oil in a wok or deep-fryer and fry the rolls in batches until pale golden in colour. Drain well, garnish with herbs and serve.

MALACCA FRIED RICE

THERE ARE MANY VERSIONS OF THIS DISH THROUGHOUT ASIA, ALL BASED UPON LEFTOVER COOKED RICE. INGREDIENTS VARY ACCORDING TO WHAT IS AVAILABLE, BUT PRAWNS ARE A POPULAR ADDITION.

SERVES FOUR TO SIX

INGREDIENTS
  2 eggs
  45ml/3 tbsp vegetable oil
  4 shallots or 1 onion, finely chopped
  5ml/1 tsp chopped fresh root ginger
  1 garlic clove, crushed
  225g/8oz raw prawns, peeled and
    deveined
  5ml/1 tsp chilli sauce (optional)
  3 spring onions, green part only,
    roughly chopped
  225g/8oz/2 cups frozen peas
  225g/8oz thickly sliced roast pork,
    diced
  45ml/3 tbsp light soy sauce
  350g/12oz/3 cups cooked white long
    grain rice, cooled
  salt and freshly ground black pepper

1 In a bowl, beat the eggs well with salt and freshly ground black pepper to taste. Heat 15ml/1 tbsp of the oil in a large, non-stick frying pan, pour in the eggs and cook until set, without stirring. This will take less than a minute. Roll up the pancake, slide it on to a plate, cut into thin strips and set aside.

COOK'S TIP
You don't have to wait until the day after you've served a Sunday roast to try this. Most delicatessens sell sliced roast pork.

2 Heat the remaining vegetable oil in a preheated wok, add the shallots or onion, ginger, garlic and prawns, and cook for 1–2 minutes, taking care that the garlic does not burn.

3 Add the chilli sauce, if using, the spring onions, peas, pork and soy sauce. Stir to heat through, then add the rice. Fry over a medium heat for 6–8 minutes. Spoon into a dish, decorate with the pancake strips and serve immediately.

CHINESE JEWELLED RICE

ANOTHER FRIED RICE MEDLEY, THIS TIME WITH CRAB MEAT AND WATER CHESTNUTS, PROVIDING CONTRASTING TEXTURES AND FLAVOURS.

SERVES FOUR

INGREDIENTS
  350g/12oz/1¾ cups white long grain rice
  45ml/3 tbsp vegetable oil
  1 onion, roughly chopped
  4 dried black Chinese mushrooms, soaked for 10 minutes in warm water to cover
  115g/4oz cooked ham, diced
  175g/6oz drained canned white crab meat
  75g/3oz/½ cup drained canned water chestnuts
  115g/4oz/1 cup peas, thawed if frozen
  30ml/2 tbsp oyster sauce
  5ml/1 tsp granulated sugar
  salt

1 Rinse the rice, then cook for about 10–12 minutes in a saucepan of lightly salted boiling water. Drain, refresh under cold water, drain again and allow to cool. Heat half the oil in a wok. When very hot, stir-fry the rice for 3 minutes. Transfer the cooked rice to a bowl and set aside.

2 Heat the remaining oil in the wok and cook the onion until softened but not coloured. Drain the mushrooms, cut off and discard the stems, then chop the caps.

3 Add the chopped mushrooms to the wok, with all the remaining ingredients except the rice. Stir-fry for 2 minutes, then add the rice and stir-fry for about 3 minutes more. Serve at once.

COOK'S TIP
When adding the oil to the hot wok, drizzle it in a "necklace" just below the rim. As it runs down, it will coat the inner surface as it heats.

THAI RICE

THIS IS A LOVELY, SOFT, FLUFFY RICE DISH, PERFUMED WITH FRESH LEMON GRASS AND LIMES.

INGREDIENTS

2 limes
1 lemon grass stalk
225g/8oz/generous 1 cup brown long
   grain rice
15ml/1 tbsp olive oil
1 onion, chopped
2.5cm/1in piece of fresh root ginger,
   peeled and finely chopped
7.5ml/1½ tsp coriander seeds
7.5ml/1½ tsp cumin seeds
750ml/1¼ pints/3 cups vegetable stock
60ml/4 tbsp chopped fresh coriander
spring onion green, toasted coconut
   strips and lime wedges, to serve

1 Pare the limes using a canelle knife or a fine grater, taking care to avoid cutting the bitter pith. Set aside the rind. Finely chop the lower portion of the lemon grass stalk and set aside.

2 Rinse the rice in plenty of cold water until the water runs clear. Tip into a sieve and drain thoroughly.

3 Heat the oil in a saucepan. Add the onion, ginger, spices, lemon grass and lime rind and fry gently over a low heat for 2–3 minutes.

4 Add the drained rice and cook for 1 minute, then pour in the stock and bring to the boil. Reduce the heat to very low and cover the pan. Cook gently for 30 minutes, then check the rice. If it is still crunchy, cover the pan and leave for 3–5 minutes more. Remove from the heat.

5 Stir in the fresh coriander, fluff up the grains, cover and leave for about 10 minutes. Garnish with spring onion green and toasted coconut strips, and serve with lime wedges.

THAI FRIED RICE

THIS SUBSTANTIAL DISH IS BASED ON THAI FRAGRANT RICE, WHICH IS SOMETIMES KNOWN AS JASMINE RICE. CHICKEN, RED PEPPER AND SWEETCORN ADD COLOUR AND EXTRA FLAVOUR.

SERVES FOUR

INGREDIENTS
475ml/16fl oz/2 cups water
50g/2oz/½ cup coconut milk powder
350g/12oz/1¾ cups Thai fragrant rice, rinsed
30ml/2 tbsp groundnut oil
2 garlic cloves, chopped
1 small onion, finely chopped
2.5cm/1in piece of fresh root ginger, grated
225g/8oz skinless, boneless chicken breasts, cut into 1cm/½in dice
1 red pepper, seeded and sliced
115g/4oz/1 cup drained canned sweetcorn kernels
5ml/1 tsp chilli oil
5ml/1 tsp hot curry powder
2 eggs, beaten
salt
spring onion shreds, to garnish

3 Push the vegetables to the sides of the wok, add the chicken to the centre and stir-fry for 2 minutes. Add the rice and stir-fry over a high heat for about 3 minutes more.

4 Stir in the sliced red pepper, sweetcorn, chilli oil and curry powder, with salt to taste. Toss over the heat for 1 minute. Stir in the beaten eggs and cook for 1 minute more. Garnish with spring onion shreds and serve.

1 Pour the water into a saucepan and whisk in the coconut milk powder. Add the rice, bring to the boil. Lower the heat, cover and cook for 12 minutes or until the rice is tender and the liquid has been absorbed. Spread the rice on a baking sheet and leave until cold.

2 Heat the oil in a wok, add the garlic, onion and ginger and stir-fry over a medium heat for 2 minutes.

COOK'S TIP
It is important that the rice is completely cold before being fried and the oil is very hot, or the rice will absorb too much oil.

EXOTIC FRUIT AND VEGETABLE SALAD

THIS IS A VARIATION ON THE FAMOUS INDONESIAN SALAD KNOWN AS GADO GADO. CHOOSE SOME OR ALL OF THE SUGGESTED FRUITS AND VEGETABLES TO MAKE AN ATTRACTIVE CENTREPIECE FOR AN INDONESIAN OR THAI MEAL.

SERVES SIX TO EIGHT

INGREDIENTS
  115g/4oz green beans, trimmed
  2 carrots, cut into batons
  115g/4oz/2 cups bean sprouts
  ¼ head Chinese leaves, shredded
  ½ small cucumber, cut into thin strips
  8 spring onions, sliced diagonally
  6 cherry tomatoes or small tomatoes,
    halved
  12–16 cooked tiger prawns
  1 small mango
  1 small papaya
  1 quantity Lontong (compressed rice)
  4 hard-boiled eggs, quartered
  fresh coriander
For the peanut dressing
  120ml/8 tbsp crunchy or smooth
    peanut butter, preferably unsalted
  1 garlic clove, crushed
  300ml/½ pint/1¼ cups coconut milk
  15ml/1 tbsp tamarind water (see
    Cook's Tip) or juice of ½ lemon
  15–30ml/1–2 tbsp light soy sauce
  hot chilli sauce, to taste

1 First, make the peanut dressing. Place all the ingredients except the chilli sauce in a pan and heat the mixture, stirring all the time, until it is very hot and smooth. Stir in chilli sauce to taste. Keep the dressing warm, or allow to cool and reheat before serving.

2 Cook the beans and carrots in boiling water for 3–4 minutes until just tender but still firm. Drain, then refresh under cold water and drain again. Cook the bean sprouts in boiling water for 2 minutes, then drain and refresh.

3 Arrange the carrots, beans and bean sprouts on a large, attractive platter, with the shredded Chinese leaves, cucumber strips, spring onions, tomatoes, and prawns.

4 Peel the mango and cut the flesh into cubes. Quarter the papaya, remove the skin and seeds, then slice the flesh. Add to the salad platter, with the lontong. Garnish with the egg quarters and fresh coriander.

5 Reheat the peanut dressing, if necessary. As soon as it is warm, pour it into a serving bowl. Place the bowl in the centre of the salad and serve. Guests help themselves to the salad, adding as much dressing as they like.

COOK'S TIP
To make tamarind water, break off a 2.5cm/1in cube of tamarind and put it in a bowl. Pour in 150ml/¼ pint/⅔ cup warm water. Using your fingers, squeeze the tamarind so that the juices dissolve into the water. Strain, discarding the solid tamarind, and use as directed in the recipe. Any unused tamarind water can be kept in a container in the fridge for up to 1 week.

FESTIVE RICE

THIS PRETTY THAI DISH IS TRADITIONALLY SHAPED INTO A CONE AND SURROUNDED BY A VARIETY OF ACCOMPANIMENTS BEFORE BEING SERVED.

SERVES EIGHT

INGREDIENTS
    450g/1lb/2⅓ cups Thai fragrant rice
    60ml/4 tbsp oil
    2 garlic cloves, crushed
    2 onions, finely sliced
    2.5ml/½ tsp ground turmeric
    750ml/1¼ pints/3 cups water
    400ml/14fl oz can coconut milk
    1–2 lemon grass stalks, bruised
For the accompaniments
    omelette strips
    2 fresh red chillies, shredded
    cucumber chunks
    tomato wedges
    deep-fried onions
    prawn crackers

1 Put the rice in a strainer and rinse thoroughly under cold water. Drain well.

2 Heat the oil in a frying pan which has a lid. Fry the garlic, onions and turmeric over a low heat for a few minutes, until the onions are softened but not browned. Add the rice and stir well so that each grain is coated in oil.

3 Pour in the water and coconut milk and add the lemon grass. Bring to the boil, stirring well. Cover the pan and cook gently for 12 minutes, or until all the liquid has been absorbed.

COOK'S TIP
Look out for fresh turmeric at Asian markets or food stores.

4 Remove the pan from the heat and lift the lid. Cover with a clean dish towel, replace the lid and leave to stand in a warm place for 15 minutes. Remove the lemon grass, mound the rice mixture in a cone on a serving platter and garnish with the accompaniments. Serve immediately.

THAI CRISPY NOODLES WITH BEEF

RICE VERMICELLI ARE VERY FINE, DRY, WHITE NOODLES BUNDLED IN LARGE FRAGILE LOOPS AND SOLD IN PACKETS. THEY ARE DEEP-FRIED BEFORE BEING ADDED TO THIS DISH, AND IN THE PROCESS THEY EXPAND TO AT LEAST FOUR TIMES THEIR ORIGINAL SIZE.

SERVES FOUR

INGREDIENTS
  about 450g/1lb rump or sirloin steak
  teriyaki sauce, for sprinkling
  175g/6oz rice vermicelli
  groundnut oil for deep-frying and
    stir-frying
  8 spring onions, diagonally sliced
  2 garlic cloves, crushed
  4–5 carrots, cut into julienne strips
  1–2 fresh red chillies, seeded and
    finely sliced
  2 small courgettes, diagonally sliced
  5ml/1 tsp grated fresh root ginger
  60ml/4 tbsp white or yellow rice
    vinegar
  90ml/6 tbsp light soy sauce
  about 475ml/16fl oz/2 cups spicy
    stock

1 Beat out the steak, if necessary, to about 2.5cm/1in thick. Place in a shallow dish, brush generously with the teriyaki sauce and set aside for 2–4 hours to marinate.

2 Separate the rice vermicelli into manageable loops and spread several layers of kitchen paper on a very large plate. Add the oil to a depth of about 5cm/2in in a large wok, and heat until a strand of vermicelli cooks as soon as it is lowered into the oil.

3 Carefully add a loop of vermicelli to the oil. It should immediately expand and become opaque. Turn the noodles over so that the strands cook on both sides and then transfer the cooked noodles to the plate. Repeat the process until all the noodles are cooked. Transfer the cooked noodles to a separate wok or deep serving bowl and keep them warm while you cook the steak and vegetables.

4 Strain the oil from the wok into a heatproof bowl and set it aside. Heat 15ml/1 tbsp groundnut oil in the clean wok. When it sizzles, fry the steak for about 30 seconds on each side until browned. Transfer to a board and cut into thick slices. The meat should be well browned on the outside but still pink inside. Set aside.

5 Add a little extra oil to the wok and stir-fry the spring onions, garlic and carrots over a medium heat for 5–6 minutes until the carrots are slightly soft and have a glazed appearance. Add the chillies, courgettes and ginger and stir-fry for 1–2 minutes more.

6 Stir in the rice vinegar, soy sauce and stock. Cook for about 4 minutes until the sauce has slightly thickened. Add the steak and cook for a further 1–2 minutes (or longer, if you prefer your meat well done).

7 Pour the steak, vegetables and all the mixture over the noodles and toss lightly and carefully to mix. Serve at once.

COOK'S TIP
As soon as you add the meat mixture to the noodles, they will soften. If you wish to keep a few crispy noodles, stir some to the surface so they do not come into contact with the hot liquid.

RICE NOODLES WITH PORK

RICE NOODLES HAVE LITTLE FLAVOUR THEMSELVES BUT THEY HAVE A WONDERFUL ABILITY TO TAKE ON THE FLAVOUR OF OTHER INGREDIENTS.

SERVES FOUR TO SIX

INGREDIENTS
- 450g/1lb pork fillet
- 225g/8oz dried rice noodles
- 115g/4oz/1 cup broccoli florets
- 1 red pepper, quartered and seeded
- about 45ml/3 tbsp groundnut oil
- 2 garlic cloves, crushed
- 10 spring onions, trimmed and cut
  into 5cm/2in diagonal slices
- 1 lemon grass stalk, finely chopped
- 1–2 fresh red chillies, seeded and
  finely chopped
- 300ml/½ pint/1¼ cups coconut milk
- 15ml/1 tbsp tomato purée
- 3 kaffir lime leaves (optional)

For the marinade
- 45ml/3 tbsp light soy sauce
- 15ml/1 tbsp rice wine
- 30ml/2 tbsp groundnut oil
- 2.5cm/1in piece of fresh root ginger

1 Cut the pork into thin strips, about 2.5cm/1in long and 1cm/½in wide. Mix all the marinade ingredients in a bowl, add the pork, stir to coat and leave to marinate for about 1 hour.

2 Spread out the noodles in a shallow dish, pour over hot water to cover and soak for 20 minutes until soft. Drain. Blanch the broccoli in a small pan of boiling water for 2 minutes, then drain and refresh under cold water. Set aside.

3 Place the pepper pieces under a hot grill for a few minutes until the skin blackens and blisters. Put in a plastic bag for about 10 minutes and then, when cool enough to handle, peel away the skin and slice the flesh thinly.

4 Drain the pork, reserving the marinade. Heat 30ml/2 tbsp of the oil in a large frying pan. Stir-fry the pork, in batches if necessary, for 3–4 minutes until the meat is tender. Transfer to a plate and keep warm.

5 Add a little more oil to the pan if necessary and fry the garlic, spring onions, lemon grass and chillies over a low to medium heat for 2–3 minutes. Add the broccoli and pepper and stir-fry for a few minutes more.

6 Stir in the reserved marinade, coconut milk and tomato purée, with the kaffir lime leaves, if using. Simmer gently until the broccoli is nearly tender, then add the pork and noodles. Toss over the heat, for 3–4 minutes until completely heated through.

CHICKEN AND BASIL COCONUT RICE

FOR THIS DISH, THE RICE IS PARTIALLY BOILED BEFORE BEING SIMMERED WITH COCONUT SO THAT IT FULLY ABSORBS THE FLAVOUR OF THE CHILLIES, BASIL AND SPICES.

SERVES FOUR

INGREDIENTS

350g/12oz/1¾ cups Thai fragrant
  rice, rinsed
30–45ml/2–3 tbsp groundnut oil
1 large onion, finely sliced into rings
1 garlic clove, crushed
1 fresh red chilli, seeded and finely
  sliced
1 fresh green chilli, seeded and
  finely sliced
generous handful of basil leaves
3 skinless, boneless chicken breasts,
  about 350g/12oz, finely sliced
5mm/¼in piece of lemon grass,
  pounded or finely chopped
50g/2oz piece of creamed coconut
  dissolved in 600ml/1 pint/2½ cups
  boiling water
salt and freshly ground black pepper

1 Bring a saucepan of lightly salted water to the boil. Add the rice to the pan and boil for about 6 minutes, until partially cooked. Drain.

2 Heat the oil in a frying pan and fry the onion rings for 5–10 minutes until golden and crisp. Lift out, drain on kitchen paper and set aside.

3 Fry the garlic and chillies in the oil remaining in the pan for 2–3 minutes, then add the basil leaves and fry briefly until they begin to wilt. Remove a few leaves and set them aside for the garnish, then add the chicken slices with the lemon grass and fry for 2–3 minutes until golden.

4 Add the rice. Stir-fry for a few minutes to coat the grains, then pour in the coconut liquid. Cook for 4–5 minutes or until the rice is tender, adding a little more water if necessary. Adjust the seasoning. Pile the rice into a warmed serving dish, scatter with the fried onion rings and basil leaves, and serve immediately.

INDONESIAN PINEAPPLE RICE

THIS WAY OF PRESENTING RICE NOT ONLY LOOKS SPECTACULAR, IT ALSO TASTES SO GOOD THAT IT CAN EASILY BE SERVED SOLO.

SERVES FOUR

INGREDIENTS

75g/3oz/¾ cup natural peanuts
1 large pineapple
45ml/3 tbsp groundnut or sunflower
  oil
1 onion, chopped
1 garlic clove, crushed
2 chicken breasts, about 225g/8oz,
  cut into strips
225g/8oz/generous 1 cup Thai
  fragrant rice, rinsed
600ml/1 pint/2½ cups chicken stock
1 lemon grass stalk, bruised
2 thick slices of ham, cut into
  julienne strips
1 fresh red chilli, seeded and very
  finely sliced
salt

1 Dry-fry the peanuts in a non-stick frying pan until golden. When cool, grind one-sixth of them in a coffee or herb mill and chop the remainder.

2 Cut a lengthways slice of pineapple, slicing through the leaves, then cut out the flesh to leave a neat shell. Chop 115g/4oz of the pineapple into cubes; saving the remainder for another dish.

3 Heat the oil in a saucepan and fry the onion and garlic for 3–4 minutes until soft. Add the chicken strips and stir-fry over a medium heat for a few minutes until evenly brown.

4 Add the rice to the pan. Toss with the chicken mixture for a few minutes, then pour in the stock, with the lemon grass and a little salt. Bring to just below boiling point, then lower the heat, cover the pan and simmer gently for 10–12 minutes until both the rice and the chicken pieces are tender.

5 Stir the chopped peanuts, the pineapple cubes and the ham into the rice, then spoon the mixture into the pineapple shell. Sprinkle the ground peanuts and the sliced chilli over the top and serve.

NASI GORENG

ONE OF THE MOST POPULAR AND BEST-KNOWN INDONESIAN DISHES, THIS IS A MARVELLOUS WAY TO USE UP LEFTOVER RICE, CHICKEN AND MEATS SUCH AS PORK.

SERVES FOUR TO SIX

INGREDIENTS
   350g/12oz/1¾ cups basmati rice (dry
     weight), cooked and cooled
   2 eggs
   30ml/2 tbsp water
   105ml/7 tbsp sunflower oil
   225g/8oz pork fillet or fillet of beef
   2–3 fresh red chillies, seeded and
     sliced
   1cm/½in cube terasi (blachan)
   2 garlic cloves, crushed
   1 onion, sliced
   115g/4oz cooked, peeled prawns
   225g/8oz cooked chicken, chopped
   30ml/2 tbsp dark soy sauce
   salt and freshly ground black pepper
   deep-fried onions, to garnish

1 Separate the grains of the cold, cooked rice with a fork. Cover and set aside until needed.

COOK'S TIP
Make the terasi paste using a pestle and mortar, if you prefer.

2 Beat the eggs with the water and a little seasoning. Heat 15ml/1 tbsp of the oil in a frying pan, pour in about half the mixture and cook until set, without stirring. Roll up the omelette, slide it on to a plate, cut into strips and set aside. Make another omelette in the same way.

3 Cut the pork or beef fillet into neat strips. Finely shred one of the chillies and set aside. Put the terasi into a food processor, add the remaining chilli, the garlic and the onion. Process to a paste.

4 Heat the remaining oil in a wok. Fry the paste, without browning, until it gives off a spicy aroma. Add the strips of pork or beef and toss the meat over the heat, to seal in the juices. Cook the meat in the wok for about 2 minutes, stirring constantly.

5 Add the prawns, cook for 2 minutes, then add the chicken, rice, and soy sauce, with salt and pepper to taste, stirring constantly. Serve in individual bowls, garnished with omelette strips, shredded chilli and deep-fried onions.

INDONESIAN COCONUT RICE

THIS WAY OF COOKING RICE IS VERY POPULAR THROUGHOUT THE WHOLE OF SOUTH-EAST ASIA.
COCONUT RICE GOES PARTICULARLY WELL WITH FISH, CHICKEN AND PORK.

SERVES FOUR TO SIX

INGREDIENTS
  350g/12oz/1¾ cups Thai fragrant rice
  400ml/14fl oz can coconut milk
  300ml/½ pint/1¼ cups water
  2.5ml/½ tsp ground coriander
  5cm/2in cinnamon stick
  1 lemon grass stalk, bruised
  1 bay leaf
  salt
  deep-fried onions, to garnish

1 Put the rice in a strainer and rinse thoroughly under cold water. Drain well, then put in a pan. Pour in the coconut milk and water. Add the coriander, cinnamon stick, lemon grass and bay leaf. Season with salt. Bring to the boil, then lower the heat, cover and simmer for 8–10 minutes.

2 Lift the lid and check that all the liquid has been absorbed, then fork the rice through carefully, removing the cinnamon stick, lemon grass and bay leaf.

3 Cover the pan with a tight-fitting lid and continue to cook over the lowest possible heat for 3–5 minutes more.

4 Pile the rice on to a warm serving dish and serve garnished with the crisp, deep-fried onions.

COOK'S TIP
When bringing the rice to the boil, stir it frequently to prevent it from settling on the bottom of the pan. Once the rice is nearly tender, continue to cook over a very low heat or just leave to stand for 5 minutes. The important thing is to cover the pan tightly.

LEMON GRASS AND COCONUT RICE WITH GREEN CHICKEN CURRY

USE ONE OR TWO FRESH GREEN CHILLIES IN THIS DISH, ACCORDING TO HOW HOT YOU LIKE YOUR CURRY. THE MILD AROMATIC FLAVOUR OF THE RICE OFFSETS THE SPICINESS OF THE CURRY.

SERVES THREE TO FOUR

INGREDIENTS
- 4 spring onions, trimmed and roughly chopped
- 1–2 fresh green chillies, seeded and roughly chopped
- 2cm/¾in piece of fresh root ginger, peeled
- 2 garlic cloves
- 5ml/1 tsp Thai fish sauce
- large bunch of fresh coriander
- small handful of fresh parsley
- 30–45ml/2–3 tbsp water
- 30ml/2 tbsp sunflower oil
- 4 skinless, boneless chicken breasts, cubed
- 1 green pepper, seeded and finely sliced
- 75g/3oz piece of creamed coconut dissolved in 400ml/14fl oz/1⅔ cups boiling water
- salt and freshly ground black pepper

For the rice
- 225g/8oz/generous 1 cup Thai fragrant rice, rinsed
- 75g/3oz piece of creamed coconut dissolved in 400ml/14fl oz/1⅔ cups boiling water
- 1 lemon grass stalk, quartered and bruised

1 Put the spring onions, chillies, ginger, garlic, fish sauce and fresh herbs in a food processor or blender. Pour in the water and process to a smooth paste.

2 Heat half the oil in large frying pan. Fry the chicken cubes until evenly browned. Transfer to a plate.

3 Heat the remaining oil in the pan. Stir-fry the green pepper for 3–4 minutes, then add the chilli and ginger paste. Fry, stirring, for 3–4 minutes until the mixture becomes fairly thick.

4 Return the chicken to the pan and add the coconut liquid. Season and bring to the boil, then lower the heat; half cover the pan and simmer for 8–10 minutes.

5 When the chicken is cooked, transfer it with the peppers to a plate. Boil the cooking liquid remaining in the pan for 10–12 minutes until it is well reduced and fairly thick.

6 Meanwhile, put the rice in a large saucepan. Add the coconut liquid and the bruised pieces of lemon grass. Stir in a little salt, bring to the boil, then lower the heat, cover and simmer very gently for 10 minutes, or for the time recommended on the packet. When the rice is tender, discard the pieces of lemon grass and fork the rice on to a warmed serving plate.

7 Return the chicken and peppers to the green curry sauce, stir well and cook gently for a few minutes to heat through. Spoon the curry over the rice, and serve immediately.

COOK'S TIP
Lemon grass features in many Asian dishes, and makes the perfect partner for coconut, especially when used with chicken. In this recipe, bruise the tough, top end of the lemon grass stem in a pestle and mortar before use.

COCONUT CREAM DESSERT

USE THAI FRAGRANT RICE FOR THIS DISH. DESSERTS LIKE THESE ARE SERVED IN COUNTRIES ALL OVER THE FAR EAST, OFTEN WITH MANGOES, PINEAPPLE OR GUAVAS. ALTHOUGH COMMERCIALLY GROUND RICE CAN BE USED FOR THIS DISH, GRINDING THE RICE YOURSELF — IN A FOOD PROCESSOR — GIVES A MUCH BETTER RESULT.

SERVES FOUR TO SIX

INGREDIENTS
  75g/3oz/scant ½ cup Thai fragrant
    rice, soaked overnight in 175ml/
    6fl oz/¾ cup water
  350ml/12fl oz/1½ cups coconut milk
  150ml/¼ pint/⅔ cup single cream
  50g/2oz/¼ cup caster sugar
  fresh raspberries and mint leaves, to
    decorate
For the coulis
  75g/3oz/¾ cup blackcurrants, stalks
    removed
  30ml/2 tbsp caster sugar
  75g/3oz/½ cup fresh or frozen
    raspberries

1 Put the rice and its soaking water into a food processor and process for a few minutes until the mixture is soupy.

2 Heat the coconut milk and cream in a non-stick saucepan. When the mixture is on the point of boiling, stir in the rice mixture.

3 Cook over a very gentle heat for 10 minutes, stirring constantly, then stir in the sugar and continue cooking for 10–15 minutes more, or until the mixture is thick and creamy.

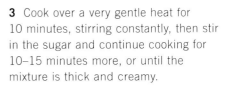

4 Pour the rice mixture into a rectangular pan that has been lined with non-stick baking paper. Cool, then chill in the fridge until the pudding is firm.

5 To make the coulis, put the blackcurrants in a bowl and sprinkle with the sugar. Set aside for about 30 minutes. Tip into a wire sieve with the raspberries and press the fruit against the sides of the sieve so that the juices collect in a bowl underneath. Taste and add more sugar if necessary.

6 Carefully cut the coconut cream into diamonds. Spoon a little of the coulis on to each dessert plate, arrange the coconut cream diamonds on top and decorate with fresh raspberries and mint leaves.

THAI RICE CAKE

NOT A DRY SNACK FROM THE HEALTH FOOD SHOP, BUT A SUMPTUOUS CELEBRATION GATEAU, MADE FROM THAI FRAGRANT RICE, TANGY CREAM AND WITH A FRESH FRUIT TOPPING.

SERVES EIGHT TO TEN

INGREDIENTS
    225g/8oz/generous 1 cup Thai
       fragrant rice, rinsed
    1 litre/1¾ pints/4 cups milk
    115g/4oz/scant ½ cup caster sugar
    6 green cardamom pods, crushed
    2 bay leaves
    300ml/½ pint/1¼ cups whipping
       cream
    6 eggs, separated
    red and white currants, sliced star
       fruit and kiwi fruit, to decorate
For the topping
    250ml/8fl oz/1 cup double cream
    150g/5oz/⅔ cup Quark or low-fat soft
       cheese
    5ml/1 tsp vanilla essence
    grated rind of 1 lemon
    40g/1½oz/3 tbsp caster sugar

1 Grease and line a 25cm/10in round, deep cake tin. Cook the rice in a pan of boiling unsalted water for 3 minutes, then drain, return to the pan and pour in the milk. Stir in the caster sugar, cardamoms and bay leaves. Bring to the boil, then lower the heat and simmer the rice for 20 minutes, stirring occasionally. Allow the mixture to cool, then remove the bay leaves and cardamom husks.

2 Preheat the oven to 180°C/350°F/ Gas 4. Spoon the rice mixture into a bowl. Beat in the cream and then the egg yolks. Whisk the egg whites until they form soft peaks, then fold them into the rice mixture.

3 Spoon into the prepared tin and bake for 45–50 minutes until risen and golden brown. Chill overnight in the tin. Turn the cake out on to a large serving plate.

4 Whip the cream until stiff, then gently fold in the Quark or soft cheese, vanilla essence, lemon rind and sugar.

5 Cover the top of the cake with the cream mixture, swirling it attractively. Decorate with red and white currants, sliced star fruit and kiwi fruit.

COOK'S TIP
Do not worry if the centre of the cake is slightly wobbly when you take it out of the oven. It will firm up as the cake starts to cool.

GREECE, TURKEY AND THE MIDDLE EAST

The people of the Middle East learned about rice from their eastern neighbours and have loved it ever since: rice is almost as much of a staple here as it is in parts of Asia. Rich Arabian spices and luscious Mediterranean produce are the inspiration for the feast of dishes from this region — many of which are now world classics.

AVGOLEMONO

THIS IS A GREAT FAVOURITE IN GREECE AND IS A FINE EXAMPLE OF HOW A FEW INGREDIENTS CAN MAKE A MARVELLOUS DISH IF CAREFULLY CHOSEN AND COOKED. IT IS ESSENTIAL TO USE A WELL-FLAVOURED STOCK. ADD AS LITTLE OR AS MUCH RICE AS YOU LIKE.

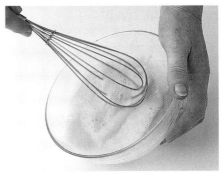

2 Whisk the egg yolks in a bowl, then add about 30ml/2 tbsp of the lemon juice, whisking constantly until the mixture is smooth and bubbly. Add a ladleful of soup and whisk again.

3 Remove the soup from the heat and slowly add the egg mixture, whisking all the time. The soup will turn a pretty lemon colour and will thicken slightly.

4 Taste and add more lemon juice if necessary. Stir in the parsley. Serve at once, without reheating, garnished with lemon slices and parsley sprigs.

SERVES FOUR

INGREDIENTS
  900ml/1½ pints/3¾ cups chicken
    stock, preferably home-made
  50g/2oz/generous ⅓ cup long grain
    rice
  3 egg yolks
  30–60ml/2–4 tbsp lemon juice
  30ml/2 tbsp finely chopped fresh
    parsley
  salt and freshly ground black pepper
  lemon slices and parsley sprigs,
    to garnish

1 Pour the stock into a pan, bring to simmering point, then add the drained rice. Half cover and cook for about 12 minutes until the rice is just tender. Season with salt and pepper.

COOK'S TIP
The trick here is to add the egg mixture to the soup without it curdling. Avoid whisking the mixture into boiling liquid. It is safest to remove the soup from the heat entirely and then whisk in the mixture in a slow but steady stream. Do not reheat as curdling would be almost inevitable.

DOLMADES

NOW POPULAR THE WORLD OVER, THESE STUFFED VINE LEAVES ORIGINATED IN GREECE. IF YOU CAN'T LOCATE FRESH VINE LEAVES, USE A PACKET OR CAN OF BRINED VINE LEAVES. SOAK THE LEAVES IN HOT WATER FOR 20 MINUTES, THEN RINSE AND DRY WELL ON KITCHEN PAPER BEFORE USE.

MAKES 20 TO 24

INGREDIENTS

24–28 fresh young vine leaves,
  soaked
30ml/2 tbsp olive oil
1 large onion, finely chopped
1 garlic clove, crushed
225g/8oz/2 cups cooked long grain
  rice, or mixed white and wild rice
about 45ml/3 tbsp pine nuts
15ml/1 tbsp flaked almonds
40g/1½oz/¼ cup sultanas
15ml/1 tbsp snipped fresh chives
15ml/1 tbsp finely chopped fresh
  mint
juice of ½ lemon
150ml/¼ pint/⅔ cup white wine
hot vegetable stock
salt and freshly ground black pepper
fresh mint sprig, to garnish
garlic yogurt and pitta bread,
  to serve (optional)

1 Bring a large pan of water to the boil and cook the vine leaves for about 2–3 minutes. They will darken and go limp after about 1 minute and simmering for a further minute or so will ensure they are pliable. If using leaves from a packet or can, place them in a large bowl, cover with boiling water and leave for a few minutes until the leaves can be easily separated. Rinse them under cold water and drain on kitchen paper.

2 Heat the oil in a small frying pan and fry the onion and garlic for 3–4 minutes over a gentle heat until soft. Spoon the mixture into a large bowl and add the cooked rice.

3 Stir in 30ml/2 tbsp of the pine nuts, the almonds, sultanas, chives and mint. Squeeze in the lemon juice. Add salt and pepper to taste and mix well.

4 Set aside four large vine leaves. Lay a vine leaf on a clean work surface, veined side uppermost. Place a spoonful of filling near the stem, fold the lower part of the vine leaf over it and roll up, folding in the sides as you go. Stuff the rest of the vine leaves in the same way.

5 Line the base of a deep frying pan with the reserved vine leaves. Place the dolmades close together in the pan, seam side down, in a single layer. Pour over the wine and enough stock to just cover. Anchor the dolmades by placing a plate on top of them, then cover the pan and simmer gently for 30 minutes.

6 Transfer the dolmades to a plate. Cool, chill, then garnish with the remaining pine nuts and the mint. Serve with a little garlic yogurt and pitta bread, if you like.

COOK'S TIP
Check the pan frequently when cooking the dolmades, to make sure that the pan does not boil dry.

GREEK PICNIC PIE

AUBERGINES LAYERED WITH SPINACH, FETA CHEESE AND RICE MAKE A MARVELLOUS FILLING FOR A PIE THAT IS PERFECT FOR PICNICS. IT CAN BE SERVED WARM OR COLD AND MAKES A GOOD VEGETARIAN DISH FOR A BUFFET LUNCH.

SERVES SIX

INGREDIENTS
    375g/13oz shortcrust pastry, thawed
       if frozen
    45–60ml/3–4 tbsp olive oil
    1 large aubergine, sliced into rounds
    1 onion, chopped
    1 garlic clove, crushed
    175g/6oz spinach, washed
    4 eggs
    75g/3oz/½ cup crumbled feta cheese
    40g/1½oz/½ cup freshly grated
       Parmesan cheese
    60ml/4 tbsp natural yogurt
    90ml/6 tbsp creamy milk
    225g/8oz/2 cups cooked white or
       brown long grain rice
    salt and freshly ground black pepper

1 Preheat the oven to 180°C/350°F/Gas 4. Roll out the pastry thinly and line a 25cm/10in flan ring. Prick the base all over and bake in the oven for 10–12 minutes until the pastry is pale golden. (Alternatively, bake blind, having lined the pastry with baking parchment and weighted it with a handful of baking beans.)

COOK'S TIP
If making your own pastry, add 5ml/1 tsp dried basil to the flour before rubbing in the butter, margarine or lard.

2 Heat 30–45ml/2–3 tbsp of the oil in a frying pan and fry the aubergine slices for 6–8 minutes on each side until golden. You may need to add a little more oil at first, but this will be released as the flesh softens. Lift out and drain on kitchen paper.

3 Add the onion and garlic to the oil remaining in the pan and fry over a gentle heat for 4–5 minutes until soft, adding a little extra oil if necessary.

4 Chop the spinach finely, by hand or in a food processor. Beat the eggs in a large mixing bowl, then add the spinach, feta, Parmesan, yogurt, milk and the onion mixture. Season well with salt and pepper and stir thoroughly to mix.

5 Spread the rice in an even layer over the bottom of the part-baked pie. Reserve a few aubergine slices for the top, and arrange the rest in an even layer over the rice.

6 Spoon the spinach and feta mixture over the aubergines and place the remaining slices on top. Bake for 30–40 minutes until lightly browned. Serve the pie warm, or cool completely before transferring to a serving plate or wrapping and packing for a picnic.

VARIATION
Courgettes could be used in place of aubergines, if you prefer. Fry the sliced courgettes in a little oil for 3–4 minutes until golden. You will need three to four medium-size courgettes, or use baby courgettes and slice them horizontally: these would look particularly attractive arranged on top of the pie.

TURKISH LAMB ON A BED OF RICE

IN TURKEY, THE TRADITIONAL WAY OF COOKING MEAT — OVER HOT CHARCOAL OR IN A WOOD-BURNING STOVE — RESULTS IN A CRUSTY, ALMOST CHARRED EXTERIOR ENCLOSING BEAUTIFULLY MOIST, TENDER MEAT. IN THIS RECIPE, THE MEAT JUICES FLAVOUR THE RICE BENEATH.

SERVES SIX

INGREDIENTS
    half leg of lamb, about
        1.5kg/3–3½lb, boned
    bunch of fresh parsley
    small bunch of fresh coriander
    50g/2oz/½ cup cashew nuts
    2 garlic cloves
    15ml/1 tbsp sunflower oil
    1 small onion, finely chopped
    200g/7oz/1¾ cups cooked white long
        grain rice
    75g/3oz/scant ½ cup ready-to-eat
        dried apricots, finely chopped
    salt and freshly ground black pepper
    fresh parsley or coriander sprigs, to
        garnish
    tzatziki, black olives and pitta bread,
        to serve (optional)

3 Crush 1 of the garlic cloves. Heat the oil in a frying pan and fry the onion and crushed garlic for 3–4 minutes until softened but not browned.

4 Put the rice in a bowl. Using a spatula, scrape all the parsley and cashew nut mixture into the rice. Add the fried onion mixture and the chopped apricots. Season with salt and pepper, stir well, then spoon into the bottom of a roasting tin, which is just large enough to hold the lamb.

5 Cut the remaining garlic clove in half and rub the cut sides over the meat. Season with pepper, then lay the meat on top of the rice, tucking all the rice under the meat, so that no rice is visible.

6 Roast the lamb for 30 minutes, then lower the oven temperature to 180°C/350°F/Gas 4. Cook for 35–45 minutes more or until the meat is cooked to your taste.

7 Cover the lamb and rice with foil and leave to rest for 5 minutes, then lift the lamb on to a board and slice it thickly. Spoon the rice mixture on to a platter, arrange the meat slices on top and garnish with fresh parsley or coriander. Serve at once, with a bowl of tzatziki, black olives and pitta bread, if liked.

1 Preheat the oven to 200°C/400°F/Gas 6. Remove the excess fat from the lamb, then trim the joint, if necessary, so that it lies flat. (If the leg has been tunnel boned, you will need to cut the meat before it will lie flat.)

2 Put the parsley and coriander in a food processor or blender and process until finely chopped. Add the cashew nuts and pulse until roughly chopped.

COOK'S TIP
In Turkey, the meat would be cooked until very well done, but it can also be served slightly pink, in the French style. For a doner kebab, split warmed pitta breads (preferably home-made) and stuff with meat, yogurt and a spicy tomato sauce. Alternatively, serve this dish with rice and a broad bean salad.

YOGURT CHICKEN AND RICE CAKE

THIS MIDDLE-EASTERN SPECIALITY IS TRADITIONALLY FLAVOURED WITH SMALL, DRIED BERRIES CALLED ZERESHK, BUT IS JUST AS DELICIOUS WITH FRESH CRANBERRIES.

SERVES SIX

INGREDIENTS

40g/1½oz/3 tbsp butter
1 chicken, about 1.5kg/3–3½lb, cut into pieces
1 large onion, chopped
250ml/8fl oz/1 cup chicken stock
2 eggs, beaten
475ml/16fl oz/2 cups natural yogurt
2–3 saffron strands, dissolved in 15ml/1 tbsp warm water
5ml/1 tsp ground cinnamon
450g/1lb/2⅓ cups basmati rice, soaked
1.2 litres/2 pints/5 cups boiling water
75g/3oz/¾ cup cranberries or zereshk (see Cook's Tip)
50g/2oz/½ cup flaked almonds
salt and freshly ground black pepper

1 Melt two-thirds of the butter in a flameproof casserole. Fry the chicken pieces with the onion for 4–5 minutes, until the onion is softened and the chicken has browned. Add the stock and season with salt and pepper. Bring to the boil, lower the heat and simmer for 45 minutes, or until the chicken is cooked and the stock has reduced by half.

2 Drain the chicken, reserving the stock. Cut the flesh into large pieces, discarding the skin and bones, and place in a large bowl. In a separate bowl, mix the eggs with the yogurt. Add the saffron water and cinnamon. Season lightly. Pour over the chicken and stir to coat. Cover and leave to marinate for up to 2 hours.

3 Preheat the oven to 160°C/325°F/ Gas 3. Grease a large baking dish, about 10cm/4in deep. Drain the rice and put it in a saucepan. Add the boiling water and a little salt, bring back to the boil and then lower the heat and simmer gently for 10 minutes. Drain, rinse thoroughly in warm water and drain once more.

4 Using a slotted spoon, lift the chicken pieces out of the yogurt marinade and put them on a plate. Mix half the rice into the marinade. Spread the mixture on the bottom of the baking dish. Arrange the chicken pieces in a single layer on top, then cover evenly with about half the plain rice. Sprinkle over the cranberries or zereshk, then cover with the rest of the rice.

COOK'S TIP
If you are lucky enough to locate zereshk, wash them thoroughly before use. Heat the berries before layering them with the rice.

5 Pour the reserved chicken stock over the rice. Sprinkle with flaked almonds and dot with the remaining butter. Cover tightly with foil and bake in the oven for 35–45 minutes.

6 Leave the dish to cool for a few minutes, then place it on a cold, damp dish towel (this will help to lift the rice from the bottom of the dish). Run a knife around the inside rim of the dish. Invert a large, flat plate over the dish and turn out the rice "cake". Cut into six wedges and serve hot, with a herb and radicchio salad, if you like.

STUFFED VEGETABLES

COLOURFUL, EASY TO PREPARE AND UTTERLY DELICIOUS, THIS MAKES A POPULAR SUPPER DISH, AND WITH A CHOICE OF VEGETABLES INCLUDED IN THE RECIPE, THERE'S BOUND TO BE SOMETHING TO APPEAL TO EVERY MEMBER OF THE FAMILY.

SERVES FOUR

INGREDIENTS

1 aubergine
1 green pepper
2 beefsteak tomatoes
45ml/3 tbsp olive oil
1 onion, chopped
2 garlic cloves, crushed
115g/4oz/1–1½ cups button
  mushrooms, chopped
1 carrot, grated
225g/8oz/2 cups cooked white long
  grain rice
15ml/1 tbsp chopped fresh dill
90g/3½oz/scant ½ cup feta cheese,
  crumbled
75g/3oz/¾ cup pine nuts, lightly
  toasted
30ml/2 tbsp currants
salt and freshly ground black pepper

1 Preheat the oven to 190°C/375°F/ Gas 5. Lightly grease a shallow baking dish. Cut the aubergine in half, through the stalk, and scoop out the flesh from each half to leave two hollow "boats". Dice the aubergine flesh. Cut the pepper in half lengthways and remove the cores and seeds.

2 Cut off the tops from the tomatoes and hollow out the centres with a spoon. Chop the flesh and add it to the diced aubergine. Place the tomatoes upside down on kitchen paper to drain.

3 Bring a pan of water to the boil, add the aubergine halves and blanch for 3 minutes. Add the pepper halves to the boiling water and blanch for 3 minutes more. Drain the vegetables, then place, hollow up, in the baking dish.

4 Heat 30ml/2 tbsp oil in a saucepan and fry the onion and garlic for about 5 minutes. Stir in the diced aubergine and tomato mixture with the mushrooms and carrot. Cover, cook for 5 minutes until softened, then mix in the rice, dill, feta, pine nuts and currants. Season to taste.

5 Divide the mixture among the vegetable shells, sprinkle with the remaining olive oil and bake for 20 minutes until the topping has browned. Serve hot or cold.

PERSIAN RICE WITH A TAHDEEG

PERSIAN OR IRANIAN CUISINE IS EXOTIC AND DELICIOUS, AND THE FLAVOURS ARE INTENSE. A TAHDEEG IS THE GLORIOUS, GOLDEN RICE CRUST OR "DIG" THAT FORMS ON THE BOTTOM OF THE SAUCEPAN AS THE RICE COOKS.

SERVES SIX TO EIGHT

INGREDIENTS

   450g/1lb/2⅓ cups basmati rice,
     soaked
   150ml/¼ pint/⅔ cup sunflower oil
   2 garlic cloves, crushed
   2 onions, 1 chopped, 1 finely sliced
   150g/5oz/⅔ cup green lentils, soaked
   600ml/1 pint/2½ cups stock
   50g/2oz/⅓ cup raisins
   10ml/2 tsp ground coriander
   45ml/3 tbsp tomato purée
   a few saffron strands
   1 egg yolk, beaten
   10ml/2 tsp natural yogurt
   75g/3oz/6 tbsp melted ghee or
     clarified butter
   salt and freshly ground black pepper

1 Drain the rice, then cook it in plenty of boiling salted water for 10–12 minutes or until tender. Drain again.

2 Heat 30ml/2 tbsp of the oil in a large saucepan and fry the garlic and the chopped onion for 5 minutes. Stir in the lentils, stock, raisins, ground coriander and tomato purée, with salt and pepper to taste. Bring to the boil, then lower the heat, cover and simmer for about 20 minutes.

3 Soak the saffron strands in a little hot water. Mix the egg yolk and yogurt in a bowl. Spoon in about 120ml/4 fl oz/ ½ cup of the cooked rice and mix thoroughly. Season well.

4 Heat about two-thirds of the remaining oil in a large saucepan. Scatter the egg and yogurt rice evenly over the bottom of the pan.

COOK'S TIP
In Iran, aromatic white basmati rice would traditionally be used for this dish, but you could use any long grain rice, or a brown rice, if you prefer.

5 Scatter the remaining rice into the pan, alternating it with the lentil mixture. Build up in a pyramid shape away from the sides of the pan, finishing with a layer of plain rice. With a long wooden spoon handle, make three holes down to the bottom of the pan; drizzle over the melted ghee or butter. Bring to a high heat, then wrap the pan lid in a clean, wet dish towel and place firmly on top. When a good head of steam appears, turn the heat down to low. Cook slowly for about 30 minutes.

6 Meanwhile, fry the onion slices in the remaining oil until browned and crisp. Drain well. Remove the rice pan from the heat, keeping it covered, and plunge the base briefly into a sink of cold water to loosen the rice on the bottom. Strain the saffron water into a bowl and stir in a few spoons of the white rice.

7 Toss the rice and lentils together in the pan and spoon out on to a serving dish, mounding the mixture. Scatter the saffron rice on top. Break up the rice crust on the bottom of the pan and place pieces of it around the mound. Scatter over the crispy fried onions and serve.

ROASTED SQUASH

Gem squash has a sweet, subtle flavour that contrasts well with olives and sun-dried tomatoes in this recipe. The rice adds substance without changing any of the flavours.

2 Mix the rice, tomatoes, olives, cheese, half the olive oil and basil in a bowl.

3 Oil a shallow baking dish with the remaining oil, just large enough to hold the squash side by side. Divide the rice mixture among the squash and place them in the dish.

SERVES FOUR AS A STARTER

INGREDIENTS
    4 whole gem squashes
    225g/8oz/2 cups cooked white
      long grain rice
    75g/3oz/1½ cups sun-dried tomatoes,
      chopped
    50g/2oz/½ cup pitted black olives,
      chopped
    60ml/4 tbsp soft goat's cheese
    30ml/2 tbsp olive oil
    15ml/1 tbsp chopped fresh basil
      leaves, plus basil sprigs, to serve
    yogurt and mint dressing or green
      salad, to serve (optional)

1 Preheat the oven to 180ºC/350ºF/ Gas 4. Trim away the base of each squash, slice off the top and scoop out and discard the seeds.

4 Cover with foil and bake for 45–50 minutes until the squash is tender when pierced with a skewer. Garnish with basil sprigs and serve with a yogurt and mint dressing or with a green salad.

AUBERGINE ROLLS

AS WELL AS MAKING AN ORIGINAL STARTER, THESE LITTLE ROLLS OF AUBERGINE WRAPPED AROUND A FILLING OF RICOTTA AND RICE ARE TASTY SERVED AS PART OF A BUFFET OR FOR A TURKISH-STYLE MEZE.

SERVES FOUR

INGREDIENTS
  2 aubergines
  olive oil, for shallow frying
  75g/3oz/scant ½ cup ricotta cheese
  75g/3oz/scant ½ cup soft goat's
    cheese
  225g/8oz/2 cups cooked white long
    grain rice
  15ml/1 tbsp chopped fresh basil
  5ml/1 tsp chopped fresh mint, plus
    mint sprigs, to garnish
  salt and freshly ground black pepper
For the tomato sauce
  15ml/1 tbsp olive oil
  1 red onion, finely chopped
  1 garlic clove, crushed
  400g/14oz can chopped tomatoes
  120ml/4fl oz/½ cup chicken stock
    or white wine or a mixture
  15ml/1 tbsp chopped fresh parsley

2 Meanwhile, cut the aubergines lengthways into four or five slices. Heat the oil in a large frying pan and fry the aubergine slices in batches until they are golden brown on both sides. Drain on kitchen paper. Mix the ricotta, goat's cheese, rice, basil and mint in a bowl. Season well with salt and pepper.

3 Place a generous spoonful of the cheese and rice mixture at one end of each aubergine slice and roll up. Arrange the rolls side by side in a shallow baking dish. Pour the tomato sauce over the top and bake for 10–15 minutes until heated through. Garnish with the mint sprigs and serve.

1 Preheat the oven to 190°C/375°F/Gas 5. Make the tomato sauce. Heat the oil in a small saucepan and fry the onion and garlic for 3–4 minutes until softened. Add the tomatoes, chicken stock and wine, if using, and sprinkle in the parsley. Season with salt and pepper. Bring to the boil, then lower the heat and simmer for 10–12 minutes until slightly thickened, stirring.

COOK'S TIP
Cut off and discard the skin on the two outer slices of aubergine. If you prefer to use less oil for the aubergines, brush each slice with a little oil, then grill until evenly browned.

RICE WITH DILL AND BROAD BEANS

THIS IS A FAVOURITE RICE DISH IN IRAN, WHERE IT IS CALLED BAGHALI POLO. *THE COMBINATION OF BROAD BEANS, DILL AND WARM SPICES WORKS VERY WELL, AND THE SAFFRON RICE ADDS A SPLASH OF BRIGHT COLOUR.*

SERVES FOUR

INGREDIENTS
275g/10oz/1½ cups basmati rice,
   soaked
750ml/1¼ pints/3 cups water
40g/1½oz/3 tbsp melted butter
175g/6oz/1½ cups frozen baby broad
   beans, thawed and peeled
90ml/6 tbsp finely chopped fresh
   dill, plus 1 fresh dill sprig, to
   garnish
5ml/1 tsp ground cinnamon
5ml/1 tsp ground cumin
2–3 saffron strands, soaked in
   15ml/1 tbsp boiling water
salt

1 Drain the rice, tip it into a saucepan and pour in the water. Add a little salt. Bring to the boil, then lower the heat and simmer very gently for 5 minutes. Drain, rinse well in warm water and drain once again.

2 Melt the butter in a non-stick saucepan. Pour two-thirds of the melted butter into a small jug and set aside. Spoon enough rice into the pan to cover the bottom. Add a quarter of the beans and a little dill. Spread over another layer of rice, then a layer of beans and dill. Repeat the layers until all the beans and dill have been used up, ending with a layer of rice. Cook over a gentle heat for 8 minutes until nearly tender.

3 Pour the reserved melted butter over the rice. Sprinkle with the ground cinnamon and cumin. Cover the pan with a clean dish towel and a tight-fitting lid, lifting the corners of the cloth back over the lid. Cook over a low heat for 25–30 minutes.

4 Spoon about 45ml/3 tbsp of the cooked rice into the bowl of saffron water; mix well. Mound the remaining rice mixture on a large serving plate and spoon the saffron rice on one side to decorate. Serve at once, decorated with the sprig of dill.

SWEET AND SOUR RICE

THIS POPULAR MIDDLE EASTERN RICE DISH IS FLAVOURED WITH FRUIT AND SPICES. IT IS OFTEN SERVED WITH LAMB OR CHICKEN.

SERVES FOUR

INGREDIENTS

50g/2oz/$\frac{1}{2}$ cup zereshk (see Cook's Tip)
45g/1$\frac{1}{2}$oz/3 tbsp butter
50g/2oz/$\frac{1}{3}$ cup raisins
50g/2oz/$\frac{1}{4}$ cup granulated sugar
5ml/1 tsp ground cinnamon
5ml/1 tsp ground cumin
350g/12oz/1$\frac{3}{4}$ cups basmati rice, soaked
2–3 saffron strands, soaked in 15ml/1 tbsp boiling water
pinch of salt

1 Thoroughly wash the zereshk in cold water at least four or five times to rinse off any bits of grit. Drain well.

2 Melt 15g/$\frac{1}{2}$oz/1 tbsp of the butter in a frying pan and fry the raisins for about 1–2 minutes.

3 Add the zereshk, fry for a few seconds, and then add the sugar, with half of the cinnamon and cumin. Cook briefly and then set aside.

4 Drain the rice, then put it in a pan with plenty of boiling, lightly salted water. Bring back to the boil, reduce the heat and simmer for 4 minutes. Drain and rinse once again, if you like.

COOK'S TIP
Zereshk are small dried berries. Look for them in Middle Eastern markets and shops. If you cannot locate them, use fresh cranberries instead.

5 Melt half the remaining butter in the clean pan, add 15ml/1 tbsp water and stir in half the cooked rice. Sprinkle with half the raisin and zereshk mixture and top with all but 45ml/3 tbsp of the rice. Sprinkle over the remaining raisin and zereshk mixture.

6 Mix the remaining cinnamon and cumin with the reserved rice, and scatter this mixture evenly over the layered mixture. Melt the remaining butter, drizzle it over the surface, then cover the pan with a clean dish towel. Cover with a tight-fitting lid, lifting the corners of the cloth back over the lid. Steam the rice over a very low heat for about 20–30 minutes.

7 Just before serving, mix 45ml/3 tbsp of the rice with the saffron water. Spoon the sweet and sour rice on to a large, flat serving dish and scatter the saffron rice over the top, to garnish.

SWEET RICE

IN IRAN, SWEET RICE IS A TRADITIONAL DISH WHICH IS SERVED AT WEDDING BANQUETS AND ON OTHER SPECIAL FEASTING OCCASIONS. IT CAN BE SERVED SOLO OR TO ACCOMPANY A MEAT DISH.

3 Melt 15g/½oz/1 tbsp of the butter in a pan and fry the carrots for 2–3 minutes. Add the remaining sugar and 60ml/4 tbsp water. Simmer for 10 minutes, shaking the pan frequently, until most of the liquid has evaporated.

4 Stir the carrots and half of the nuts into the orange peel in the pan and set aside. Drain the rice and cook in salted water for about 5 minutes. Drain once more and rinse thoroughly in plenty of cold water.

SERVES FOUR TO SIX

INGREDIENTS
   2 oranges
   45ml/3 tbsp granulated sugar
   40g/1½oz/3 tbsp butter
   3 carrots, cut into julienne strips
   50g/2oz/½ cup mixed chopped
     pistachios, almonds and pine nuts
   350g/12oz/1¾ cups basmati rice,
     soaked
   2–3 saffron strands, soaked in
     15ml/1 tbsp warm water
   salt, to taste

1 Pare the rind from the oranges in wide strips, using a potato peeler and taking care to avoid including the white pith. Cut the rind into thin shreds. Place in a saucepan with enough water to cover and bring to the boil. Simmer for a few minutes, then drain. Repeat until the rind no longer tastes bitter.

2 Return the orange rind to the pan. Add half the sugar, then pour in 60ml/ 4 tbsp water. Bring to the boil, then simmer until the syrup is reduced by half. Set aside.

5 Melt half the remaining butter in the clean pan. Add 45ml/3 tbsp water. Fork a little of the rice into the pan and spoon on some of the carrot mixture. Repeat these layers until all the mixture has been used up. Cook gently for 10 minutes. Melt the remaining butter, pour it over the sweet rice and cover the pan with a clean dish towel and a tight-fitting lid. Steam for 30–45 minutes. Mound on plates, garnish with the remaining nuts, drizzle with the saffron water, and serve.

ALMA-ATA

THIS DISH COMES FROM CENTRAL ASIA AND IS A SPECTACULAR COMBINATION OF THE FRUITS AND NUTS FROM THAT REGION.

SERVES FOUR

INGREDIENTS

75g/3oz/¾ cup blanched almonds
60ml/4 tbsp sunflower oil
225g/8oz carrots, cut into julienne
   strips
2 onions, chopped
115g/4oz/½ cup ready-to-eat dried
   apricots, chopped
50g/2oz/⅓ cup raisins
350g/12oz/1¾ cups basmati rice,
   soaked
600ml/1 pint/2½ cups vegetable stock
150ml/¼ pint/⅔ cup orange juice
grated rind of 1 orange
25g/1oz/⅓ cup pine nuts
1 red eating apple, chopped
salt and freshly ground black pepper

3 Pour in the vegetable stock and orange juice, stirring constantly, then stir in the orange rind. Reserve a few toasted almonds for the garnish and stir in the remainder with the pine nuts. Cover the pan with a double piece of foil and fit the casserole lid securely. Transfer to the oven and bake for 30–35 minutes, until the rice is tender and all the liquid has been absorbed.

4 Remove from the oven, season to taste and stir in the chopped apple. Serve from the casserole or spoon into a warmed serving dish. Garnish with the reserved almonds.

1 Preheat the oven to 160°C/325°F/ Gas 3. Toast the almonds in a dry frying pan for 4–5 minutes until golden.

2 Heat the oil in a heavy, flameproof casserole and fry the carrots and onions over a moderately high heat for 6–8 minutes until both are slightly glazed. Add the apricots, raisins and rice and cook over a medium heat for a few minutes, stirring all the time, until the grains of rice are coated in the oil.

VARIATION
For a one-dish meal, add 450g/1lb lamb, cut into cubes. Brown in the casserole in a little oil, then transfer to a dish while you cook the onion and carrots. Stir the meat back into the casserole when you add the stock and orange juice.

SWEET BASMATI DESSERT

*YOU WILL FIND VARIATIONS ON THIS SWEET AND CREAMY DESSERT IN TURKEY, EGYPT, LEBANON AND
SYRIA. THE BASMATI AROMA IS DISTINCTIVE WITHOUT BEING INTRUSIVE.*

SERVES SIX TO EIGHT

INGREDIENTS
   275g/10oz/1½ cups basmati rice,
     soaked
   1.2 litres/2 pints/5 cups milk
   pinch of saffron strands dissolved in
     warm milk or water
   about 2.5ml/½ tsp ground cardamom
     seeds
   75–115g/3–4oz/½ cup granulated
     sugar
   400g/14oz can evaporated milk
To serve
   1 papaya
   25g/1oz/¼ cup flaked almonds
     (optional)

1 Drain the rice and cook it in plenty
of water, using a non-stick saucepan.

2 Drain the rice again, return to the
pan and pour in the milk. Heat very
gently until barely simmering and cook
for 30–45 minutes, stirring occasionally.

3 Stir in the saffron milk or water, the
ground cardamom seeds and the sugar.
Cook for 3–4 minutes more, then stir in
the evaporated milk.

4 Cut the papaya in half, remove the
skin and scoop out the seeds. Slice the
flesh and arrange it on a platter. Spoon
the sweet basmati rice into individual
bowls, sprinkle with flaked almonds
and top each portion with two small
slices of papaya, if you like. Serve the
dessert at once.

COOK'S TIP
If you cook the pudding on top of the
stove, it is essential to use a non-stick
pan. If you haven't got one, bake the
pudding instead. Spoon the cooked rice
into a baking dish. Bring the milk to the
boil, pour it over the rice, stir and cover
tightly. Bake at 150ºC/300ºF/Gas 2 for
45 minutes, then stir in the remaining
ingredients and bake for 15 minutes
more. Cool slightly before serving.

FRUITED RICE RING

THIS UNUSUAL RICE PUDDING LOOKS BEAUTIFUL TURNED OUT OF A RING MOULD, BUT IF YOU PREFER, YOU CAN STIR THE FRUIT INTO THE RICE AND SERVE IT IN INDIVIDUAL DISHES.

SERVES FOUR

INGREDIENTS

65g/2½oz/⅓ cup short grain pudding rice
900ml/1½ pints/3¾ cups semi-skimmed milk
5cm/2in cinnamon stick
175g/6oz/1½ cups dried fruit salad
175ml/6fl oz/¾ cup orange juice
45ml/3 tbsp caster sugar
finely grated rind of 1 small orange
sunflower oil, for greasing

1 Mix the rice and milk in a saucepan. Add the cinnamon stick and bring to the boil. Lower the heat, cover the saucepan and simmer, stirring occasionally, for about 1½ hours, until all the liquid has been absorbed.

2 Meanwhile, put the dried fruit salad in a separate pan, pour over the orange juice and bring to the boil. Lower the heat, cover and simmer very gently for about 1 hour, until the fruit is tender and no liquid remains.

3 Remove the cinnamon stick from the rice and gently stir in the caster sugar and grated orange rind.

COOK'S TIP
When spooning the dried fruit into the tin, bear in mind that this will be the topping when the ring is turned out. Try to balance colours and varieties of fruit.

4 Lightly oil a 1.5 litre/2½ pint/6¼ cup ring tin. Spoon in the fruit so that it covers the bottom of the tin evenly. Top with the rice, smooth it down firmly, then chill until firm.

5 Run a knife around the edge of the ring tin, then invert a serving plate on top. Turn tin and plate over together, then lift off the tin. Serve in slices.

SPAIN AND PORTUGAL

Spain is one of Europe's most
important rice-growing countries,
and has grown rice for over 1000
years. It is not surprising, then,
to find in Spain and neighbouring
Portugal a wealth of superb rice
recipes, most famously the noble
paella. Other traditional dishes
include Moors and Christians,
which dates back over 1200 years.

FLAMENCO EGGS

*THIS ADAPTATION OF A CLASSIC SPANISH RECIPE WORKS VERY WELL WITH CAMARGUE RED RICE,
ALTHOUGH ANY LONG GRAIN RICE — BROWN OR WHITE — COULD BE USED.*

SERVES FOUR

INGREDIENTS
   175g/6oz/scant 1 cup Camargue red
      rice
   chicken or vegetable stock or water
   45ml/3 tbsp olive oil
   1 Spanish onion, chopped
   1 garlic clove, crushed
   350g/12oz lean minced beef
   75g/3oz chorizo sausage, cut into
      small cubes
   5ml/1 tsp paprika, plus extra for
      dusting
   10ml/2 tsp tomato purée
   15–30ml/1–2 tbsp chopped fresh
      parsley
   2 red peppers, seeded and sliced
   3 tomatoes, peeled, seeded and
      chopped
   120ml/4fl oz/½ cup passata or
      tomato juice
   4 eggs
   40ml/8 tsp single cream
   salt and freshly ground black pepper

1 Preheat the oven to 180°C/350°F/Gas 4.
Cook the rice in stock or water, following
the instructions on the packet. Heat
30ml/2 tbsp of oil and fry the onion and
garlic for 5 minutes until the onion is
tinged with brown, stirring occasionally.

2 Add the minced beef and cook,
stirring occasionally, until browned. Stir
in the chorizo and paprika and continue
cooking over a low heat for 4–5 minutes.
Stir in the tomato purée and parsley and
season with salt and pepper.

3 Heat the remaining oil in a saucepan
and fry the peppers until they begin to
sizzle. Cover and cook over a moderate
heat, shaking the pan occasionally, for
4–5 minutes until the peppers are
singed in places. Add the tomatoes and
continue cooking for 3–4 minutes until
they are very soft. Remove the pan from
the heat, stir in the passata or tomato
juice and add salt to taste.

4 Drain the rice, and divide it among
four shallow ovenproof dishes. Spread
the meat mixture over the rice and top
with the peppers and tomatoes. Make
a hole in the centre of each portion
and break in an egg. Spoon 10ml/2 tsp
of the cream over each egg yolk, dust
with paprika, and bake for about
12–15 minutes until the whites of the
eggs are set. Serve at once.

ORANGE CHICKEN SALAD

WITH THEIR TANGY FLAVOUR, ORANGE SEGMENTS ARE THE PERFECT PARTNER FOR TENDER CHICKEN IN THIS TASTY RICE SALAD. TO APPRECIATE ALL THE FLAVOURS FULLY, SERVE IT AT ROOM TEMPERATURE.

SERVES FOUR

INGREDIENTS

  3 large seedless oranges
  175g/6oz/scant 1 cup white long
    grain rice
  475ml/16fl oz/2 cups water
  10ml/2 tsp Dijon mustard
  2.5ml/½ tsp caster sugar
  175ml/6fl oz/¾ cup vinaigrette
    dressing (see Cook's Tip)
  450g/1lb cooked chicken, diced
  45ml/3 tbsp snipped fresh chives
  75g/3oz/¾ cup cashew nuts, toasted
  salt and freshly ground black pepper
  mixed salad leaves, to serve

1 Pare 1 of the oranges thinly, taking care to remove only the coloured part of the rind and avoiding the bitter pith.

2 Put the pieces of orange rind in a saucepan and add the rice. Pour in the water, add a pinch of salt and bring to the boil. Cover and steam over a very low heat for about 15 minutes, or until the rice is tender and all the water has been absorbed.

3 Meanwhile, peel all the oranges. Working over a plate to catch the juices, cut them into segments. Add the orange juice, mustard and sugar to the vinaigrette dressing and whisk to combine well. Taste and add more salt and pepper if needed.

4 When the rice is cooked, remove it from the heat and discard the orange rind. Spoon the rice into a bowl, let it cool slightly, then add half the dressing. Toss well and cool completely.

5 Add the chicken, chives, cashew nuts and orange segments to the rice in the bowl. Add the remaining dressing and toss gently. Serve on a bed of mixed salad leaves.

COOK'S TIP

To make the dressing, whisk 45ml/3 tbsp red wine vinegar with salt and pepper to taste. Gradually whisk in 90ml/6 tbsp corn oil and 60ml/4 tbsp olive oil.

MOORS AND CHRISTIANS

THIS DISH IS THE TRADITIONAL CENTREPIECE OF THE MOYOS E CRISTIANOS FESTIVAL, WHICH IS HELD IN SPAIN EVERY YEAR TO REMEMBER THE CONQUEST OF THE CHRISTIANS OVER THE MOORS. THE BLACK BEANS REPRESENT THE DARK-SKINNED MOORS, AND THE WHITE RICE THE WHITE CHRISTIANS.

SERVES SIX

INGREDIENTS
 400g/14oz/2 cups black beans,
  soaked overnight
 1 onion, quartered
 1 carrot, sliced
 1 stalk celery, sliced
 1 garlic clove, crushed
 1 bay leaf
 5ml/1 tsp paprika
 45ml/3 tbsp olive oil
 juice of 1 orange
 300g/11oz/1¾ cups long grain rice
 salt and cayenne pepper
For the garnish
 chopped fresh parsley, sliced orange,
  sliced red onion, 2 hard-boiled
  eggs, cut into wedges

1 Put the beans in a saucepan with the onion, carrot, celery, garlic and bay leaf and 1.75 litres/3 pints/7½ cups water. Bring to the boil and cook rapidly for 10 minutes, then reduce the heat and simmer for 1 hour, topping up the water if necessary. When the beans are almost tender, drain, discarding the vegetables. Return the beans to a clean saucepan.

2 Blend together the paprika, oil and cayenne pepper and stir into the beans with the orange juice. Top up with a little extra water, if necessary. Heat gently until barely simmering, then cover and cook for 10–15 minutes until the beans are completely tender. Remove from the heat and allow to stand in the liquid for 15 minutes. Add salt to taste.

3 Meanwhile, cook the rice until tender, either by boiling or by the absorption method. Drain, then pack into a buttered bowl and allow to stand for 10 minutes.

4 Unmould the rice onto a serving plate, placing the black beans around the edge of the plate. Garnish with chopped parsley, orange slices, red onion and egg wedges.

ALICANTE OMELETTE RICE

THIS IS A REALLY UNUSUAL DISH, FLAVOURED WITH GARLICKY SPANISH SAUSAGE AND TOPPED WITH BEATEN EGG SO THAT THE EFFECT SUGGESTS AN OMELETTE OR EVEN A SOUFFLE. IF YOU CANNOT GET BUTIFARRA, USE CHORIZO OR ANY SIMILAR SPANISH SAUSAGE INSTEAD.

SERVES SIX

INGREDIENTS
 45ml/3 tbsp sunflower oil
 200g/7oz butifarra or other Spanish
  sausage, sliced
 2 tomatoes, peeled, seeded and
  chopped
 175g/6oz lean pork, cut into bite-
  size pieces
 175g/6oz skinless, boneless chicken
  breast or rabbit, cut into chunks
 350g/12oz/1¾ cups Spanish rice or
  risotto rice
 900ml–1 litre/1½–1¾ pints/
  3¾–4 cups hot chicken stock
 pinch of saffron strands, crushed
 115g/4oz/⅔ cup cooked chick-peas
 6 eggs
 salt and freshly ground black pepper

1 Preheat the oven to 190°C/375°F/ Gas 5. Heat the oil in a flameproof casserole and fry the sausage for a few minutes. Transfer to a plate.

2 Add the tomatoes and fry for a few minutes until slightly thickened. Stir in the pork and chicken or rabbit pieces and cook for 2–3 minutes until the meat has browned lightly, stirring frequently. Add the rice, stir over the heat for about a minute, then pour in the hot stock. Add the saffron, with salt and pepper to taste, and stir well.

3 Bring to the boil, then lower the heat and add the sausage and chick-peas. Cover tightly with the lid and cook over a low heat for about 15 minutes until the rice is tender.

4 Beat the eggs with a little water and a pinch of salt and pour over the rice. Place the casserole, uncovered, in the oven and cook for about 10 minutes, until the eggs have set and browned slightly on top.

BAKED TROUT WITH RICE, SUN-DRIED TOMATOES AND NUTS

TROUT IS VERY POPULAR IN SPAIN, PARTICULARLY IN THE NORTH. IF YOU FILLET THE TROUT BEFORE YOU COOK IT, IT COOKS MORE EVENLY, AND IS EASIER TO SERVE BECAUSE THERE ARE NO BONES TO GET IN THE WAY OF THE STUFFING.

SERVES FOUR

INGREDIENTS

2 fresh trout, each about 500g/1¼lb
75g/3oz/¾ cup mixed unsalted
  cashew nuts, pine nuts, almonds or
  hazelnuts
25ml/1½ tbsp olive oil, plus extra for
  drizzling
1 small onion, finely chopped
10ml/2 tsp grated fresh root ginger
175g/6oz/1½ cups cooked white long
  grain rice
4 tomatoes, peeled and very finely
  chopped
4 sun-dried tomatoes in oil, drained
  and chopped
30ml/2 tbsp chopped fresh tarragon
2 fresh tarragon sprigs
salt and freshly ground black pepper
dressed green leaves, to serve

1 Unless the fishmonger has already filleted the trout, use a sharp knife to do so, leaving as little flesh on the bones as possible. Check the cavity for any tiny bones remaining and remove these with tweezers.

2 Preheat the oven to 190°C/375°F/ Gas 5. Spread out the nuts in a shallow baking tin and bake for 3–4 minutes until golden, shaking the tin occasionally. Chop the nuts roughly.

3 Heat the oil in a small frying pan and fry the onion for 3–4 minutes until soft. Stir in the ginger, cook for 1 minute more, then spoon into a mixing bowl.

4 Stir in the rice, chopped tomatoes, sun-dried tomatoes, toasted nuts and tarragon. Season the stuffing well.

5 Place each of the two trout in turn on a large piece of oiled foil and spoon the stuffing into the cavity. Add a sprig of tarragon and a drizzle of olive oil.

6 Fold the foil over to enclose each trout completely, and put the parcels in a large roasting tin. Bake for 20–25 minutes until the fish is just tender. Cut the fish into thick slices. Serve with dressed green leaves.

SEVILLE CHICKEN

ORANGES AND ALMONDS ARE A FAVOURITE INGREDIENT IN SOUTHERN SPAIN, ESPECIALLY AROUND SEVILLE, WHERE THE ORANGE AND ALMOND TREES ARE A FAMILIAR AND WONDERFUL SIGHT.

SERVES FOUR

INGREDIENTS

1 orange
8 chicken thighs
plain flour, seasoned with salt and pepper
45ml/3 tbsp olive oil
1 large Spanish onion, roughly chopped
2 garlic cloves, crushed
1 red pepper, seeded and sliced
1 yellow pepper, seeded and sliced
115g/4oz chorizo sausage, sliced
50g/2oz/½ cup flaked almonds
225g/8oz/generous 1 cup brown basmati rice
about 600ml/1 pint/2½ cups chicken stock
400g/14oz can chopped tomatoes
175ml/6fl oz/¾ cup white wine
generous pinch of dried thyme
salt and freshly ground black pepper
fresh thyme sprigs, to garnish

1 Pare a thin strip of peel from the orange and set it aside. Peel the orange, then cut it into segments, working over a bowl to catch the juice. Dust the chicken thighs with seasoned flour.

2 Heat the oil in a large frying pan and fry the chicken pieces on both sides until nicely brown. Transfer to a plate. Add the onion and garlic to the pan and fry for 4–5 minutes until the onion begins to brown. Add the red and yellow peppers and fry, stirring occasionally, until slightly softened.

3 Add the chorizo, stir-fry for a few minutes, then sprinkle over the almonds and rice. Cook, stirring, for 1–2 minutes.

4 Pour in the chicken stock, tomatoes and wine and add the orange strip and thyme. Season well. Bring to simmering point, stirring, then return the chicken pieces to the pan.

5 Cover tightly and cook over a very low heat for 1–1¼ hours until the rice and chicken are tender. Just before serving, add the orange segments and allow to cook briefly to heat through. Garnish with fresh thyme and serve.

COOK'S TIP
Cooking times for this dish will depend largely on the heat. If the rice seems to be drying out too quickly, add a little more stock or wine and reduce the heat. If, after 40 minutes or so, the rice is still barely cooked, increase the heat a little. Make sure the rice is kept below the liquid (the chicken can lie on the surface) and stir the rice occasionally if it seems to be cooking unevenly.

CELEBRATION PAELLA

*THIS PAELLA IS A MARVELLOUS MIXTURE OF SOME OF THE FINEST SPANISH INGREDIENTS. CHICKEN
AND RABBIT, SEAFOOD AND VEGETABLES ARE MIXED WITH RICE TO MAKE A COLOURFUL PARTY DISH.*

SERVES SIX TO EIGHT

INGREDIENTS
  450g/1lb fresh mussels
  90ml/6 tbsp white wine
  150g/5oz French beans, cut into
    2.5cm/1in lengths
  115g/4oz/1 cup frozen broad beans
  6 small skinless, boneless chicken
    breasts, cut into large pieces
  30ml/2 tbsp plain flour, seasoned
    with salt and pepper
  about 90ml/6 tbsp olive oil
  6–8 large raw prawns, tailed and
    deveined, or 12 smaller raw prawns
  150g/5oz pork fillet, cut into bite-
    size pieces
  2 onions, chopped
  2–3 garlic cloves, crushed
  1 red pepper, seeded and sliced
  2 ripe tomatoes, peeled, seeded and
    chopped
  900ml/1½ pints/3¾ cups well-
    flavoured chicken stock
  good pinch of saffron, dissolved in
    30ml/2 tbsp hot water
  350g/12oz/1¾ cups Spanish rice or
    risotto rice
  225g/8oz chorizo sausage, thickly
    sliced
  115g/4oz/1 cup frozen peas
  6–8 stuffed green olives, thickly
    sliced

COOK'S TIP
Ideally, you need to use a paella pan
for this dish and, strictly speaking, the
paella shouldn't be stirred during
cooking. You may find, though, that –
because of the distribution of heat – the
rice cooks in the centre but not around
the outside. (This doesn't happen if
paella is cooked traditionally – outdoors,
on a large wood fire.) To make sure your
paella cooks evenly, you could break the
rule and stir occasionally, or cook the
paella on the sole of a hot 190°C/375°F/
Gas 5 oven for about 15–18 minutes.
The result should be practically identical,
but in Spain this would be termed an
arroz – a rice – rather than paella.

1 Scrub the mussels, discarding any
that do not close when sharply tapped.
Place in a large saucepan with the
wine, bring to the boil, then cover the
pan tightly and cook for 3–4 minutes
until all the mussels have opened,
shaking the pan occasionally. Drain,
reserving the liquid and discarding any
mussels that have not opened.

2 Briefly cook the green beans and
broad beans in separate pans of boiling
water for 2–3 minutes. Drain. As soon
as the broad beans are cool enough to
handle, pop them out of their skins.

3 Dust the chicken with the seasoned
flour. Heat half the oil in a paella pan or
deep frying pan and fry the chicken
until evenly browned. Transfer to a
plate. Fry the prawns briefly, adding
more oil if needed, then use a slotted
spoon to transfer them to a plate. Heat
a further 30ml/2 tbsp of the oil in the
pan and brown the pork evenly.
Transfer to a separate plate.

4 Heat the remaining oil and fry the
onions and garlic for 3–4 minutes until
golden brown. Add the red pepper,
cook for 2–3 minutes, then add the
chopped tomatoes and cook until the
mixture is fairly thick.

5 Stir in the chicken stock, the
reserved mussel liquid and the saffron
liquid. Season well with salt and pepper
and bring to the boil. When the liquid is
bubbling, throw in all the rice. Stir once,
then add the chicken pieces, pork,
prawns, beans, chorizo and peas. Cook
over a moderately high heat for 12
minutes, then lower the heat and leave
to cook for 8–10 minutes more, until all
the liquid has been absorbed.

6 Add the mussels and olives and
continue cooking for a further 3–4
minutes to heat through. Remove the
pan from the heat, cover with a clean
damp dish towel and leave to stand for
10 minutes before serving from the pan.

SEAFOOD PAELLA

*THIS IS A GREAT DISH TO SERVE TO GUESTS ON A SPECIAL OCCASION BECAUSE IT LOOKS SPECTACULAR.
BRING THE PAELLA PAN TO THE TABLE AND LET EVERYONE HELP THEMSELVES.*

SERVES FOUR

INGREDIENTS
60ml/4 tbsp olive oil
225g/8oz monkfish or cod fillets,
   skinned and cut into chunks
3 prepared baby squid, body cut into
   rings and tentacles chopped
1 red mullet, filleted, skinned and
   cut into chunks (optional)
1 onion, chopped
3 garlic cloves, finely chopped
1 red pepper, seeded and sliced
4 tomatoes, peeled and roughly
   chopped
225g/8oz/generous 1 cup risotto rice
450ml/¾ pint/scant 2 cups fish stock
150ml/¼ pint/⅔ cup white wine
4–5 saffron strands soaked in
   30ml/2 tbsp hot water
115g/4oz cooked, peeled prawns,
   thawed if frozen
75g/3oz/¾ cup frozen peas
8 fresh mussels, scrubbed
salt and freshly ground black pepper
4 Mediterranean prawns, in the shell,
   and fresh parsley sprigs, to garnish
lemon wedges, to serve

1 Heat half the oil in paella pan or a
large frying pan and add the monkfish
or cod, the squid and the red mullet, if
using. Stir-fry for 2 minutes, then tip
the contents of the pan into a bowl and
set aside.

2 Heat the remaining oil in the pan
and add the onion, garlic and pepper.
Fry for 6–7 minutes, stirring frequently,
until softened.

3 Stir in the tomatoes and fry for
2 minutes, then add the rice. Stir to
coat the grains with oil, then cook for
2–3 minutes. Pour over the fish stock,
wine and saffron water. Season with
salt and freshly ground black pepper,
and mix well.

COOK'S TIP
Before adding the mussels to the rice
mixture, check that they are all closed.
Any that are open should close when
sharply tapped; any that fail to do this
must be discarded.

4 Gently stir in the reserved cooked fish
(with all the juices), then the peeled
prawns and the peas. Push the mussels
into the rice. Cover and cook over a
gentle heat for about 30 minutes, or
until the stock has been absorbed but
the rice mixture is still relatively moist.
All the mussels should have opened;
discard any that remain closed.

5 Remove from the heat, and leave the
paella to stand, covered, for 5 minutes.
Arrange the whole prawns on top.
Sprinkle the paella with parsley and
serve with the lemon wedges.

CHICKEN PIRI-PIRI

THIS IS A CLASSIC PORTUGUESE DISH, BASED ON A HOT SAUCE MADE FROM ANGOLAN CHILLIES. IT IS POPULAR WHEREVER THERE ARE PORTUGUESE COMMUNITIES, AND IS OFTEN SERVED IN SOUTH AFRICA.

SERVES FOUR

INGREDIENTS

4 chicken breast portions
30–45ml/2–3 tbsp olive oil
1 large onion, finely sliced
2 carrots, cut into thin strips
1 large parsnip or 2 small parsnips, cut into thin strips
1 red pepper, seeded and sliced
1 yellow pepper, seeded and sliced
1 litre/1¾ pints/4 cups chicken stock
3 tomatoes, peeled, seeded and chopped
generous dash of piri-piri sauce
15ml/1 tbsp tomato purée
½ cinnamon stick
1 fresh thyme sprig, plus extra fresh thyme, to garnish
1 bay leaf
275g/10oz/1½ cups white long grain rice
15ml/1 tbsp lime or lemon juice
salt and freshly ground black pepper

1 Preheat the oven to 180°C/350°F/ Gas 4. Rub the chicken skin with a little salt and pepper. Heat 30ml/2 tbsp of the oil in a large frying pan and brown the chicken portions on all sides. Transfer to a plate.

2 Add some more oil if necessary and fry the onion for 2–3 minutes until slightly softened. Add the carrots, parsnip and peppers, stir-fry for a few minutes and then cover and sweat for 4–5 minutes until quite soft.

3 Pour in the chicken stock, then add the tomatoes, piri-piri sauce, tomato purée and cinnamon stick. Stir in the thyme and bay leaf. Season to taste and bring to the boil. Using a ladle, spoon off 300ml/½ pint/1¼ cups of the liquid and set aside in a small pan.

4 Put the rice in the bottom of a casserole. Using a slotted spoon, scoop the vegetables out of the pan and spread them over the rice. Arrange the chicken pieces on top. Pour over the spicy chicken stock from the pan, cover the casserole tightly and cook in the oven for about 45 minutes, until both the rice and chicken are completely tender.

5 Meanwhile, heat the reserved chicken stock, adding a few more drops of piri-piri sauce and the lime or lemon juice.

6 To serve, spoon the piri-piri chicken and rice on to warmed serving plates. Serve the remaining sauce separately or poured over the chicken.

SPANISH RICE SALAD

RICE AND A CHOICE OF CHOPPED SALAD VEGETABLES ARE SERVED IN A WELL-FLAVOURED DRESSING.

SERVES SIX

INGREDIENTS
   275g/10oz/1½ cups white long grain
      rice
   1 bunch spring onions, finely sliced
   1 green pepper, seeded and finely
      diced
   1 yellow pepper, seeded and finely
      diced
   225g/8oz tomatoes, peeled, seeded
      and chopped
   30ml/2 tbsp chopped fresh coriander
For the dressing
   75ml/5 tbsp mixed sunflower and
      olive oil
   15ml/1 tbsp rice vinegar
   5ml/1 tsp Dijon mustard
   salt and freshly ground black pepper

COOK'S TIP
Cooked garden peas, cooked diced carrot
and drained, canned sweetcorn can be
added to this versatile salad.

1 Cook the rice in plenty of boiling
water for 10–12 minutes until tender
but still *al dente*. Do not overcook.
Drain, rinse under cold water and drain
again. Leave to cool completely.

2 Place the rice in a large serving bowl.
Add the spring onions, peppers,
tomatoes and coriander.

3 Make the dressing. Mix all the
ingredients in a jar with a tight-fitting lid
and shake vigorously until well mixed.
Stir 60–75ml/4–5 tbsp of the dressing
into the rice and adjust the seasoning.

4 Cover and chill for about 1 hour
before serving. Offer the remaining
dressing separately.

PRAWN, MELON AND CHORIZO SALAD

THIS IS A RICH AND COLOURFUL SALAD. IT TASTES BEST WHEN MADE WITH FRESH PRAWNS.

SERVES FOUR

INGREDIENTS
   450g/1lb/4 cups cooked white long
      grain rice
   1 avocado
   15ml/1 tbsp lemon juice
   ½ small melon, cut into wedges
   15g/½oz/1 tbsp butter
   ½ garlic clove
   115g/4oz raw prawns, peeled and
      deveined
   25g/1oz chorizo sausage, finely
      sliced
   flat leaf parsley, to garnish
For the dressing
   75ml/5 tbsp natural yogurt
   45ml/3 tbsp mayonnaise
   15ml/1 tbsp olive oil
   3 fresh tarragon sprigs
   freshly ground black pepper

1 Put the cooked rice in a large salad
bowl, breaking it up with your fingers if
necessary.

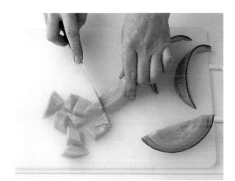

2 Peel the avocado and cut it into
chunks. Place in a mixing bowl and toss
lightly with the lemon juice. Slice the
melon off the rind, cut the flesh into
chunks and add to the avocado.

3 Melt the butter in a small pan and
fry the garlic for 30 seconds. Add the
prawns and cook for about 3 minutes
until evenly pink. Add the chorizo and
stir-fry for 1 minute more, then tip the
mixture into the bowl with the avocado
and melon chunks. Mix lightly, then
leave to cool.

4 Make the dressing by whizzing
together all the ingredients in a food
processor or blender. Stir half of the
mixture into the rice and the remainder
into the prawn and avocado mixture.
Pile the salad on top of the rice. Chill
for about 30 minutes before serving,
garnished with flat leaf parsley sprigs.

PORTUGUESE RICE PUDDING

THIS IS POPULAR ALL OVER PORTUGAL AND IF YOU VISIT THAT COUNTRY YOU'RE LIKELY TO FIND IT ON MOST MENUS. TRADITIONALLY IT IS SERVED COLD, BUT IS ACTUALLY DELICIOUS WARM AS WELL.

2 Drain well, then return to the clean pan. Add the milk, lemon rind and butter. Bring to the boil over a moderately low heat, then cover, reduce the heat to the lowest setting and simmer for about 20 minutes or until the rice is thick and creamy.

3 Remove the pan from the heat and allow the rice to cool a little. Remove and discard the lemon rind, then stir in the sugar and the egg yolks. Mix well.

SERVES FOUR TO SIX

INGREDIENTS
  175g/6oz/scant 1 cup short grain
    pudding rice
  600ml/1 pint/2½ cups creamy milk
  2 or 3 strips pared lemon rind
  65g/2½oz/5 tbsp butter, in pieces
  115g/4oz/½ cup caster sugar
  4 egg yolks
  salt
  ground cinnamon, for dusting
  lemon wedges, to serve

1. Cook the rice in plenty of lightly salted water for about 5 minutes, by which time it will have lost its brittleness.

4 Divide among four to six serving bowls and dust with ground cinnamon. Serve cool, with lemon wedges for squeezing.

RICE CONDE SUNDAE

COOKING RICE PUDDING ON TOP OF THE HOB INSTEAD OF IN THE OVEN GIVES IT A LIGHT, CREAMY TEXTURE, ESPECIALLY IF YOU REMEMBER TO STIR IT FREQUENTLY. IT IS PARTICULARLY GOOD SERVED COLD WITH A TOPPING OF FRUIT AND TOASTED NUTS OR A TRICKLE OF HOT CHOCOLATE SAUCE.

SERVES FOUR

INGREDIENTS
   50g/2oz/generous ¼ cup short grain
     pudding rice
   5ml/1 tsp vanilla essence
   2.5ml/½ tsp ground cinnamon
   45ml/3 tbsp granulated sugar
   600ml/1 pint/2½ cups milk
For the toppings
   soft berry fruits such as
     strawberries, raspberries and
     cherries
   chocolate sauce and flaked toasted
     almonds (optional)

3 When the grains are soft, remove the pan from the heat. Allow the rice to cool, stirring it occasionally, then chill.

4 Before serving, stir the rice pudding and spoon it into four sundae dishes. Top with fresh fruits, and with chocolate sauce and almonds, if using.

VARIATION
For a special occasion, use single cream instead of milk, and glaze the fruit with a little melted redcurrant jelly. (Add a splash of port if you like.)

1 Mix the rice, vanilla essence, cinnamon and sugar in a saucepan. Pour in the milk. Bring to the boil, stirring constantly, then reduce the heat so that the mixture barely simmers.

2 Cook the rice over a low heat for 30–40 minutes, stirring frequently. Add extra milk to the rice if it begins to dry out.

ITALY

In Italy, especially in the north,
rice is more than just a useful
accompaniment to meat and fish.
Risottos are one of the few rice
dishes that are entirely native to
Europe, and, like the rice eaten in
the east, the rice here is loved for
its own merits. Other ingredients
are added for flavour, but the star
of the risotto is the rice itself.

FRIED RICE BALLS STUFFED WITH MOZZARELLA

THESE DEEP-FRIED BALLS OF RISOTTO GO BY THE NAME OF SUPPLI AL TELEFONO IN THEIR NATIVE ITALY. STUFFED WITH MOZZARELLA CHEESE, THEY ARE VERY POPULAR SNACKS, WHICH IS HARDLY SURPRISING AS THEY ARE QUITE DELICIOUS.

SERVES FOUR

INGREDIENTS
  1 quantity Risotto with Parmesan
    Cheese or Mushroom Risotto
  3 eggs
  breadcrumbs and plain flour, to coat
  115g/4oz/⅔ cup mozzarella cheese,
    cut into small cubes
  oil, for deep-frying
  dressed curly endive and cherry
    tomatoes, to serve

1 Put the risotto in a bowl and allow it to cool completely. Beat two of the eggs, and stir them into the cold risotto until well mixed.

2 Use your hands to form the rice mixture into balls the size of a large egg. If the mixture is too moist to hold its shape well, stir in a few tablespoons of breadcrumbs. Poke a hole into the centre of each ball with your finger, then fill it with a few small cubes of mozzarella, and close the hole over again with the rice mixture.

3 Heat the oil for deep-frying until a small piece of bread sizzles as soon as it is dropped in.

4 Spread some flour on a plate. Beat the remaining egg in a shallow bowl. Sprinkle another plate with breadcrumbs. Roll the balls in the flour, then in the egg, and finally in the breadcrumbs.

5 Fry them a few at a time in the hot oil until golden and crisp. Drain on kitchen paper while the remaining balls are being fried. Serve hot, with a simple salad of dressed curly endive leaves and cherry tomatoes.

COOK'S TIP
These provide the perfect solution as to what to do with leftover risotto, as they are best made with a cold mixture, cooked the day before.

SPINACH AND RICE SOUP

USE VERY YOUNG SPINACH LEAVES TO PREPARE THIS LIGHT AND FRESH-TASTING SOUP.

SERVES FOUR

INGREDIENTS

675g/1½lb fresh spinach leaves, washed
45ml/3 tbsp extra virgin olive oil
1 small onion, finely chopped
2 garlic cloves, finely chopped
1 small fresh red chilli, seeded and finely chopped
225g/8oz/generous 1 cup risotto rice
1.2 litres/2 pints/5 cups vegetable stock
salt and freshly ground black pepper
shavings of pared Parmesan or Pecorino cheese, to serve

1 Place the spinach in a large pan with just the water that clings to its leaves after washing. Add a large pinch of salt. Heat gently until the spinach has wilted, then remove from the heat and drain, reserving any liquid.

2 Either chop the spinach finely using a large kitchen knife or place in a food processor and process the leaves to a fairly coarse purée.

3 Heat the oil in a large saucepan and gently cook the onion, garlic and chilli for 4–5 minutes until softened. Stir in the rice until well coated, then pour in the stock and reserved spinach liquid. Bring to the boil, lower the heat and simmer for 10 minutes.

4 Add the spinach, with salt and pepper to taste. Cook for 5–7 minutes, until the rice is tender. Check the seasoning. Serve in heated bowls, topped with the shavings of cheese.

COOK'S TIP
Buy Parmesan or Pecorino cheese in the piece from a reputable supplier, and it will be full of flavour and easy to grate or shave with a vegetable peeler.

TROUT AND PARMA HAM RISOTTO ROLLS

THIS MAKES A DELICIOUS AND ELEGANT MEAL. THE RISOTTO — MADE WITH PORCINI MUSHROOMS AND PRAWNS — IS A FINE MATCH FOR THE ROBUST FLAVOUR OF THE TROUT ROLLS.

SERVES FOUR

INGREDIENTS
   4 trout fillets, skinned
   4 slices Parma ham
   caper berries, to garnish
For the risotto
   30ml/2 tbsp olive oil
   8 large raw prawns, peeled and
     deveined
   1 medium onion, chopped
   225g/8oz/generous 1 cup risotto
     rice
   about 105ml/7 tbsp white wine
   about 750ml/1¼ pints/3 cups
     simmering fish or chicken stock
   15g/½oz/2 tbsp dried porcini or
     chanterelle mushrooms, soaked
     for 10 minutes in warm water to
     cover
   salt and freshly ground black pepper

2 Add the chopped onion to the oil remaining in the pan and fry over a gentle heat for 3–4 minutes until soft. Add the rice and stir for 3–4 minutes until the grains are evenly coated in oil. Add 75ml/5 tbsp of the wine and then the stock, a little at a time, stirring over a gentle heat and allowing the rice to absorb the liquid before adding more.

4 Remove the pan from the heat and stir in the prawns. Preheat the oven to 190°C/375°F/Gas 5.

5 Take a trout fillet, place a spoonful of risotto at one end and roll up. Wrap each fillet in a slice of Parma ham and place in a greased ovenproof dish.

1 First make the risotto. Heat the oil in a heavy-based saucepan or deep frying pan and fry the prawns very briefly until flecked with pink. Lift out on a slotted spoon and transfer to a plate.

3 Drain the mushrooms, reserving the liquid, and cut the larger ones in half. Towards the end of cooking, stir the mushrooms into the risotto with 15ml/ 1 tbsp of the reserved mushroom liquid. If the rice is not yet *al dente*, add a little more stock or mushroom liquid and cook for 2–3 minutes more. Season to taste with salt and pepper.

6 Spoon any remaining risotto around the fish fillets and sprinkle over the rest of the wine. Cover loosely with foil and bake for 15–20 minutes until the fish is tender. Spoon the risotto on to a platter, top with the trout rolls and garnish with caper berries. Serve at once.

COOK'S TIP
There are no hard and fast rules about which type of risotto to use for this dish. Almost any risotto recipe could be used, although a vegetable or seafood risotto would be particularly suitable.

STUFFED CHICKEN ROLLS

THESE DELICIOUS CHICKEN ROLLS ARE SIMPLE TO MAKE, BUT SOPHISTICATED ENOUGH TO SERVE AT A DINNER PARTY, ESPECIALLY IF YOU ARRANGE SLICES ON A BED OF TAGLIATELLE TOSSED WITH FRIED WILD MUSHROOMS.

SERVES FOUR

INGREDIENTS
25g/1oz/2 tbsp butter
1 garlic clove, chopped
150g/5oz/1¼ cups cooked white long
   grain rice
45ml/3 tbsp ricotta cheese
10ml/2 tsp chopped fresh flat leaf
   parsley
5ml/1 tsp chopped fresh tarragon
4 skinless, boneless chicken breasts
3–4 slices Parma ham
15ml/1 tbsp olive oil
120ml/4fl oz/½ cup white wine
salt and freshly ground black pepper
fresh flat leaf parsley sprigs, to
   garnish
cooked tagliatelle and sautéed blewit
   mushrooms, to serve (optional)

2 Add the rice, ricotta, parsley and tarragon and season with salt and pepper. Stir to mix.

5 Place a spoonful of the rice stuffing at the wider end of each ham-topped breast. Roll up carefully and tie in place with cooking string or secure with a cocktail stick.

3 Place each chicken breast in turn between two sheets of clear film and flatten by beating lightly, but firmly, with a rolling pin.

6 Heat the oil and the remaining butter in a frying pan and lightly fry the chicken rolls until browned on all sides. Place side by side in a shallow baking dish and pour over the white wine.

7 Cover the dish with greaseproof paper and cook in the oven for 30–35 minutes until the chicken is tender.

8 Cut the rolls into slices and serve on a bed of tagliatelle with sautéed blewit mushrooms and a generous grinding of black pepper, if you like. Garnish with sprigs of flat leaf parsley.

1 Preheat the oven to 180°C/350°F/ Gas 4. Melt about 10g/¼oz/2 tsp of the butter in a small pan and fry the garlic for a few seconds without browning. Spoon into a bowl.

4 Divide the slices of Parma ham between the chicken breasts, trimming the ham to fit, if necessary.

COOK'S TIP
Risotto rice could be used in place of white long grain in this dish. Risotto rice has a different consistency to long grain, and will make a much denser stuffing for the chicken rolls.

PUMPKIN AND PISTACHIO RISOTTO

Vegetarians tired of the standard dinner party fare will love this elegant combination of creamy, golden rice and orange pumpkin, and so will everyone else. It would look particularly impressive served in the hollowed-out pumpkin shell.

SERVES FOUR

INGREDIENTS

1.2 litres/2 pints/5 cups vegetable
    stock or water
generous pinch of saffron strands
30ml/2 tbsp olive oil
1 onion, chopped
2 garlic cloves, crushed
900g/2lb pumpkin, peeled, seeded
    and cut into 2cm/¾in cubes (about
    7 cups)
400g/14oz/2 cups risotto rice
200ml/7fl oz/scant 1 cup dry white
    wine
30ml/2 tbsp freshly grated Parmesan
    cheese
50g/2oz/½ cup pistachios, coarsely
    chopped
45ml/3 tbsp chopped fresh marjoram
    or oregano, plus leaves to garnish
salt, freshly grated nutmeg and
    freshly ground black pepper

1 Bring the stock or water to the boil and reduce to a low simmer. Ladle a little of it into a small bowl. Add the saffron strands and leave to infuse.

2 Heat the oil in a large, heavy-based saucepan or deep frying pan. Add the onion and garlic and cook gently for about 5 minutes until softened. Add the pumpkin and rice and stir to coat everything in oil. Cook for a few more minutes until the rice looks transparent.

3 Pour in the wine and allow it to bubble hard. When it has been absorbed, add a quarter of the hot stock or water and the saffron liquid. Stir until all the liquid has been absorbed. Gradually add the remaining stock or water, a little at a time, allowing the rice to absorb the liquid before adding more, and stirring constantly. After 20–30 minutes the rice should be golden yellow, creamy and *al dente*.

4 Stir in the Parmesan cheese, cover the pan and leave the risotto to stand for 5 minutes. To finish, stir in the pistachios and marjoram or oregano. Season to taste with a little salt, nutmeg and pepper, scatter over a few marjoram or oregano leaves and serve.

RISOTTO WITH PARMESAN

THIS TRADITIONAL RISOTTO IS SIMPLY FLAVOURED WITH GRATED PARMESAN CHEESE AND GOLDEN, FRIED CHOPPED ONION.

SERVES THREE TO FOUR

INGREDIENTS
1.2 litres/2 pints/5 cups beef,
    chicken or vegetable stock
65g/2½oz/5 tbsp butter
1 small onion, finely chopped
275g/10oz/1½ cups risotto rice
120ml/4fl oz/½ cup dry white wine
75g/3oz/1 cup freshly grated Parmesan
    cheese, plus extra to garnish
basil leaves, to garnish
salt and freshly ground black pepper

1 Heat the stock in a saucepan, and leave to simmer until needed.

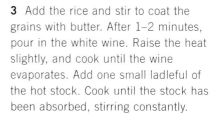

2 Melt two-thirds of the butter in a large heavy-based saucepan or deep frying pan. Stir in the onion, and cook gently until soft and golden.

3 Add the rice and stir to coat the grains with butter. After 1–2 minutes, pour in the white wine. Raise the heat slightly, and cook until the wine evaporates. Add one small ladleful of the hot stock. Cook until the stock has been absorbed, stirring constantly.

4 Gradually add the remaining stock, a little at a time, allowing the rice to absorb the liquid before adding more, and stirring constantly. After 20–30 minutes the rice should be creamy and *al dente*. Season to taste.

5 Remove the pan from the heat. Stir in the remaining butter and the Parmesan cheese. Taste again for seasoning. Allow the risotto to rest for 3–4 minutes before serving, garnished with basil leaves and shavings of Parmesan, if you like.

COOK'S TIP
If you run out of stock when cooking the risotto, use hot water, but do not worry if the rice is done before you have used up all the stock.

RISOTTO WITH RICOTTA AND BASIL

THIS IS A WELL-FLAVOURED RISOTTO, WHICH BENEFITS FROM THE DISTINCT PUNGENCY OF BASIL, MELLOWED WITH SMOOTH RICOTTA.

SERVES THREE TO FOUR

INGREDIENTS
  45ml/3 tbsp olive oil
  1 onion, finely chopped
  275g/10oz/1½ cups risotto rice
  1 litre/1¾ pints/4 cups hot chicken
    or vegetable stock
  175g/6oz/¾ cup ricotta cheese
  50g/2oz/generous 1 cup fresh basil
    leaves, finely chopped, plus extra
    to garnish
  75g/3oz/1 cup freshly grated
    Parmesan cheese
  salt and freshly ground black pepper

1 Heat the oil in a large saucepan or flameproof casserole and fry the onion over a gentle heat until soft.

2 Tip in the rice. Cook for a few minutes, stirring, until the rice is coated with oil and is slightly translucent.

3 Pour in about a quarter of the stock. Cook, stirring, until all the stock has been absorbed, then add another ladleful. Continue in this manner, adding more stock when the previous ladleful has been absorbed, until the risotto has been cooking for about 20 minutes and the rice is just tender.

4 Spoon the ricotta into a bowl and break it up a little with a fork. Stir into the risotto along with the basil and Parmesan. Taste and adjust the seasoning, then cover and let stand for 2–3 minutes before serving, garnished with basil leaves.

RISOTTO FRITTATA

*HALF OMELETTE, HALF RISOTTO, THIS MAKES A DELIGHTFUL LIGHT LUNCH OR SUPPER DISH.
IF POSSIBLE, COOK EACH FRITTATA SEPARATELY, AND PREFERABLY IN A SMALL, CAST IRON PAN,
SO THAT THE EGGS COOK QUICKLY UNDERNEATH BUT STAY MOIST ON TOP.*

SERVES FOUR

INGREDIENTS
  30–45ml/2–3 tbsp olive oil
  1 small onion, finely chopped
  1 garlic clove, crushed
  1 large red pepper, seeded and cut
    into thin strips
  150g/5oz/¾ cup risotto rice
  400–475ml/14–16fl oz/1⅔–2 cups
    simmering chicken stock
  25–40g/1–1½oz/2–3 tbsp butter
  175g/6oz/2½ cups button
    mushrooms, finely sliced
  60ml/4 tbsp freshly grated Parmesan
    cheese
  6–8 eggs
  salt and freshly ground black pepper

1 Heat 15ml/1 tbsp oil in a large frying pan and fry the onion and garlic over a gentle heat for 2–3 minutes until the onion begins to soften but does not brown. Add the pepper and cook, stirring, for 4–5 minutes, until soft.

2 Stir in the rice and cook gently for 2–3 minutes, stirring all the time, until the grains are evenly coated with oil.

3 Add a quarter of the chicken stock and season. Stir over a low heat until the stock has been absorbed. Continue to add more stock, a little at a time, allowing the rice to absorb the liquid before adding more. Continue cooking in this way until the rice is *al dente*.

4 In a separate small pan, heat a little of the remaining oil and some butter and quickly fry the mushrooms until golden. Transfer to a plate.

5 When the rice is tender, remove from the heat and stir in the mushrooms and Parmesan cheese.

6 Beat together the eggs with 40ml/8 tsp cold water and season well. Heat the remaining oil and butter in an omelette pan and add the risotto mixture. Spread the mixture out in the pan, then immediately add the beaten egg, tilting the pan so that the omelette cooks evenly. Fry over a moderately high heat for 1–2 minutes, then transfer to a warmed plate and serve.

COOK'S TIP
This will make a more substantial dish for two, using five or six eggs. If preferred, the frittata could be cooked as individual portions.

PORCINI AND PARMESAN RISOTTO

THE SUCCESS OF A GOOD RISOTTO DEPENDS ON BOTH THE QUALITY OF THE RICE USED AND THE TECHNIQUE. ADD THE STOCK GRADUALLY AND STIR CONSTANTLY TO COAX A CREAMY TEXTURE FROM THE STARCH GRAINS. THIS VARIATION ON THE CLASSIC RISOTTO ALLA MILANESE INCLUDES SAFFRON, PORCINI MUSHROOMS AND PARMESAN.

SERVES FOUR

INGREDIENTS

15g/½oz/2 tbsp dried porcini
  mushrooms
150ml/¼ pint/⅔ cup warm water
1 litre/1¾ pints/4 cups vegetable stock
generous pinch of saffron strands
30ml/2 tbsp olive oil
1 onion, finely chopped
1 garlic clove, crushed
350g/12oz/1¾ cups Arborio or
  Carnaroli rice
150ml/¼ pint/⅔ cup dry white wine
25g/1oz/2 tbsp butter
50g/2oz/⅔ cup freshly grated
  Parmesan cheese
salt and freshly ground black pepper
pink and yellow oyster mushrooms,
  to serve (optional)

1 Put the dried porcini in a bowl and pour over the warm water. Leave the mushrooms to soak for 20 minutes, then lift out with a slotted spoon. Filter the soaking water through a layer of kitchen paper in a sieve, then place it in a saucepan with the stock. Bring the liquid to a gentle simmer.

2 Spoon about 45ml/3 tbsp of the hot stock into a cup and stir in the saffron strands. Set aside. Finely chop the porcini. Heat the oil in a separate pan and lightly sauté the onion, garlic and mushrooms for 5 minutes. Gradually add the rice, stirring to coat the grains in oil. Cook for 2 minutes, stirring constantly. Season with salt and pepper.

3 Pour in the white wine. Cook, stirring, until it has been absorbed, then ladle in a quarter of the stock. Cook, stirring, until the stock has been absorbed. Gradually add the remaining stock, a little at a time, allowing the rice to absorb the liquid before adding more, and stirring constantly.

4 After about 20 minutes, when all the stock has been absorbed and the rice is cooked but still has a "bite", stir in the butter, saffron water (with the strands) and half the Parmesan. Serve, sprinkled with the remaining Parmesan. Garnish with pink and yellow oyster mushrooms, if you like.

VARIATIONS
There are endless variations on this delectable dish. The proportion of stock to rice, onions, garlic and butter must remain constant but you can ring the changes with the flavourings and cheese.

RISOTTO <u>WITH</u> FOUR VEGETABLES

THIS IS ONE OF THE PRETTIEST RISOTTOS, ESPECIALLY WHEN MADE WITH ACORN SQUASH.

<u>SERVES THREE TO FOUR</u>

INGREDIENTS
115g/4oz/1 cup shelled fresh peas
115g/4oz/1 cup green beans, cut
  into short lengths
30ml/2 tbsp olive oil
75g/3oz/6 tbsp butter
1 acorn squash, skin and seeds
  removed, flesh cut into matchsticks
1 onion, finely chopped
275g/10oz/1½ cups risotto rice
120ml/4fl oz/½ cup Italian dry white
  vermouth
1 litre/1¾ pints/4 cups boiling
  chicken stock
75g/3oz/1 cup freshly grated
  Parmesan cheese
salt and freshly ground black pepper

1 Bring a saucepan of lightly salted water to the boil, add the peas and beans and cook for 2–3 minutes, until the vegetables are just tender. Drain, refresh under cold running water, drain again and set aside.

2 Heat the oil with 25g/1oz/2 tbsp of the butter in a medium saucepan until foaming. Add the squash and cook gently for 2–3 minutes or until just softened. Remove with a slotted spoon and set aside. Add the onion to the pan and cook gently for about 3 minutes, stirring frequently, until softened.

3 Stir in the rice until the grains start to swell and burst, then add the vermouth. Stir until the vermouth stops sizzling and most of it has been absorbed by the rice, then add a few ladlefuls of the stock, with salt and pepper to taste. Stir over a low heat until the stock has been absorbed.

4 Gradually add the remaining stock, a few ladlefuls at a time, allowing the rice to absorb the liquid before adding more, and stirring all the time.

VARIATIONS
Shelled broad beans can be used instead of the peas, and asparagus tips instead of the green beans. Use courgettes if acorn squash is not available.

5 After about 20 minutes, when all the stock has been absorbed and the rice is cooked and creamy but still has a "bite", gently stir in the vegetables, the remaining butter and about half the grated Parmesan. Heat through, then taste for seasoning and serve with the remaining grated Parmesan served separately.

GREEN RISOTTO

You could use spinach-flavoured risotto rice to give this stunning dish even greater dramatic impact. However, white risotto rice makes a pretty contrast to the spinach.

SERVES THREE TO FOUR

INGREDIENTS
30ml/2 tbsp olive oil
1 onion, finely chopped
275g/10oz/1½ cups risotto rice
1 litre/1¾ pints/4 cups hot chicken
  stock
75ml/5 tbsp white wine
about 400g/14oz tender baby
  spinach leaves
15ml/1 tbsp chopped fresh basil
5ml/1 tsp chopped fresh mint
60ml/4 tbsp freshly grated Parmesan
  cheese
salt and freshly ground black pepper
knob of butter or more grated
  Parmesan cheese, to serve

1 Heat the oil and fry the onion for 3–4 minutes until soft. Add the rice and stir to coat each grain. Pour in the stock and wine, a little at a time, stirring constantly over a gentle heat until all the liquid has been absorbed.

2 Stir in the spinach leaves and herbs with the last of the liquid, and add a little seasoning. Continue cooking until the rice is tender and the spinach leaves have wilted. Stir in the Parmesan cheese, with a knob of butter, if you like, or serve with extra Parmesan.

COOK'S TIP
The secret with risotto is to add the hot liquid gradually, about a ladleful at a time, and to stir constantly until the liquid has been absorbed before adding more.

RISOTTO WITH BACON, BABY COURGETTES AND PEPPERS

This would make the perfect dish to come home to after an early show at the theatre. Creamy risotto topped with vegetables and crisp bacon is irresistible and easy to make.

SERVES FOUR

INGREDIENTS
30ml/2 tbsp olive oil
115g/4oz rindless streaky bacon
  rashers, cut into thick strips
350g/12oz/1¾ cups risotto rice
1.2 litres/2 pints/5 cups hot
  vegetable or chicken stock
30ml/2 tbsp single cream
45ml/3 tbsp dry sherry
50g/2oz/⅔ cup freshly grated
  Parmesan cheese
50g/2oz/⅔ cup chopped fresh parsley
salt and freshly ground black pepper
For the vegetables
1 small red pepper, seeded
1 small green pepper, seeded
25g/1oz/2 tbsp butter
75g/3oz horse mushrooms, sliced
225g/8oz baby courgettes, halved
1 onion, halved and sliced
1 garlic clove, crushed

1 Heat half the oil in a frying pan. Add the bacon and heat gently until the fat runs. Increase the heat and fry until crisp, then drain on kitchen paper and set aside.

2 Heat the remaining oil in a heavy-based saucepan. Add the rice, stir to coat the grains, then ladle in a little of the hot stock. Stir until it has been absorbed. Gradually add the rest of the stock, stirring constantly.

3 Cut the peppers into chunks. Melt the butter in a separate pan and fry the peppers, mushrooms, courgettes, onion and garlic until the onion is just tender. Season well, then stir in the bacon.

4 When all the stock has been absorbed by the rice, stir in the cream, sherry, Parmesan, parsley and seasoning. Spoon the risotto on to individual plates and top each portion with fried vegetables and bacon. Serve immediately.

RISOTTO WITH ASPARAGUS

FRESH FARM ASPARAGUS ONLY HAS A SHORT SEASON, SO IT IS SENSIBLE TO MAKE THE MOST OF IT. THIS ELEGANT RISOTTO IS ABSOLUTELY DELICIOUS.

SERVES THREE TO FOUR

INGREDIENTS
225g/8oz fresh asparagus
750ml/1¼ pints/3 cups vegetable or chicken stock
65g/2½oz/5 tbsp butter
1 small onion, finely chopped
275g/10oz/1½ cups risotto rice, such as Arborio or Carnaroli
75g/3oz/1 cup freshly grated Parmesan cheese
salt and freshly ground black pepper

1 Bring a pan of water to the boil. Cut off any woody pieces on the ends of the asparagus stalks, peel the lower portions, then cook in the water for 5 minutes. Drain the asparagus, reserving the cooking water, refresh under cold water and drain again. Cut the asparagus diagonally into 4cm/1½in pieces. Keep the tip and next-highest sections separate from the stalks.

2 Place the stock in a saucepan and add 450ml/¾ pint/scant 2 cups of the asparagus cooking water. Heat to simmering point, and keep it hot.

3 Melt two-thirds of the butter in a large, heavy-based saucepan or deep frying pan. Add the onion and fry until it is soft and golden. Stir in all the asparagus except the top two sections. Cook for 2–3 minutes. Add the rice and cook for 1–2 minutes, mixing well to coat it with butter. Stir in a ladleful of the hot liquid. Using a wooden spoon, stir until the stock has been absorbed.

4 Gradually add the remaining stock, a little at a time, allowing the rice to absorb the liquid before adding more, and stirring all the time.

5 After 10 minutes, add the remaining asparagus sections. Continue to cook as before, for about 15 minutes, until the rice is *al dente* and the risotto is creamy. Off the heat, stir in the remaining butter and the Parmesan. Grind in a little black pepper, and taste again for salt. Serve at once.

RISOTTO WITH FOUR CHEESES

THIS IS A VERY RICH DISH. SERVE IT FOR A SPECIAL DINNER-PARTY FIRST COURSE, WITH A LIGHT, DRY SPARKLING WHITE WINE.

SERVES FOUR

INGREDIENTS

40g/1½oz/3 tbsp butter
1 small onion, finely chopped
1.2 litres/2 pints/5 cups chicken stock, preferably home-made
350g/12oz/1¾ cups risotto rice
200ml/7fl oz/scant 1cup dry white wine
50g/2oz/½ cup grated Gruyère cheese
50g/2oz/½ cup diced taleggio cheese
50g/2oz/½ cup diced Gorgonzola cheese
50g/2oz/⅔ cup freshly grated Parmesan cheese
salt and freshly ground black pepper
chopped fresh flat leaf parsley, to garnish

1 Melt the butter in a large, heavy-based saucepan or deep frying pan and fry the onion over a gentle heat for about 4–5 minutes, stirring frequently, until softened and lightly browned. Pour the stock into another pan and heat it to simmering point.

2 Add the rice to the onion mixture, stir until the grains start to swell and burst, then add the wine. Stir until it stops sizzling and most of it has been absorbed by the rice, then pour in a little of the hot stock. Add salt and pepper to taste. Stir over a low heat until the stock has been absorbed.

3 Gradually add the remaining stock, a little at a time, allowing the rice to absorb the liquid before adding more, and stirring constantly. After 20–25 minutes the rice will be *al dente* and the risotto creamy.

4 Turn off the heat under the pan, then add the Gruyère, taleggio, Gorgonzola and 30ml/2 tbsp of the Parmesan cheese. Stir gently until the cheeses have melted, then taste for seasoning. Spoon into a serving bowl and garnish with parsley. Serve the remaining Parmesan separately.

TIMBALLO OF RICE WITH PEAS

THE TIMBALLO GETS ITS NAME FROM THE FACT THAT IT LOOKS LIKE AN INVERTED KETTLEDRUM
(TIMBALLO OR TIMPANO). IT IS MADE LIKE A RISOTTO, BUT IS GIVEN A FINAL BAKING IN THE OVEN.

SERVES THREE TO FOUR

INGREDIENTS
  75g/3oz/6 tbsp butter
  30ml/2 tbsp olive oil
  1 small onion, finely chopped
  50g/2oz ham, cut into small dice
  45ml/3 tbsp finely chopped fresh
    parsley, plus a few sprigs to garnish
  2 garlic cloves, very finely chopped
  225g/8oz/2 cups shelled peas,
    thawed if frozen
  60ml/4 tbsp water
  1.3 litres/2¼ pints/5½ cups chicken
    or vegetable stock
  350g/12oz/1¾ cups risotto rice,
    preferably Arborio
  75g/3oz/1 cup freshly grated
    Parmesan cheese
  175g/6oz fontina cheese, very
    thinly sliced

1 Preheat the oven to 180°C/350°F/
Gas 4. Heat half the butter and all the
oil in a large, heavy-based pan. Cook
the onion until soft, then add the ham
and stir over a medium heat for 3–4
minutes. Stir in the parsley and garlic.
Cook for 2 minutes. Add the peas, then
season and add the water.

2 Cover the pan, and cook for
8 minutes for fresh peas, or 4 minutes
for frozen peas. Remove the lid and cook
until the liquid has evaporated. Spoon
half the mixture into a dish. Heat the
stock and keep it simmering. Butter
a flat-based baking dish and line
with non-stick baking paper.

3 Stir the rice into the pea mixture
in the pan. Heat through, then add
a ladleful of stock. Cook until this has
been absorbed, stirring constantly.
Add the remaining stock in the same
way, adding more liquid only when the
previous quantity has been absorbed.

4 After about 20 minutes, when the
rice is just tender, remove it from the
heat. Season and mix in most of the
remaining butter and half the Parmesan.

5 Assemble the timballo. Sprinkle the
bottom of the dish with Parmesan, and
spoon in half the rice. Add a layer of
fontina slices and spoon over the
reserved pea and ham mixture. Smooth
level, and sprinkle with Parmesan.

6 Cover with the remaining fontina
slices and end with the remaining rice.
Sprinkle with the last of the Parmesan,
and dot with butter. Bake for 10–15
minutes. Remove from the oven, and
allow to stand for 10 minutes.

7 To unmould, slip a knife around the
timballo between the rice and the dish.
Place a serving plate upside down on
top. Wearing oven gloves, turn over dish
and plate together. Peel off the lining
paper. Serve by cutting into wedges.

LEMON AND HERB RISOTTO CAKE

THIS UNUSUAL DISH CAN BE SERVED AS A MAIN COURSE WITH SALAD, OR AS A SATISFYING SIDE DISH.
IT IS ALSO GOOD SERVED COLD, AND PACKS WELL FOR PICNICS.

SERVES FOUR

INGREDIENTS
  1 small leek, finely sliced
  600ml/1 pint/2½ cups chicken stock
  225g/8oz/generous 1 cup risotto rice
  finely grated rind of 1 lemon
  30ml/2 tbsp snipped fresh chives
  30ml/2 tbsp chopped fresh parsley
  75g/3oz/¾ cup grated mozzarella
    cheese
  salt and freshly ground black pepper

1 Preheat the oven to 200°C/400°F/
Gas 6. Lightly oil a 21cm/8½ in round
loose-based cake tin.

2 Put the leek in a large pan with
45ml/3 tbsp of the stock. Cook over a
medium heat, stirring occasionally, until
softened. Stir in the rice, then add the
remaining stock.

3 Bring to the boil. Lower the heat,
cover the pan and simmer gently,
stirring occasionally, for about 20
minutes, or until all the liquid has
been absorbed.

4 Stir in the lemon rind, herbs, cheese,
and seasoning. Spoon the mixture into
the tin, cover with foil and bake for
30–35 minutes or until lightly browned.
Leave to stand for 5 minutes, then turn
out. Serve hot or cold, in slices.

COOK'S TIP
This risotto uses less liquid than normal
and therefore has a drier consistency.

RISOTTO WITH PRAWNS

THIS PRAWN RISOTTO IS GIVEN A SOFT PINK COLOUR BY THE ADDITION OF A LITTLE TOMATO PURÉE.

SERVES THREE TO FOUR

INGREDIENTS
  350g/12oz large raw prawns, in
    the shells
  1 litres/1¾ pints/4 cups water
  1 bay leaf
  1–2 fresh parsley sprigs
  5ml/1 tsp whole peppercorns
  2 garlic cloves, peeled and left whole
  65g/2½oz/5 tbsp butter
  2 shallots, finely chopped
  275g/10oz/1½ cups risotto rice
  15ml/1 tbsp tomato purée softened
    in 120ml/4fl oz/½ cup dry white
    wine
  salt and freshly ground black pepper

1 Put the prawns in a large saucepan and add the water, herbs, peppercorns and garlic. Bring to the boil over a medium heat. As soon as the prawns turn pink, lift them out, peel them and return the shells to the saucepan. Boil the stock with the shells for 10 minutes more, then strain. Return the stock to the clean pan, and simmer gently until needed.

2 Slice the prawns in half lengthways, removing the dark vein along the back. Set four halves aside for the garnish, and roughly chop the rest.

3 Heat two-thirds of the butter in a flameproof casserole and fry the shallots until golden. Add the rice, mixing well to coat it with butter. Pour in the tomato purée and wine and cook until it has been absorbed. Add the simmering stock, a ladleful at a time, allowing it to be absorbed before adding more.

4 When all the stock has been absorbed and the rice is creamy, stir in the chopped prawns, the remaining butter and seasoning. Cover and let the risotto rest for 3–4 minutes. Spoon into a bowl, garnish with the reserved prawns and serve.

MUSHROOM RISOTTO

MUSHROOM RISOTTO IS EASY TO MAKE AND APPEALS TO ALMOST EVERYONE. WILD MUSHROOMS WILL GIVE A MORE INTENSE FLAVOUR, BUT YOU CAN USE WHATEVER MUSHROOMS ARE AVAILABLE.

SERVES THREE TO FOUR

INGREDIENTS
  25g/1oz/⅓ cup dried wild
    mushrooms, preferably porcini
  350ml/12fl oz/1½ cups warm water
  900ml/1½ pints/3¾ cups beef or
    chicken stock
  175g/6oz/1½–2 cups button
    mushrooms, sliced
  juice of ½ lemon
  75g/3oz/6 tbsp butter
  30ml/2 tbsp finely chopped fresh
    parsley
  30ml/2 tbsp olive oil
  1 small onion, finely chopped
  275g/10oz/1½ cups risotto rice
  120ml/4fl oz/½ cup dry white wine
  45ml/3 tbsp freshly grated Parmesan
    cheese
  salt and freshly ground black pepper
  fresh herbs, to garnish

1 Put the dried mushrooms in a bowl with the warm water. Soak them for at least 40 minutes, then lift them out and rinse them thoroughly. Filter the soaking water through a strainer lined with kitchen paper, and pour into a saucepan. Add the stock to the pan and bring to simmering point.

2 Toss the button mushrooms with the lemon juice in a bowl. Melt a third of the butter in a saucepan and fry the button mushrooms until they give up their juices and begin to brown. Stir in the parsley, cook for 30 seconds more, then transfer to a bowl.

3 Heat the olive oil and half the remaining butter in the saucepan and fry the onion until soft. Add the rice and stir constantly, so that the grains are evenly coated in the oil.

4 Stir in all of the mushrooms, add the wine, and cook over a medium heat until it has been absorbed. Add the stock, a ladleful at a time, making sure each is absorbed before adding more. When all the liquid has been absorbed, remove the pan from the heat, stir in the remaining butter, the Parmesan and seasoning. Cover the pan and allow to rest for 3–4 minutes before serving.

RISOTTO ALLA MILANESE

THIS CLASSIC RISOTTO IS ALWAYS SERVED WITH THE HEARTY BEEF STEW, OSSO BUCO, BUT ALSO MAKES A DELICIOUS FIRST COURSE OR LIGHT SUPPER DISH IN ITS OWN RIGHT.

SERVES THREE TO FOUR

INGREDIENTS
    about 1.2 litres/2 pints/5 cups beef
      or chicken stock
    good pinch of saffron strands
    75g/3oz/6 tbsp butter
    1 onion, finely chopped
    275g/10oz/1½ cups risotto rice
    75g/3oz/1 cup freshly grated
      Parmesan cheese
    salt and freshly ground black pepper

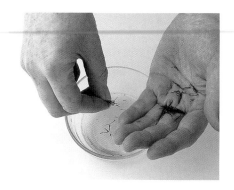

1 Bring the stock to the boil, then reduce to a low simmer. Ladle a little stock into a small bowl. Add the saffron strands and leave to infuse.

2 Melt 50g/2oz/4 tbsp of the butter in a large saucepan until foaming. Add the onion and cook gently for about 3 minutes, stirring frequently, until softened but not browned.

3 Add the rice. Stir until the grains start to swell and burst, then add a few ladlefuls of the stock, with the saffron liquid and salt and pepper to taste. Stir over a low heat until the stock has been absorbed. Add the remaining stock, a few ladlefuls at a time, allowing the rice to absorb all the liquid before adding more, and stirring constantly. After 20–25 minutes, the rice should be just tender and the risotto golden yellow, moist and creamy.

4 Gently stir in about two-thirds of the grated Parmesan and the remaining butter. Heat through until the butter has melted, then taste for seasoning. Transfer the risotto to a warmed serving bowl or platter and serve hot, with the remaining grated Parmesan served separately.

RISI E BISI

A CLASSIC PEA AND HAM RISOTTO FROM THE VENETO. ALTHOUGH THIS IS TRADITIONALLY SERVED AS A STARTER IN ITALY, IT ALSO MAKES AN EXCELLENT SUPPER DISH WITH HOT, CRUSTY BREAD.

SERVES FOUR

INGREDIENTS
75g/3oz/6 tbsp butter
1 small onion, finely chopped
about 1 litre/1¾ pints/4 cups
  simmering chicken stock
275g/10oz/1½ cups risotto rice
150ml/¼ pint/⅔ cup dry white wine
225g/8oz/2 cups frozen petits pois,
  thawed
115g/4oz cooked ham, diced
salt and freshly ground black pepper
50g/2oz/⅔ cup freshly grated
  Parmesan cheese, to serve

1 Melt 50g/2oz/4 tbsp of the butter in a saucepan until foaming. Add the onion and cook gently for about 3 minutes, stirring frequently, until softened. Have the hot stock ready in an adjacent pan.

2 Add the rice to the onion mixture. Stir until the grains start to swell, then pour in the wine. Stir until it stops sizzling and most of it has been absorbed, then pour in a little hot stock, with salt and pepper to taste. Stir continuously, over a low heat, until all the stock has been absorbed.

3 Add the remaining stock, a little at a time, allowing the rice to absorb all the liquid before adding more, and stirring constantly. Add the peas after about 20 minutes. After 25–30 minutes, the rice should be *al dente* and the risotto moist and creamy.

4 Gently stir in the diced cooked ham and the remaining butter. Heat through until the butter has melted, then taste for seasoning. Transfer to a warmed serving bowl. Grate or shave a little Parmesan over the top and serve the rest separately.

COOK'S TIP
Always use fresh Parmesan cheese, grated off a block. It has a far superior flavour to the ready-grated Parmesan.

Risotto-stuffed Aubergines with Spicy Tomato Sauce

Aubergines are a challenge to the creative cook and allow for some unusual recipe ideas. Here, they are filled with a rice stuffing and baked with a cheese and pine nut topping.

SERVES FOUR

INGREDIENTS
    4 small aubergines
    105ml/7 tbsp olive oil
    1 small onion, chopped
    175g/6oz/scant 1 cup risotto rice
    750ml/1¼ pints/3 cups hot vegetable
      stock
    15ml/1 tbsp white wine vinegar
    25g/1oz/⅓ cup freshly grated
      Parmesan cheese
    15g/½oz/2 tbsp pine nuts
For the tomato sauce
    300ml/½ pint/1¼ cups thick passata
      or puréed tomatoes
    5ml/1 tsp mild curry paste
    pinch of salt

1 Preheat the oven to 200°C/400°F/
Gas 6. Cut the aubergines in half
lengthways, and remove the flesh with
a small knife. Brush the shells with
30ml/2 tbsp of the oil and bake on a
baking sheet, supported by crumpled
foil, for 6–8 minutes.

2 Chop the aubergine flesh. Heat the
remaining oil in a medium pan. Add
the aubergine flesh and the onion, and
cook over a gentle heat for 3–4 minutes
until soft. Add the rice and stock, and
leave to simmer, uncovered, for about
15 minutes. Add the vinegar.

COOK'S TIP
If the aubergine shells do not stand
level, cut a thin slice from the bottom.

3 Increase the oven temperature to
230°C/450°F/Gas 8. Spoon the rice
mixture into the aubergine skins, top
with the cheese and pine nuts, return
to the oven and brown for 5 minutes.

4 To make the sauce, mix the passata
or puréed tomatoes with the curry paste
in a small pan. Heat through and add
salt to taste. Spoon the sauce on to four
individual serving plates and arrange
two aubergine halves on each one.

LEEK, MUSHROOM AND LEMON RISOTTO

LEEKS AND LEMON GO TOGETHER BEAUTIFULLY IN THIS LIGHT RISOTTO, WHILE MUSHROOMS ADD TEXTURE AND EXTRA FLAVOUR.

SERVES FOUR

INGREDIENTS

225g/8oz trimmed leeks
225g/8oz/2–3 cups brown cap
  mushrooms
30ml/2 tbsp olive oil
3 garlic cloves, crushed
75g/3oz/6 tbsp butter
1 large onion, roughly chopped
350g/12oz/1¾ cups risotto rice
1.2 litres/2 pints/5 cups simmering
  vegetable stock
grated rind of 1 lemon
45ml/3 tbsp lemon juice
50g/2oz/⅔ cup freshly grated
  Parmesan cheese
60ml/4 tbsp mixed chopped fresh
  chives and flat leaf parsley
salt and freshly ground black pepper

1 Slice the leeks in half lengthways, wash them well and then slice them evenly. Wipe the mushrooms with kitchen paper and chop them roughly.

2 Heat the oil in a large saucepan and cook the garlic for 1 minute. Add the leeks, mushrooms and plenty of seasoning and cook over a medium heat for about 10 minutes, or until the leeks have softened and browned. Spoon into a bowl and set aside.

3 Add 25g/1oz/2 tbsp of the butter to the pan. As soon as it has melted, add the onion and cook over a medium heat for 5 minutes until it has softened and is golden.

4 Stir in the rice and cook for about 1 minute until the grains begin to look translucent and are coated in the fat. Add a ladleful of stock and cook gently, stirring occasionally, until the liquid has been absorbed.

5 Continue to add stock, a ladleful at a time, until all of it has been absorbed, and stirring constantly. This should take about 25–30 minutes. The risotto will turn thick and creamy and the rice should be tender but not sticky.

6 Just before serving, add the leeks and mushrooms, with the remaining butter. Stir in the grated lemon rind and juice. Add the grated Parmesan cheese and the herbs. Adjust the seasoning and serve immediately.

RISOTTO WITH CHICKEN

THIS IS A CLASSIC COMBINATION OF CHICKEN AND RICE, COOKED WITH PARMA HAM, WHITE WINE AND PARMESAN CHEESE.

SERVES SIX

INGREDIENTS

30ml/2 tbsp olive oil
225g/8oz skinless, boneless chicken
   breasts, cut into 2.5cm/1in cubes
1 onion, finely chopped
1 garlic clove, finely chopped
450g/1lb/2⅓ cups risotto rice
120ml/4fl oz/½ cup dry white wine
1.5ml/¼ tsp saffron threads
1.75 litres/3 pints/7½ cups
   simmering chicken stock
50g/2oz Parma ham, cut into thin
   strips
25g/1oz/2 tbsp butter, cubed
25g/1oz/⅓ cup freshly grated
   Parmesan cheese, plus extra to
   serve
salt and freshly ground black pepper
flat leaf parsley, to garnish

1 Heat the oil in a frying pan over a moderately high heat. Add the chicken cubes and cook, stirring, until they start to turn white.

2 Reduce the heat to low and add the onion and garlic. Cook, stirring, until the onion is soft. Stir in the rice. Sauté for 1–2 minutes, stirring constantly, until all the rice grains are coated in oil.

3 Add the wine and cook, stirring, until the wine has been absorbed. Stir the saffron into the simmering stock, then add ladlefuls of stock to the rice, allowing each ladleful to be absorbed before adding the next.

4 When the rice is three-quarters cooked, add the Parma ham and continue cooking until the rice is just tender and the risotto creamy.

5 Add the butter and the Parmesan and stir in well. Season with salt and pepper to taste. Serve the risotto hot, sprinkled with a little more Parmesan, and garnish with parsley.

RISOTTO WITH SMOKED BACON AND TOMATO

A CLASSIC RISOTTO, WITH PLENTY OF ONIONS, SMOKED BACON AND SUN-DRIED TOMATOES. YOU'LL WANT TO KEEP GOING BACK FOR MORE!

SERVES FOUR TO SIX

INGREDIENTS
  8 sun-dried tomatoes in olive oil
  275g/10oz good-quality rindless
    smoked back bacon
  75g/3oz/6 tbsp butter
  450g/1lb onions, roughly chopped
  2 garlic cloves, crushed
  350g/12oz/1¾ cups risotto rice
  300ml/½ pint/1¼ cups dry white wine
  1 litre/1¾ pints/4 cups simmering
    vegetable stock
  50g/2oz/⅔ cup freshly grated
    Parmesan cheese
  45ml/3 tbsp mixed chopped fresh
    chives and flat leaf parsley
  salt and freshly ground black pepper

1 Drain the sun-dried tomatoes and reserve 15ml/1 tbsp of the oil. Roughly chop the tomatoes and set aside. Cut the bacon into 2.5cm/1in pieces.

2 Heat the oil from the sun-dried tomatoes in a large saucepan. Fry the bacon until well cooked and golden. Remove with a slotted spoon and drain on kitchen paper.

3 Heat 25g/1oz/2 tbsp of the butter in a saucepan and fry the onions and garlic over a medium heat for 10 minutes, until soft and golden brown.

4 Stir in the rice. Cook for 1 minute, until the grains turn translucent. Stir the wine into the stock. Add a ladleful of the mixture to the rice and cook gently until the liquid has been absorbed.

5 Stir in another ladleful of the stock and wine mixture and allow it to be absorbed. Repeat this process until all the liquid has been used up. This should take 25–30 minutes. The risotto will turn thick and creamy, and the rice should be tender but not sticky.

6 Just before serving, stir in the bacon, sun-dried tomatoes, Parmesan, half the herbs and the remaining butter. Adjust the seasoning (remember that the bacon may be quite salty) and serve sprinkled with the remaining herbs.

SHELLFISH RISOTTO WITH MIXED MUSHROOMS

THIS IS A QUICK AND EASY RISOTTO, WHERE ALL THE LIQUID IS ADDED IN ONE GO. THE METHOD IS WELL-SUITED TO THIS SHELLFISH DISH, AS IT MEANS EVERYTHING COOKS TOGETHER UNDISTURBED.

SERVES SIX

INGREDIENTS
225g/8oz live mussels
225g/8oz live Venus or carpet
  shell clams
45ml/3 tbsp olive oil
1 onion, chopped
450g/1lb/2⅓ cups risotto rice
1.75 litres/3 pints/7½ cups simmering
  chicken or vegetable stock
150ml/¼ pint/⅔ cup white wine
225g/8oz/2–3 cups assorted wild and
  cultivated mushrooms, trimmed and
  sliced
115g/4oz raw peeled prawns,
  deveined
1 medium or 2 small squid, cleaned,
  trimmed and sliced
3 drops truffle oil (optional)
75ml/5 tbsp chopped mixed fresh
  parsley and chervil
celery salt and cayenne pepper

1 Scrub the mussels and clams clean and discard any that are open and do not close when tapped with a knife. Set aside. Heat the oil in a large frying pan and fry the onion for 6–8 minutes until soft but not browned.

2 Add the rice, stirring to coat the grains in oil, then pour in the stock and wine and cook for 5 minutes. Add the mushrooms and cook for 5 minutes more, stirring occasionally.

3 Add the prawns, squid, mussels and clams and stir into the rice. Cover the pan and simmer over a low heat for 15 minutes until the prawns have turned pink and the mussels and clams have opened. Discard any of the shellfish that remain closed.

4 Switch off the heat. Add the truffle oil, if using, and stir in the herbs. Cover tightly and leave to stand for 5–10 minutes to allow all the flavours to blend. Season to taste with celery salt and a pinch of cayenne, pile into a warmed dish, and serve immediately.

SALMON RISOTTO <u>WITH</u> CUCUMBER AND TARRAGON

THIS SIMPLE RISOTTO IS COOKED ALL IN ONE GO, AND IS THEREFORE SIMPLER THAN THE USUAL RISOTTO. IF YOU PREFER TO COOK THE TRADITIONAL WAY, ADD THE LIQUID GRADUALLY, ADDING THE SALMON ABOUT TWO-THIRDS OF THE WAY THROUGH COOKING.

SERVES FOUR

INGREDIENTS
25g/1oz/2 tbsp butter
small bunch of spring onions, white
   parts only, chopped
½ cucumber, peeled, seeded and
   chopped
350g/12oz/1¾ cups risotto rice
1.2 litres/2 pints/5 cups hot chicken
   or fish stock
150ml/¼ pint/⅔ cup dry white wine
450g/1lb salmon fillet, skinned and
   diced
45ml/3 tbsp chopped fresh tarragon
salt and freshly ground black pepper

1 Heat the butter in a large saucepan and add the spring onions and cucumber. Cook for 2–3 minutes without letting the spring onions colour.

2 Stir in the rice, then pour in the stock and wine. Bring to the boil, then lower the heat and simmer, uncovered, for 10 minutes, stirring occasionally.

3 Stir in the diced salmon and season to taste with salt and freshly ground black pepper. Continue cooking for a further 5 minutes, stirring occasionally, then switch off the heat. Cover and leave to stand for 5 minutes.

4 Remove the lid, add the chopped tarragon and mix lightly. Spoon into a warmed bowl and serve.

VARIATION
Carnaroli risotto rice would be excellent in this risotto, although if it is not available, Arborio can be used instead.

TRUFFLE AND LOBSTER RISOTTO

TO CAPTURE THE PRECIOUS QUALITIES OF THE FRESH TRUFFLE, PARTNER IT WITH LOBSTER AND SERVE IN A SILKY SMOOTH RISOTTO. BOTH TRUFFLE SHAVINGS AND TRUFFLE OIL ARE ADDED TOWARDS THE END OF COOKING TO PRESERVE THEIR FLAVOUR.

SERVES FOUR

INGREDIENTS

50g/2oz/4 tbsp unsalted butter
1 medium onion, chopped
350g/12oz/1¾ cups risotto rice,
    preferably Carnaroli
1 fresh thyme sprig
150ml/¼ pint/⅔ cup dry white wine
1.2 litres/2 pints/5 cups simmering
    chicken stock
1 freshly cooked lobster
45ml/3 tbsp chopped mixed fresh
    parsley and chervil
3–4 drops truffle oil
2 hard-boiled eggs
1 fresh black or white truffle
salt and freshly ground black pepper

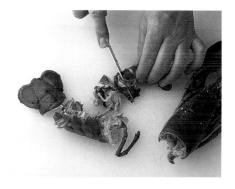

1 Melt the butter, add the onion and fry until soft. Add the rice and stir well to coat with fat. Add the thyme, then the wine, and cook until it has been absorbed. Add the chicken stock a little at a time, stirring. Let each ladleful be absorbed before adding the next.

2 Twist off the lobster tail, cut the underside with scissors and remove the white tail meat. Carefully break open the claws with a small kitchen hammer and remove the flesh. Cut half the meat into big chunks, then roughly chop the remainder.

3 Stir in the chopped lobster meat, half the chopped herbs and the truffle oil. Remove the rice from the heat, cover and leave to stand for 5 minutes.

4 Divide among warmed plates and centre the lobster chunks on top. Cut the hard-boiled eggs into wedges and arrange them around the lobster meat. Finally, shave fresh truffle over each portion and sprinkle with the remaining herbs. Serve immediately.

COOK'S TIP
To make the most of the aromatic truffle scent, keep the tuber in the rice jar for a few days before use.

PANCETTA AND BROAD BEAN RISOTTO

THIS DELICIOUS RISOTTO MAKES A HEALTHY AND FILLING MEAL, SERVED WITH COOKED FRESH SEASONAL VEGETABLES OR A MIXED GREEN SALAD.

SERVES FOUR

INGREDIENTS
15ml/1 tbsp olive oil
1 onion, chopped
2 garlic cloves, finely chopped
175g/6oz smoked pancetta, diced
350g/12oz/1¾ cups risotto rice
1.5 litres/2½ pints/6¼ cups
  simmering chicken stock
225g/8oz/2 cups frozen baby broad
  beans
30ml/2 tbsp chopped fresh mixed
  herbs, such as parsley, thyme and
  oregano
salt and freshly ground black pepper
shavings of Parmesan cheese, to
  serve

1 Heat the oil in a large saucepan. Add the onion, garlic and pancetta and cook gently for about 5 minutes, stirring occasionally. Do not allow the onion and garlic to brown.

2 Add the rice to the pan and cook for 1 minute, stirring. Add a ladleful of stock and cook, stirring all the time, until the liquid has been absorbed.

3 Continue adding the stock, a ladleful at a time, until the rice is tender, and almost all the liquid has been absorbed. This will take 30–35 minutes.

4 Meanwhile, cook the broad beans in a saucepan of lightly salted, boiling water for about 3 minutes until tender. Drain well and stir into the risotto, with the mixed herbs. Add salt and pepper to taste. Spoon into a bowl and serve, sprinkled with shavings of fresh Parmesan cheese.

COOK'S TIP
If the broad beans are large, or if you prefer skinned beans, remove the outer skin after cooking.

Brown Rice Risotto with Mushrooms and Parmesan

A classic risotto of mixed mushrooms, herbs and fresh Parmesan cheese, but made using brown long grain rice. Serve simply, with a mixed leaf salad tossed in a light dressing.

SERVES FOUR

INGREDIENTS

- 15ml/1 tbsp olive oil
- 4 shallots, finely chopped
- 2 garlic cloves, crushed
- 15g/½oz/2 tbsp dried porcini mushrooms, soaked in 150ml/ ¼ pint/⅔ cup hot water for 20 minutes
- 250g/9oz/1⅓ cups brown long grain rice
- 900ml/1½ pints/3¾ cups well-flavoured vegetable stock
- 450g/1lb/6 cups mixed mushrooms, such as closed cup, chestnut and field mushrooms, sliced if large
- 30–45ml/2–3 tbsp chopped fresh flat leaf parsley
- 50g/2oz/⅔ cup freshly grated Parmesan cheese
- salt and freshly ground black pepper

1 Heat the oil in a large saucepan, add the shallots and garlic and cook gently for 5 minutes, stirring. Drain the porcini, reserving their liquid, and chop roughly. Add the brown rice to the shallot mixture and stir to coat the grains in oil.

2 Stir the vegetable stock and the porcini soaking liquid into the rice mixture in the saucepan. Bring to the boil, lower the heat and simmer, uncovered, for about 20 minutes or until most of the liquid has been absorbed, stirring frequently.

3 Add all the mushrooms, stir well, and cook the risotto for 10–15 minutes more until the liquid has been absorbed.

4 Season with salt and pepper to taste, stir in the chopped parsley and grated Parmesan and serve at once.

CRAB RISOTTO

THIS IS A FRESH-FLAVOURED RISOTTO WHICH MAKES A WONDERFUL MAIN COURSE OR STARTER.
YOU WILL NEED TWO CRABS FOR THIS RECIPE, AND IT IS THEREFORE A GOOD DISH TO FOLLOW
A VISIT TO THE SEASIDE, WHERE CRABS ARE CHEAP AND PLENTIFUL.

SERVES THREE TO FOUR

INGREDIENTS
2 large cooked crabs
15ml/1 tbsp olive oil
25g/1oz/2 tbsp butter
2 shallots, finely chopped
275g/10oz/1½ cups risotto rice,
  preferably Carnaroli
75ml/5 tbsp Marsala or brandy
1 litre/1¾ pints/4 cups simmering
  fish stock
5ml/1 tsp chopped fresh tarragon
5ml/1 tsp chopped fresh parsley
60ml/4 tbsp double cream
salt and freshly ground black pepper

1 First remove the crab meat from each of the shells in turn. Hold the crab firmly in one hand and hit the back underside firmly with the heel of your hand. This should loosen the shell from the body. Using your thumbs, push against the body and pull away from the shell. From the inside of the shell, remove and discard the intestines.

2 Discard the grey gills (dead man's fingers). Break off the claws and legs from the body, then use a small hammer or crackers to break them open. Using a pick, remove the meat from the claws and legs. Place the meat on a plate.

3 Using a pick or a skewer, pick out the white meat from the body cavities and place on the plate with the meat from the claws and legs, reserving some white meat to garnish. Scoop out the brown meat from inside the shell and set aside with the white meat on the plate.

4 Heat the oil and butter in a pan and gently fry the shallots until soft but not browned. Add the rice. Cook for a few minutes, stirring, until the rice is slightly translucent, then add the Marsala or brandy, bring to the boil, and cook, stirring, until the liquid has evaporated.

5 Add a ladleful of hot stock and cook, stirring, until all the stock has been absorbed. Continue cooking in this way until about two-thirds of the stock has been added, then carefully stir in all the crab meat and the herbs.

6 Continue to cook the risotto, adding the remaining stock. When the rice is almost cooked but still has a slight "bite", remove it from the heat, stir in the cream and adjust the seasoning. Cover and leave to stand for 3 minutes to finish cooking. Serve garnished with the reserved white crab meat.

MONKFISH RISOTTO

MONKFISH IS A VERSATILE, FIRM-TEXTURED FISH WITH A SUPERB FLAVOUR, WHICH IS ACCENTUATED WITH LEMON GRASS IN THIS SOPHISTICATED RISOTTO.

SERVES THREE TO FOUR

INGREDIENTS
  seasoned flour
  about 450g/1lb monkfish, cut into
    cubes
  30ml/2 tbsp olive oil
  40g/1½oz/3 tbsp butter
  2 shallots, finely chopped
  1 lemon grass stalk, finely chopped
  275g/10oz/1½ cups risotto rice,
    preferably Carnaroli
  175ml/6fl oz/¾ cup dry white wine
  1 litre/1¾ pints/4 cups simmering
    fish stock
  30ml/2 tbsp chopped fresh parsley
  salt and white pepper
  dressed salad leaves, to serve

4 Tip in the rice. Cook for 2–3 minutes, stirring, until the rice is coated with oil and is slightly translucent. Gradually add the wine and the hot stock, stirring and waiting until each ladleful has been absorbed before adding the next.

5 When the rice is about three-quarters cooked, stir in the monkfish. Continue to cook the risotto, adding the remaining stock and stirring constantly until the grains of rice are tender, but still retain a bit of "bite". Season with salt and white pepper.

6 Remove the pan from the heat, stir in the parsley and cover with the lid. Leave the risotto to stand for a few minutes before serving with a garnish of dressed salad leaves.

COOK'S TIP
Lemon grass adds a subtle flavour to this dish. Remove the tough outer skin and chop the inner flesh finely.

1 Spoon the seasoned flour over the monkfish cubes in a bowl. Toss the monkfish until coated.

2 Heat 15ml/1 tbsp of the oil with half the butter in a frying pan. Fry the monkfish cubes over a medium to high heat for 3–4 minutes until cooked, turning occasionally. Transfer to a plate and set aside.

3 Heat the remaining oil and butter in a saucepan and fry the shallots over a low heat for about 4 minutes until soft but not brown. Add the lemon grass and cook for 1–2 minutes more.

SCALLOP RISOTTO

TRY TO BUY FRESH SCALLOPS FOR THIS DISH, WHICH TASTE MUCH BETTER THAN FROZEN ONES.
FRESH SCALLOPS COME WITH THE CORAL ATTACHED, WHICH ADDS FLAVOUR, TEXTURE AND COLOUR.

SERVES THREE TO FOUR

INGREDIENTS
   about 12 scallops, with their corals
   50g/2oz/4 tbsp butter
   15ml/1 tbsp olive oil
   30ml/2 tbsp Pernod
   2 shallots, finely chopped
   275g/10oz/1½ cups risotto rice
   1 litre/1¾ pints/4 cups simmering
     fish stock
   generous pinch of saffron strands,
     dissolved in 15ml/1 tbsp warm milk
   30ml/2 tbsp chopped fresh parsley
   60ml/4 tbsp double cream
   salt and freshly ground black pepper

1 Separate the scallops from their corals. Cut the white flesh in half or into 2cm/¾in slices.

2 Melt half the butter with 5ml/1 tsp oil. Fry the white parts of the scallops for 2–3 minutes. Pour over the Pernod, heat for a few seconds, then ignite and allow to flame for a few seconds. When the flames have died down, remove the pan from the heat.

3 Heat the remaining butter and olive oil in a pan and fry the shallots for about 3–4 minutes, until soft but not browned. Add the rice and cook for a few minutes, stirring, until the rice is coated with oil and is beginning to turn translucent around the edges.

4 Gradually add the hot stock, a ladleful at a time, stirring constantly and waiting for each ladleful of stock to be absorbed before adding the next.

5 When the rice is very nearly cooked, add the scallops and all the juices from the pan, together with the corals, the saffron milk, parsley and seasoning. Stir well to mix. Continue cooking, adding the remaining stock and stirring occasionally, until the risotto is thick and creamy.

6 Remove the pan from the heat, stir in the double cream and cover. Leave the risotto to rest for about 3 minutes to complete the cooking, then pile it into a warmed bowl and serve.

SQUID RISOTTO WITH CHILLI AND CORIANDER

SQUID NEEDS TO BE COOKED EITHER VERY QUICKLY OR VERY SLOWLY. HERE THE SQUID IS MARINATED IN LIME AND KIWI FRUIT — A POPULAR METHOD IN NEW ZEALAND FOR TENDERISING SQUID.

SERVES THREE TO FOUR

INGREDIENTS
    about 450g/1lb squid
    about 45ml/3 tbsp olive oil
    15g/½oz/1 tbsp butter
    1 onion, finely chopped
    2 garlic cloves, crushed
    1 fresh red chilli, seeded and finely
      sliced
    275g/10oz/1½ cups risotto rice
    175ml/6fl oz/¾ cup dry white wine
    1 litre/1¾ pints/4 cups simmering
      fish stock
    30ml/2 tbsp chopped fresh coriander
    salt and freshly ground black pepper
For the marinade
    2 ripe kiwi fruit, chopped and mashed
    1 fresh red chilli, seeded and finely
      sliced
    30ml/2 tbsp fresh lime juice

1 If not already cleaned, prepare the squid by cutting off the tentacles at the base and pulling to remove the quill. Discard the quill and intestines, if necessary, and pull away the thin outer skin. Rinse the body and cut into thin strips: cut the tentacles into short pieces, discarding the beak and eyes.

2 Mash the kiwi fruit for the marinade in a bowl, then stir in the chilli and lime juice. Add the squid, stirring to coat all the strips in the mixture. Season with salt and freshly ground black pepper, cover with clear film and set aside in the fridge for 4 hours or overnight.

3 Drain the squid. Heat 15ml/1 tbsp of the olive oil in a frying pan and cook the strips, in batches if necessary, for about 30–60 seconds over a high heat. It is important that the squid cooks very quickly. Transfer the cooked squid to a plate and set aside. Don't worry if some of the marinade clings to the squid, but if too much juice accumulates in the pan, pour this into a jug and add more olive oil when cooking the next batch, so that the squid fries rather than simmers. Reserve the accumulated juices in a jug.

4 Heat the remaining oil with the butter in a large saucepan and gently fry the onion and garlic for 5–6 minutes until soft. Add the sliced chilli to the saucepan and fry for 1 minute more.

5 Add the rice. Cook for a few minutes, stirring, until the rice is coated with oil and is slightly translucent, then stir in the wine until it has been absorbed.

6 Gradually add the hot stock and the reserved cooking liquid from the squid, a ladleful at a time, stirring the rice constantly and waiting until each quantity of stock has been absorbed before adding the next.

7 When the rice is about three-quarters cooked, stir in the squid and continue cooking the risotto until all the stock has been absorbed and the rice is tender, but retains a bit of "bite". Stir in the chopped coriander, cover with the lid or a dish towel, and leave to rest for a few minutes before serving.

COOK'S TIP
Although fish stock underlines the flavour of the squid, a light chicken or vegetable stock would also work well in this recipe.

MUSSEL RISOTTO

FRESH ROOT GINGER AND CORIANDER ADD A DISTINCTIVE FLAVOUR TO THIS DISH, WHILE THE GREEN CHILLIES GIVE IT A LITTLE HEAT. THE CHILLIES COULD BE OMITTED FOR A MILDER DISH.

SERVES THREE TO FOUR

INGREDIENTS

900g/2lb fresh mussels
about 250ml/8fl oz/1 cup dry white
    wine
30ml/2 tbsp olive oil
1 onion, chopped
2 garlic cloves, crushed
1–2 fresh green chillies, seeded and
    finely sliced
2.5cm/1in piece of fresh root ginger,
    grated
275g/10oz/1½ cups risotto rice
900ml/1½ pints/3¾ cups simmering
    fish stock
30ml/2 tbsp chopped fresh coriander
30ml/2 tbsp double cream
salt and freshly ground black pepper

3 Add the rice and cook over a medium heat for 2 minutes, stirring, until the rice is coated in oil and becomes translucent.

4 Stir in the reserved cooking liquid from the mussels. When this has been absorbed, add the remaining wine and cook stirring, until this has been absorbed. Now add the hot fish stock, a little at a time, making sure each addition has been absorbed before adding the next.

5 When the rice is about three-quarters cooked, stir in the mussels. Add the coriander and season with salt and pepper. Continue adding stock to the risotto until it is creamy and the rice is tender but slightly firm in the centre.

6 Remove the risotto from the heat, stir in the cream, cover and leave to rest for a few minutes. Spoon into a warmed serving dish, decorate with the reserved mussels in their shells, and serve immediately.

1 Scrub the mussels, discarding any that do not close when sharply tapped. Place in a large saucepan. Add 120ml/4fl oz/½ cup of the wine and bring to the boil. Cover the pan and cook the mussels for 4–5 minutes until they have opened, shaking the pan occasionally. Drain, reserving the liquid and discarding any mussels that have not opened. Remove most of the mussels from their shells, reserving a few in their shells for decoration. Strain the mussel liquid.

2 Heat the oil and fry the onion and garlic for 3–4 minutes until beginning to soften. Add the chillies. Continue to cook over a low heat for 1–2 minutes, stirring frequently, then stir in the ginger and fry gently for 1 minute more.

SEAFOOD RISOTTO

You can use any shellfish or seafood for this risotto, as long as the total weight is similar to that used here. The risotto would also make a very good starter for eight.

SERVES FOUR TO SIX

INGREDIENTS

450g/1lb fresh mussels
about 250ml/8fl oz/1 cup dry white
  wine
225g/8oz sea bass fillet, skinned and
  cut into pieces
seasoned flour
60ml/4 tbsp olive oil
8 scallops with corals separated,
  white parts halved or sliced, if large
225g/8oz squid, cleaned and cut
  into rings
12 large raw prawns or langoustines,
  heads removed
2 shallots, finely chopped
1 garlic clove, crushed
400g/14oz/2 cups risotto rice,
  preferably Carnaroli
3 tomatoes, peeled, seeded and
  chopped
1.5 litres/2½ pints/6¼ cups
  simmering fish stock
30ml/2 tbsp chopped fresh parsley
30ml/2 tbsp double cream
salt and freshly ground black pepper

1 Scrub the mussels, discarding any that do not close when sharply tapped. Place them in a large saucepan and add 90ml/6 tbsp of the wine. Bring to the boil, cover the pan and cook for 3–4 minutes until all the mussels have opened, shaking the pan occasionally. Drain, reserving the liquid and discarding any mussels that have not opened. Set aside a few mussels in their shells for garnishing; remove the others from their shells. Strain the cooking liquid.

2 Dust the pieces of sea bass in seasoned flour. Heat 30ml/2 tbsp of the olive oil in a frying pan and fry the fish for 3–4 minutes until cooked. Transfer to a plate. Add a little more oil to the pan and fry the white parts of the scallops for 1–2 minutes on both sides until tender. Transfer to a plate.

3 Fry the squid for 3–4 minutes in the same pan, adding a little more oil if necessary, then set aside. Lastly, add the prawns or langoustines and fry for a further 3–4 minutes until pink, turning frequently. Towards the end of cooking, add a splash of wine – about 30ml/ 2 tbsp – and continue cooking so that the prawns become tender, but do not burn. Remove the prawns from the pan. As soon as they are cool enough to handle, remove the shells and legs, leaving the tails intact.

4 In a large saucepan, heat the remaining olive oil and fry the shallots and garlic for 3–4 minutes over a gentle heat until the shallots are soft but not brown. Add the rice and cook for a few minutes, stirring, until the rice is coated with oil and the grains are slightly translucent. Stir in the tomatoes, with the reserved liquid from the mussels.

5 When all the free liquid has been absorbed, add the remaining wine, stirring constantly. When it has also been absorbed, gradually add the hot stock, one ladleful at a time, continuing to stir the rice constantly and waiting until each quantity of stock has been absorbed before adding the next.

6 When the risotto is three-quarters cooked, carefully stir in all the seafood, except the mussels reserved for the garnish. Continue to cook until all the stock has been absorbed and the rice is tender but still has a bit of "bite".

7 Stir in the parsley and cream and adjust the seasoning. Cover the pan and leave the risotto to stand for 2–3 minutes. Serve in individual bowls, garnished with the reserved mussels in their shells.

CHAMPAGNE RISOTTO

THIS MAY SEEM RATHER EXTRAVAGANT, BUT IT MAKES A REALLY BEAUTIFULLY FLAVOURED RISOTTO, PERFECT FOR THAT SPECIAL ANNIVERSARY DINNER.

SERVES THREE TO FOUR

INGREDIENTS

25g/1oz/2 tbsp butter
2 shallots, finely chopped
275g/10oz/1½ cups risotto rice,
  preferably Carnaroli
½ bottle or 300ml/½ pint/1¼ cups
  champagne
750ml/1¼ pints/3 cups simmering
  light vegetable or chicken stock
150ml/¼ pint/⅔ cup double cream
40g/1½oz/½ cup freshly grated
  Parmesan cheese
10ml/2 tsp very finely chopped fresh
  chervil
salt and freshly ground black pepper
black truffle shavings, to garnish
  (optional)

1 Melt the butter in a pan and fry the shallots for 2–3 minutes until softened. Add the rice and cook, stirring all the time, until the grains are evenly coated in butter and are beginning to look translucent around the edges.

2 Pour in about two-thirds of the champagne and cook over a high heat so that the liquid bubbles fiercely. Cook, stirring, until all the liquid has been absorbed before beginning to add the hot stock.

3 Add the stock, a ladleful at a time, making sure that each addition has been completely absorbed before adding the next. The risotto should gradually become creamy and velvety and all the stock should be absorbed.

4 When the rice is tender but retains a bit of "bite", stir in the remaining champagne and the double cream and Parmesan. Adjust the seasoning. Remove from the heat, cover and leave to stand for a few minutes. Stir in the chervil. If you want to gild the lily, garnish with a few truffle shavings.

ROASTED PEPPER RISOTTO

THIS MAKES AN EXCELLENT VEGETARIAN SUPPER DISH, OR A STARTER FOR SIX.

SERVES THREE TO FOUR

INGREDIENTS
1 red pepper
1 yellow pepper
15ml/1 tbsp olive oil
25g/1oz/2 tbsp butter
1 onion, chopped
2 garlic cloves, crushed
275g/10oz/1½ cups risotto rice
1 litre/1¾ pints/4 cups simmering
  vegetable stock
50g/2oz/⅔ cup freshly grated
  Parmesan cheese
salt and freshly ground black pepper
freshly grated Parmesan cheese, to
  serve (optional)

1 Preheat the grill to high. Cut the peppers in half, remove the seeds and pith and arrange, cut side down, on a baking sheet. Place under the grill for 5–6 minutes until the skin is charred. Put the peppers in a plastic bag, tie the ends and leave for 4–5 minutes.

2 Peel the peppers when they are cool enough to handle and the steam has loosened the skin. Cut into thin strips,

3 Heat the oil and butter in a pan and fry the onion and garlic for 4–5 minutes over a low heat until the onion begins to soften. Add the peppers and cook the mixture for 3–4 minutes more, stirring occasionally.

4 Stir in the rice. Cook over a medium heat for 3–4 minutes, stirring all the time, until the rice is evenly coated in oil and the outer part of each grain has become translucent.

5 Add a ladleful of stock. Cook, stirring, until all the liquid has been absorbed. Continue to add the stock, a ladleful at a time, making sure each quantity has been absorbed before adding the next.

6 When the rice is tender but retains a bit of "bite", stir in the Parmesan, and add seasoning to taste. Cover and leave to stand for 3–4 minutes, then serve, with extra Parmesan, if using.

TWO CHEESE RISOTTO

THIS UNDENIABLY RICH AND CREAMY RISOTTO IS JUST THE THING TO SERVE ON COLD WINTER
EVENINGS WHEN EVERYONE NEEDS WARMING UP.

SERVES THREE TO FOUR

INGREDIENTS
    7.5ml/1½ tsp olive oil
    50g/2oz/4 tbsp butter
    1 onion, finely chopped
    1 garlic clove, crushed
    275g/10oz/1½ cups risotto rice,
      preferably Vialone Nano
    175ml/6fl oz/¾ cup dry white wine
    1 litre/1¾ pints/4 cups simmering
      vegetable or chicken stock
    75g/3oz/¾ cup fontina cheese, cubed
    50g/2oz/⅔ cup freshly grated
      Parmesan cheese, plus extra, to
      serve
    salt and freshly ground black pepper

1 Heat the olive oil with half the butter
in a pan and gently fry the onion and
garlic for 5–6 minutes until soft. Add
the rice and cook, stirring all the time,
until the grains are coated in fat and
have become slightly translucent
around the edges.

2 Stir in the wine. Cook, stirring, until
the liquid has been absorbed, then add
a ladleful of hot stock. Stir until the
stock has been absorbed, then add the
remaining stock in the same way,
waiting for each quantity of stock to be
absorbed before adding more.

3 When the rice is half cooked, stir
in the fontina cheese, and continue
cooking and adding stock. Keep stirring
the rice all the time.

4 When the risotto is creamy and the
grains are tender but still have a bit of
"bite", stir in the remaining butter and
the Parmesan. Season, then remove the
pan from the heat, cover and leave to
rest for 3–4 minutes before serving.

QUICK RISOTTO

THIS IS RATHER A CHEAT'S RISOTTO AS IT DEFIES ALL THE RULES THAT INSIST THE STOCK IS ADDED
GRADUALLY. INSTEAD, THE RICE IS COOKED QUICKLY IN A CONVENTIONAL WAY, AND THE OTHER
INGREDIENTS ARE SIMPLY THROWN IN AT THE LAST MINUTE. IT TASTES GOOD FOR ALL THAT.

SERVES THREE TO FOUR

INGREDIENTS
    275g/10oz/1½ cups risotto rice
    1 litre/1¾ pints/4 cups simmering
      chicken stock
    115g/4oz/1 cup mozzarella cheese,
      cut into small cubes
    2 egg yolks
    30ml/2 tbsp freshly grated Parmesan
      cheese
    75g/3oz cooked ham, cut into small
      cubes
    30ml/2 tbsp chopped fresh parsley
    salt and freshly ground black pepper
    fresh parsley sprigs, to garnish
    freshly grated Parmesan cheese, to
      serve

1 Put the rice in a pan. Pour in the
stock, bring to the boil and then cover
and simmer for about 18–20 minutes
until the rice is tender.

2 Remove the pan from the heat and
quickly stir in the mozzarella, egg yolks,
Parmesan, ham and parsley. Season
well with salt and pepper.

3 Cover the pan and stand for 2–3
minutes to allow the cheese to melt,
then stir again. Pile into warmed serving
bowls and serve immediately, with extra
Parmesan cheese.

PESTO RISOTTO

If you buy the pesto — and there are some good varieties available nowadays — this is just about as easy as a risotto gets.

SERVES THREE TO FOUR

INGREDIENTS
  30ml/2 tbsp olive oil
  2 shallots, finely chopped
  1 garlic clove, crushed
  275g/10oz/1½ cups risotto rice
  175ml/6fl oz/¾ cup dry white wine
  1 litre/1¾ pints/4 cups simmering
    vegetable stock
  45ml/3 tbsp pesto
  25g/1oz/⅓ cup freshly grated
    Parmesan cheese, plus extra, to
    serve (optional)
  salt and freshly ground black pepper

1 Heat the olive oil in a pan and fry the shallots and garlic for 4–5 minutes until the shallots are soft but not browned.

2 Add the rice and cook over a medium heat, stirring all the time, until the grains of rice are coated in oil and the outer part of the grain is translucent and the inner part opaque.

3 Pour in the wine. Cook, stirring, until all of it has been absorbed, then start adding the hot stock, a ladleful at a time, stirring constantly and waiting until each addition of stock has been absorbed before adding the next.

4 After about 20 minutes, when all the stock has been absorbed and the rice is creamy and tender, stir in the pesto and Parmesan. Taste and adjust seasoning and then cover and rest for 3–4 minutes. Spoon into a bowl and serve, with extra Parmesan, if you like.

PUMPKIN AND APPLE RISOTTO

Pumpkin and other winter squash are very popular in Italy and appear in many classic recipes. If pumpkins are out of season, use butternut or onion squash — the flavours will be slightly different, but they both work well.

SERVES THREE TO FOUR

INGREDIENTS
  225g/8oz butternut squash or
    pumpkin flesh
  1 cooking apple
  120ml/4fl oz/½ cup water
  25g/1oz/2 tbsp butter
  25ml/1½ tbsp olive oil
  1 onion, finely chopped
  1 garlic clove, crushed
  275g/10oz/1½ cups risotto rice, such
    as Vialone Nano
  175ml/6fl oz/¾ cup fruity white wine
  900ml–1 litre/1½–1¾ pints/3¾–4
    cups simmering vegetable stock
  75g/3oz/1 cup freshly grated
    Parmesan cheese
  salt and freshly ground black pepper

1 Cut the squash into small pieces. Peel, core and roughly chop the apple. Place in a pan and pour in the water. Bring to the boil, then simmer for about 15–20 minutes until the squash is very tender. Drain, return the squash mixture to the pan and add half the butter. Mash the mixture roughly with a fork to break up any large pieces, but leave the mixture chunky.

2 Heat the oil and remaining butter in a pan and fry the onion and garlic until the onion is soft. Tip in the rice. Cook, stirring constantly, over a medium heat for 2 minutes until it is coated in oil and the grains are slightly translucent.

3 Add the wine and stir into the rice. When all the liquid has been absorbed, begin to add the stock a ladleful at a time, making sure each addition has been absorbed before adding the next. This should take about 20 minutes.

4 When roughly two ladlefuls of stock are left, add the squash and apple mixture together with another addition of stock. Continue to cook, stirring well and adding the rest of the stock, until the risotto is very creamy. Stir in the Parmesan cheese, adjust the seasoning and serve immediately.

ROSEMARY RISOTTO <u>WITH</u> BORLOTTI BEANS

THIS IS A CLASSIC RISOTTO WITH A SUBTLE AND COMPLEX TASTE, FROM THE HEADY FLAVOURS OF ROSEMARY TO THE SAVOURY BEANS AND THE FRUITY-SWEET FLAVOURS OF MASCARPONE AND PARMESAN.

<u>SERVES THREE TO FOUR</u>

INGREDIENTS
  400g/14oz can borlotti beans
  30ml/2 tbsp olive oil
  1 onion, chopped
  2 garlic cloves, crushed
  275g/10oz/1½ cups risotto rice
  175ml/6fl oz/¾ cup dry white wine
  900ml–1 litre/1½–1¾ pints/
    3¾–4 cups simmering vegetable or
    chicken stock
  60ml/4 tbsp mascarpone cheese
  65g/2½oz/scant 1 cup freshly grated
    Parmesan cheese, plus extra, to
    serve (optional)
  5ml/1 tsp chopped fresh rosemary
  salt and freshly ground black pepper

1 Drain the beans, rinse under cold water and drain again. Purée about two-thirds of the beans fairly coarsely in a food processor or blender. Set the remaining beans aside.

2 Heat the olive oil in a large pan and gently fry the onion and garlic for 6–8 minutes until very soft. Add the rice and cook over a medium heat for a few minutes, stirring constantly, until the grains are thoroughly coated in oil and are slightly translucent.

VARIATION
Fresh thyme or marjoram could be used for this risotto instead of rosemary, if preferred. One of the great virtues of risotto is that it lends itself well to variations. Experiment with different herbs to make your own speciality dish.

3 Pour in the wine. Cook over a medium heat for 2–3 minutes, stirring all the time, until the wine has been absorbed. Add the stock gradually, a ladleful at a time, waiting for each quantity to be absorbed before adding more, and continuing to stir.

4 When the rice is three-quarters cooked, stir in the bean purée. Continue to cook the risotto, adding the remaining stock, until it is creamy and the rice is tender but still has a bit of "bite". Add the reserved beans, with the mascarpone, Parmesan and rosemary, then season to taste. Stir thoroughly, then cover and leave to stand for about 5 minutes so that the risotto absorbs the flavours fully and the rice completes cooking. Serve with extra Parmesan, if you like.

JERUSALEM ARTICHOKE RISOTTO

THIS IS A SIMPLE AND WARMING RISOTTO, WHICH BENEFITS FROM THE DELICIOUS AND DISTINCTIVE FLAVOUR OF JERUSALEM ARTICHOKES.

SERVES THREE TO FOUR

INGREDIENTS

400g/14oz Jerusalem artichokes
40g/1½oz/3 tbsp butter
15ml/1 tbsp olive oil
1 onion, finely chopped
1 garlic clove, crushed
275g/10oz/1½ cups risotto rice
120ml/4fl oz/½ cup fruity white wine
1 litre/1¾ pints/4 cups simmering vegetable stock
10ml/2 tsp chopped fresh thyme
40g/1½oz/½ cup freshly grated Parmesan cheese, plus extra, to serve
salt and freshly ground black pepper
fresh thyme sprigs, to garnish

1 Peel the artichokes, cut them into pieces and immediately add them to a pan of lightly salted water. Simmer them until tender, then drain and mash with 15g/½oz/1 tbsp of the butter. Add a little more salt, if needed.

2 Heat the oil and the remaining butter in a pan and fry the onion and garlic for 5–6 minutes until soft. Add the rice and cook over a medium heat for about 2 minutes until the grains are translucent around the edges.

3 Pour in the wine, stir until it has been absorbed, then start adding the simmering stock, a ladleful at a time, making sure each quantity has been absorbed before adding more.

4 When you have just one last ladleful of stock to add, stir in the mashed artichokes and the chopped thyme. Season with salt and pepper. Continue cooking until the risotto is creamy and the artichokes are hot. Stir in the Parmesan. Remove from the heat, cover the pan and leave the risotto to stand for a few minutes. Spoon into a serving dish, garnish with thyme, and serve with Parmesan cheese.

DUCK RISOTTO

THIS MAKES AN EXCELLENT STARTER FOR SIX OR COULD BE SERVED FOR HALF THAT NUMBER AS A LUNCH OR SUPPER DISH. ADD A GREEN SALAD, OR SERVE WITH MANGETOUTS AND SAUTÉED RED PEPPER SLICES.

SERVES THREE TO FOUR

INGREDIENTS
2 duck breasts
30ml/2 tbsp brandy
30ml/2 tbsp orange juice
15ml/1 tbsp olive oil (optional)
1 onion, finely chopped
1 garlic clove, crushed
275g/10oz/1½ cups risotto rice
1–1.2 litres/1¾–2 pints/4–5 cups
  simmering duck, turkey or chicken
  stock
5ml/1 tsp chopped fresh thyme
5ml/1 tsp chopped fresh mint
10ml/2 tsp grated orange rind
40g/1½oz/½ cup freshly grated
  Parmesan cheese
salt and freshly ground black pepper
strips of thinly pared orange rind, to
  garnish

1 Score the fatty side of the duck breasts and rub them with salt. Put them, fat side down, in a heavy frying pan and dry-fry over a medium heat for 6–8 minutes to render the fat. Transfer the breasts to a plate and then pull away and discard the fat. Cut the flesh into strips about 2cm/¾in wide.

2 Pour all but 15ml/1 tbsp of the rendered duck fat from the pan into a cup or jug, then reheat the fat in the pan. Fry the duck slices for 2–3 minutes over a medium high heat until evenly brown but not overcooked. Add the brandy, heat to simmering point and then ignite, either by tilting the pan or using a taper. When the flames have died down, add the orange juice and season with salt and pepper. Remove from the heat and set aside.

3 In a saucepan, heat either 15ml/ 1 tbsp of the remaining duck fat or use olive oil. Fry the onion and garlic over a gentle heat until the onion is soft but not browned. Add the rice and cook, stirring all the time, until the grains are coated in oil and have become slightly translucent around the edges.

4 Add the stock, a ladleful at a time, waiting for each quantity of stock to be absorbed completely before adding the next. Just before adding the final ladleful of stock, stir in the duck, with the thyme and mint. Continue cooking until the risotto is creamy and the rice is tender but still has a bit of "bite".

5 Add the orange rind and Parmesan. Taste and adjust the seasoning, then remove from the heat, cover the pan and leave to stand for a few minutes. Serve on individual plates, garnished with the pared orange rind.

CHICKEN LIVER RISOTTO

THE COMBINATION OF CHICKEN LIVERS, BACON, PARSLEY AND THYME GIVES THIS RISOTTO A WONDERFULLY RICH FLAVOUR. SERVE IT AS A STARTER FOR FOUR OR A LUNCH FOR TWO OR THREE.

SERVES TWO TO FOUR

INGREDIENTS
   175g/6oz chicken livers
   about 15ml/1 tbsp olive oil
   about 25g/1oz/2 tbsp butter
   about 40g/1½oz speck or 3 rindless
     streaky bacon rashers, finely
     chopped
   2 shallots, finely chopped
   1 garlic clove, crushed
   1 celery stick, finely sliced
   275g/10oz/1½ cups risotto rice
   175ml/6fl oz/¾ cup dry white wine
   900ml–1 litre/1½–1¾ pints/3¾–4
     cups simmering chicken stock
   5ml/1 tsp chopped fresh thyme
   15ml/1 tbsp chopped fresh parsley
   salt and freshly ground black pepper
   parsley and thyme sprigs to garnish

1 Clean the chicken livers carefully, removing any fat or membrane. Rinse well, pat dry with kitchen paper and cut into small, even pieces.

2 Heat the oil and butter in a frying pan and fry the speck or bacon for 2–3 minutes. Add the shallots, garlic and celery and continue frying for 3–4 minutes over a low heat until the vegetables are slightly softened. Increase the heat and add the chicken livers, stir-frying for a few minutes until they are brown all over.

3 Add the rice. Cook, stirring, for a few minutes, then pour over the wine. Allow to boil so that the alcohol is driven off. Stir frequently, taking care not to break up the chicken livers. When all the wine has been absorbed, add the hot stock, a ladleful at a time, stirring constantly.

4 About halfway through cooking, add the thyme and season with salt and pepper. Continue to add the stock as before, making sure that each quantity has been absorbed before adding more.

5 When the risotto is creamy and the rice is tender but still has a bit of "bite", stir in the parsley. Taste and adjust the seasoning. Remove the pan from the heat, cover and leave to rest for a few minutes before serving, garnished with parsley and thyme.

LEEK AND HAM RISOTTO

ANOTHER SIMPLE RISOTTO THAT MAKES AN EASY SUPPER, YET IS SPECIAL ENOUGH FOR A DINNER PARTY.

SERVES THREE TO FOUR

INGREDIENTS
7.5ml/1½ tsp olive oil
40g/1½oz/3 tbsp butter
2 leeks, cut in slices
175g/6oz prosciutto, torn into pieces
75g/3oz/generous 1 cup button
  mushrooms, sliced
275g/10oz/1½ cups risotto rice
1 litre/1¾ pints/4 cups simmering
  chicken stock
45ml/3 tbsp chopped fresh flat leaf
  parsley
40g/1½oz/½ cup freshly grated
  Parmesan cheese
salt and freshly ground black pepper

1 Heat the oil and butter in a pan and fry the leeks until soft. Set aside a few strips of prosciutto for the garnish and add the rest to the pan. Fry for 1 minute, then add the mushrooms and stir-fry for 2–3 minutes until lightly browned.

2 Add the rice. Cook, stirring, for 1–2 minutes until the grains are evenly coated in oil and have become translucent around the edges. Add a ladleful of hot stock. Stir until this has been absorbed completely, then add the next ladleful. Continue in this way until all the stock has been absorbed.

3 When the risotto is creamy and the rice is tender but still has a bit of "bite", stir in the parsley and Parmesan. Adjust the seasoning, remove from the heat and cover. Allow to rest for a few minutes. Spoon into a bowl, garnish with the reserved prosciutto and serve.

RABBIT AND LEMON GRASS RISOTTO

THE LEMON GRASS ADDS A PLEASANT TANG TO THIS RISOTTO. IF RABBIT ISN'T AVAILABLE, USE CHICKEN OR TURKEY INSTEAD.

SERVES THREE TO FOUR

INGREDIENTS
225g/8oz rabbit meat, cut into strips
seasoned flour
50g/2oz/¼ cup butter
15ml/1 tbsp olive oil
45ml/3 tbsp dry sherry
1 onion, finely chopped
1 garlic clove, crushed
1 lemon grass stalk, peeled and very
  finely sliced
275g/10oz/1½ cups risotto rice,
  preferably Carnaroli
1 litre/1¾ pints/4 cups simmering
  chicken stock
10ml/2 tsp chopped fresh thyme
45ml/3 tbsp double cream
25g/1oz/⅓ cup freshly grated
  Parmesan cheese
salt and freshly ground black pepper

1 Coat the rabbit strips in the seasoned flour. Heat half the butter and olive oil in a frying pan and fry the rabbit quickly until evenly brown. Add the sherry, and allow to boil briefly to burn off the alcohol. Season with salt and pepper and set aside.

2 Heat the remaining olive oil and butter in a large saucepan. Fry the onion and garlic over a low heat for 4–5 minutes until the onion is soft. Add the sliced lemon grass and cook for a few more minutes.

3 Add the rice and stir to coat in the oil. Add a ladleful of stock and cook, stirring, until the liquid has been absorbed. Continue adding the stock gradually, stirring constantly. When the rice is almost cooked, stir in three-quarters of the rabbit strips, with the pan juices. Add the thyme and seasoning.

4 Continue cooking until the rice is tender but still has a "bite". Stir in the cream and Parmesan, remove from the heat and cover. Leave to rest before serving, garnished with rabbit strips.

APPLE AND LEMON RISOTTO WITH POACHED PLUMS

ALTHOUGH IT'S ENTIRELY POSSIBLE TO COOK THIS BY THE CONVENTIONAL RISOTTO METHOD — BY ADDING THE LIQUID SLOWLY — IT MAKES MORE SENSE TO COOK THE RICE WITH THE MILK, IN THE SAME WAY AS FOR A RICE PUDDING.

SERVES FOUR

INGREDIENTS
  1 cooking apple
  15g/½oz/1 tbsp butter
  175g/6oz/scant 1 cup risotto rice
  600ml/1 pint/2½ cups creamy milk
  about 50g/2oz/¼ cup caster sugar
  1.5ml/¼ tsp ground cinnamon
  30ml/2 tbsp lemon juice
  45ml/3 tbsp double cream
  grated rind of 1 lemon, to decorate
For the poached plums
  50g/2oz/¼ cup light brown
    muscovado sugar
  200ml/7fl oz/scant 1 cup apple juice
  3 star anise
  cinnamon stick
  6 plums, halved and sliced

1 Peel and core the apple. Cut it into large chunks. Put these in a large, non-stick pan and add the butter. Heat gently until the butter melts.

2 Add the rice and milk and stir well. Bring to the boil over a medium heat, then simmer very gently for 20–25 minutes, stirring occasionally.

COOK'S TIP
If the apple is very sharp (acidic) the milk may curdle. There is no need to worry about this – it won't affect the look or taste of the sauce.

3 To make the poached plums, dissolve the sugar in 150ml/¼ pints/⅔ cup apple juice in a pan. Add the spices and bring to the boil. Boil for 2 minutes. Add the plums, and simmer for 2 minutes. Set aside until ready to serve.

4 Stir the sugar, cinnamon and lemon juice into the risotto. Cook for 2 minutes, stirring all the time, then stir in the cream. Taste and add more sugar if necessary. Decorate with the lemon rind and serve with the poached plums.

CHOCOLATE RISOTTO

IF YOU'VE NEVER TASTED A SWEET RISOTTO, THERE'S A TREAT IN STORE. CHOCOLATE RISOTTO IS DELECTABLE, AND CHILDREN OF ALL AGES LOVE IT.

SERVES FOUR TO SIX

INGREDIENTS

  175g/6oz/scant 1 cup risotto rice
  600ml/1 pint/2½ cups creamy milk
  75g/3oz plain chocolate, broken into
    pieces
  25g/1oz/2 tbsp butter
  about 50g/2oz/¼ cup caster sugar
  pinch of ground cinnamon
  60ml/4 tbsp double cream
  fresh raspberries and chocolate
    caraque, to decorate
  chocolate sauce, to serve

3 Remove the pan from the heat and stir in the ground cinnamon and double cream. Cover the pan and leave to stand for a few minutes.

4 Spoon the risotto into individual dishes or dessert plates, and decorate with fresh raspberries and chocolate caraque. Serve with chocolate sauce.

1 Put the rice in a non-stick pan. Pour in the milk and bring to the boil over a low to medium heat. Reduce the heat to the lowest setting and simmer very gently for about 20 minutes, stirring occasionally, until the rice is very soft.

2 Stir in the chocolate, butter and sugar. Cook, stirring all the time over a very gentle heat for 1–2 minutes, until the chocolate has melted.

FRANCE

There are many wonderful rice recipes from France, which was quick to assimilate the variety of rice dishes discovered from colonial adventures abroad. Pilaffs and rice stuffings have been favourites for years. More recently, the red rice from the Camargue region, with its unique nutty flavour, has become very popular.

PROVENÇAL FISH SOUP

THE RICE MAKES THIS A SUBSTANTIAL MAIN MEAL SOUP. BASMATI OR THAI RICE HAS THE BEST FLAVOUR, BUT ANY LONG GRAIN RICE COULD BE USED. IF USING A QUICK-COOK RICE, COOK THE VEGETABLES FOR LONGER BEFORE ADDING THE RICE.

SERVES FOUR TO SIX

INGREDIENTS

450g/1lb fresh mussels
about 250ml/8fl oz/1 cup white wine
675–900g/1½–2lb mixed white fish
   fillets such as monkfish, plaice,
   cod or haddock
6 large scallops
30ml/2 tbsp olive oil
3 leeks, chopped
1 garlic clove, crushed
1 red pepper, seeded and cut into
   2.5cm/1in pieces
1 yellow pepper, seeded and cut into
   2.5cm/1in pieces
175g/6oz fennel, cut into 4cm/1½in
   pieces
400g/14oz can chopped tomatoes
about 1.2 litres/2 pints/5 cups
   well-flavoured fish stock
generous pinch of saffron threads,
   soaked in 15ml/1 tbsp hot water
175g/6oz/scant 1 cup basmati rice,
   soaked
8 large raw prawns, peeled and
   deveined
salt and freshly ground black pepper
30–45ml/2–3 tbsp fresh dill, to
   garnish
crusty bread, to serve (optional)

1 Clean the mussels, discarding any that do not close when tapped with a knife. Place them in a heavy-based pan. Add 90ml/6 tbsp of the wine, cover, bring to the boil over a high heat and cook for about 3 minutes or until all the mussels have opened. Strain, reserving the liquid. Set aside half the mussels in their shells for the garnish; shell the rest and put them in a bowl. Discard any mussels that have not opened.

2 Cut the fish into 2.5cm/1in cubes. Detach the corals from the scallops and slice the white flesh into three or four pieces. Add the scallops to the fish and the corals to the mussels.

3 Heat the olive oil in a saucepan and fry the leeks and garlic for 3–4 minutes until softened. Add the peppers and fennel and fry for 2 minutes more.

4 Add the tomatoes, stock, saffron water, reserved mussel liquid and the remaining wine. Season well and cook for 5 minutes. Drain the rice, stir it into the mixture, cover and simmer for 10 minutes until it is just tender.

5 Carefully stir in the white fish and cook over a low heat for 5 minutes. Add the prawns, cook for 2 minutes then add the scallop corals and mussels and cook for 2–3 minutes more, until all the fish is tender. If the soup seems dry, add a little extra white wine or stock, or a little of both. Spoon into warmed soup dishes, top with the mussels in their shells and sprinkle with the dill. Serve with fresh crusty bread, if liked.

COOK'S TIP
To make your own fish stock, place about 450g/1lb white fish trimmings – bones, heads, but not gills – in a large pan. Add a chopped onion, carrot, bay leaf, parsley sprig, 6 peppercorns and a 5cm/2in piece of pared lemon rind. Pour in 1.2 litres/2 pints/5 cups water, bring to the boil, then simmer gently for 25–30 minutes. Strain through muslin.

SALMON AND RICE GRATIN

THIS ALL-IN-ONE SUPPER DISH IS IDEAL FOR INFORMAL ENTERTAINING AS IT CAN BE MADE AHEAD OF TIME AND REHEATED FOR ABOUT HALF AN HOUR BEFORE BEING SERVED WITH A TOSSED SALAD.

SERVES SIX

INGREDIENTS
 675g/1½lb fresh salmon fillet, skinned
 1 bay leaf
 a few parsley stalks
 1 litre/1¾ pints/4 cups water
 400g/14oz/2 cups basmati rice, soaked and drained
 30–45ml/2–3 tbsp chopped fresh parsley, plus extra to garnish
 175g/6oz/1½ cups Cheddar cheese, grated
 3 hard-boiled eggs, chopped
 salt and freshly ground black pepper
For the sauce
 1 litre/1¾ pints/4 cups milk
 40g/1½oz/⅓ cup plain flour
 40g/1½oz/3 tbsp butter
 5ml/1 tsp mild curry paste or French mustard

1 Put the salmon in a wide, shallow pan. Add the bay leaf and parsley stalks, with salt and pepper. Pour in the water and bring to simmering point. Poach the fish for about 12 minutes until just tender.

2 Lift the fish out of the pan using a slotted spoon, then strain the liquid into a saucepan. Leave the fish to cool, then remove any visible bones and flake the flesh gently with a fork.

3 Drain the rice and add it to the saucepan containing the fish-poaching liquid. Bring to the boil, then lower the heat, cover and simmer for 10 minutes without lifting the lid.

4 Remove the pan from the heat and, without lifting the lid, allow the rice to stand undisturbed for 5 minutes.

5 Meanwhile, make the sauce. Mix the milk, flour and butter in a saucepan. Bring to the boil over a low heat, whisking constantly until the sauce is smooth and thick. Stir in the curry paste or mustard, with salt and pepper to taste. Simmer for 2 minutes.

6 Preheat the grill. Remove the sauce from the heat and stir in the chopped parsley and rice, with half the cheese. Using a large metal spoon, fold in the flaked fish and eggs. Spoon into a shallow gratin dish and sprinkle with the rest of the cheese. Heat under the grill until the topping is golden brown and bubbling. Serve in individual dishes, garnished with chopped parsley.

VARIATIONS
Prawns could be substituted for the salmon, and other hard cheeses, such as Lancashire or Red Leicester, could be used instead of the Cheddar.

RED RICE SALAD NIÇOISE

RED RICE, WITH ITS SWEET NUTTINESS, GOES WELL IN THIS CLASSIC SALAD. THE TUNA OR SWORDFISH COULD BE BARBECUED OR PAN-FRIED BUT TAKE CARE THAT IT DOES NOT OVERCOOK.

SERVES SIX

INGREDIENTS
    about 675g/1½lb fresh tuna or
    swordfish, sliced into 2cm/¾in thick
    steaks
    350g/12oz/1¾ cups Camargue red
    rice
    fish or vegetable stock or water
    450g/1lb French beans
    450g/1lb broad beans, shelled
    1 cos lettuce
    450g/1lb cherry tomatoes, halved
    unless very tiny
    30ml/2 tbsp coarsely chopped fresh
    coriander
    3 hard-boiled eggs
    175g/6oz/1½ cups stoned black
    olives
    olive oil, for brushing
For the marinade
    1 red onion, roughly chopped
    2 garlic cloves
    ½ bunch fresh parsley
    ½ bunch fresh coriander
    10ml/2 tsp paprika
    45ml/3 tbsp olive oil
    45ml/3 tbsp water
    30ml/2 tbsp white wine vinegar
    15ml/1 tbsp fresh lime or lemon
    juice
    salt and freshly ground black pepper
For the dressing
    30ml/2 tbsp fresh lime or lemon
    juice
    5ml/1 tsp Dijon mustard
    ½ garlic clove, crushed (optional)
    60ml/4 tbsp olive oil
    60ml/4 tbsp sunflower oil

COOK'S TIP
A good salad Niçoise is a feast for the eyes as well as the palate. Arrange the ingredients with care, either on a large serving dish or individual salad plates.

1 Make the marinade by mixing all the ingredients in a food processor and processing them for 30–40 seconds until the vegetables and herbs are finely chopped.

2 Prick the tuna or swordfish steaks all over with a fork, lay them side by side in a shallow dish and pour over the marinade, turning the fish to coat each piece. Cover with clear film and leave in a cool place for 2–4 hours.

3 Cook the rice in stock or water, following the instructions on the packet, then drain, tip into a bowl and set aside.

4 Make the dressing. Mix the citrus juice, mustard and garlic (if using) in a bowl. Whisk in the oils, then add salt and freshly ground black pepper to taste. Stir 60ml/4 tbsp of the dressing into the rice, then spoon the rice into the centre of a large serving dish.

5 Cook the French beans and broad beans in boiling salted water until tender. Drain, refresh under cold water and drain again. Remove the outer shell from the broad beans and add them to the rice.

6 Discard the outer leaves from the lettuce and tear the inner leaves into pieces. Add to the salad with the tomatoes and coriander. Shell the hard-boiled eggs and cut them into sixths. Preheat the grill.

7 Arrange the tuna or swordfish steaks on a grill pan. Brush with the marinade and a little extra olive oil. Grill for 3–4 minutes on each side, until the fish is tender and flakes easily when tested with the tip of a sharp knife. Brush with marinade and more olive oil when turning the fish over.

8 Allow the fish to cool a little, then break the steaks into large pieces. Toss into the salad with the olives and the remaining dressing. Decorate with the eggs and serve.

BEEF IN PASTRY WITH WILD MUSHROOMS AND RICE

A TASTY LAYER OF RICE AND JUICY WILD MUSHROOMS TOPS EACH FILLET STEAK BEFORE IT IS WRAPPED IN PUFF PASTRY. THIS COOKS TO CRISP AND FLAKY PERFECTION, THE PERFECT FOIL FOR THE FILLING.

SERVES FOUR

INGREDIENTS
  20g/¾oz/¼ cup dried wild
    mushrooms, soaked for 10 minutes
    in warm water to cover
  115g/4oz/1½–1¾ cups morel
    mushrooms
  about 45ml/3 tbsp olive oil
  4 shallots, finely chopped
  1 garlic clove, crushed
  20g/¾oz/1½ tbsp butter
  175g/6oz/1½ cups cooked white long
    grain rice
  10ml/2 tsp chopped fresh marjoram
  15ml/1 tbsp finely chopped fresh
    parsley
  275g/10oz puff pastry, thawed if
    frozen
  4 fillet steaks, each about 90g/3½oz
    and 2.5cm/1in thick
  10ml/2 tsp Dijon mustard
  1 egg, beaten with 15ml/1 tbsp water
  salt and freshly ground black pepper
  roast potatoes and patty pan squash,
    to serve (optional)

1 Preheat the oven to 220°C/425°F/ Gas 7. Drain the dried mushrooms, reserving the liquid, and chop finely. Trim the morels and chop them.

2 Heat 15ml/1 tbsp of the olive oil in a frying pan and fry the shallots and garlic for 2–3 minutes until soft, stirring occasionally. Add the butter to the pan. When it begins to foam, add the mushrooms and cook for 3–4 minutes more, stirring occasionally.

3 Scrape the mixture into the bowl of rice and stir in the marjoram and parsley. Season to taste.

4 Cut the pastry into four and roll out each piece into an 18cm/7in circle. Trim the top and bottom edges.

5 Heat the remaining olive oil in the pan and fry the steaks for about 30 seconds on each side until browned. Spread a little mustard over each steak, then place on one side of a piece of pastry. Spoon a quarter of the mushroom and rice mixture on top of each steak.

6 Fold the pastry over to make a pasty, sealing the join with a little of the egg wash. Repeat to make four pasties, then place them on an oiled baking sheet. Slit the top of each pasty, decorate with the pastry trimmings, and glaze with more egg wash. Bake in the oven for about 15 minutes, until the pastry is golden.

CHICKEN PILAFF

THE FRENCH MARMITE POT IS IDEAL FOR THIS RECIPE. THE TALL SIDES SLANT INWARDS, REDUCING EVAPORATION AND ENSURING THAT THE RICE COOKS SLOWLY WITHOUT BECOMING DRY.

SERVES THREE TO FOUR

INGREDIENTS
- 15–20 dried chanterelle mushrooms
- 15–30ml/1–2 tbsp olive oil
- 15g/½oz/1 tbsp butter
- 4 thin rashers rindless smoked streaky bacon, chopped
- 3 skinless, boneless chicken breasts, cut into thin slices
- 4 spring onions, sliced
- 225g/8oz/generous 1 cup basmati rice, soaked
- 450ml/¾ pint/scant 2 cups hot chicken stock
- salt and freshly ground black pepper

1 Preheat the oven to 180°C/350°F/ Gas 4. Soak the mushrooms for 10 minutes in warm water. Drain, reserving the liquid. Slice the mushrooms, discarding the stalks.

2 Heat the olive oil and butter in a frying pan. Fry the bacon for 2–3 minutes. Add the chicken and stir-fry until the pieces are golden brown all over. Transfer the chicken and bacon mixture to a bowl using a slotted spoon.

3 Briefly fry the mushrooms and spring onions in the fat remaining in the pan, then add them to the chicken pieces. Drain the rice and add it to the pan, with a little olive oil if necessary. Stir-fry for 2–3 minutes. Spoon the rice into an earthenware marmite pot or casserole.

4 Pour the hot chicken stock and reserved mushroom liquid over the rice in the marmite pot or casserole. Stir in the reserved chicken and mushroom mixture and season.

5 Cover with a double piece of foil and secure with a lid. Cook in the oven for 30–35 minutes until the rice is tender.

RED RICE AND ROASTED RED PEPPER SALAD

PEPPERS, SUN-DRIED TOMATOES AND GARLIC GIVE A DISTINCTLY MEDITERRANEAN FLAVOUR TO THIS SALAD DISH. IT MAKES AN EXCELLENT ACCOMPANIMENT TO SPICY SAUSAGES OR FISH.

SERVES FOUR

INGREDIENTS
225g/8oz/generous 1 cup Camargue
    red rice
vegetable or chicken stock or water
    (see method)
45ml/3 tbsp olive oil
3 red peppers, seeded and sliced into
    strips
4–5 sun-dried tomatoes
4–5 whole garlic cloves, unpeeled
1 onion, chopped
30ml/2 tbsp chopped fresh parsley,
    plus extra to garnish
15ml/1 tbsp chopped fresh coriander
10ml/2 tsp balsamic vinegar
salt and freshly ground black pepper

1 Cook the rice in stock or water, following instructions on the packet. Heat the oil in a frying pan and add the peppers. Cook over a medium heat for 4 minutes, shaking occasionally.

2 Lower the heat, add the sun-dried tomatoes, whole garlic cloves and onion, cover the pan and cook for 8–10 minutes more, stirring occasionally. Remove the lid and cook for 3 minutes more.

3 Off the heat, stir in the parsley, coriander and vinegar, and season. Spread the rice out on a serving dish and spoon the pepper mixture on top. Peel the whole garlic cloves, cut the flesh into slices and scatter these over the salad. Serve at room temperature, garnished with more fresh parsley.

CREAMY FISH PILAU

THIS DISH IS INSPIRED BY A FUSION OF CUISINES — THE METHOD COMES FROM INDIA AND USES THAT COUNTRY'S FAVOURITE RICE, BASMATI, BUT THE DELICIOUS WINE AND CREAM SAUCE IS VERY MUCH FRENCH IN FLAVOUR.

SERVES FOUR TO SIX

INGREDIENTS
450g/1lb fresh mussels, scrubbed
350ml/12fl oz/1½ cups white wine
fresh parsley sprig
about 675g/1½lb salmon
225g/8oz scallops
about 15ml/1 tbsp olive oil
40g/1½oz/3 tbsp butter
2 shallots, finely chopped
225g/8oz/3 cups button mushrooms,
    halved if large
275g/10oz/1½ cups basmati rice,
    soaked
300ml/½ pint/1¼ cups fish stock
150ml/¼ pint/⅔ cup double cream
15ml/1 tbsp chopped fresh parsley
225g/8oz large cooked prawns,
    peeled and deveined
salt and freshly ground black pepper
fresh flat leaf parsley sprigs, to
    garnish

1 Preheat the oven to 160°C/325°F/ Gas 3. Place the mussels in a pan with 90ml/6 tbsp of the wine and parsley, cover and cook for 4–5 minutes until they have opened. Drain, reserving the cooking liquid. Remove the mussels from their shells, discarding any that have not opened.

2 Cut the fish into bite-size pieces. Detach the corals from the scallops and cut the white scallop flesh into thick pieces.

3 Heat half the olive oil and butter and fry the shallots and mushrooms for 3–4 minutes. Transfer to a large bowl. Heat the remaining oil in the frying pan and fry the rice for 2–3 minutes, stirring until it is coated in oil. Spoon the rice into a deep casserole.

4 Pour the stock, remaining wine and reserved mussel liquid into the frying pan, and bring to the boil. Off the heat, stir in the cream and parsley; season lightly. Pour over the rice and then add the salmon and the scallop flesh, together with the mushroom mixture. Stir carefully to mix.

5 Cover the casserole tightly. Bake for 30–35 minutes, then add the corals, replace the cover and cook for 4 minutes more. Add the mussels and prawns, cover and cook for 3–4 minutes until the seafood is heated through and the rice is tender. Serve garnished with the parsley sprigs.

COURGETTE ROULADE

THIS MAKES A REALLY IMPRESSIVE BUFFET SUPPER OR DINNER PARTY DISH, OR CAN BE WRAPPED AND SERVED CHILLED AS THE PIÈCE DE RÉSISTANCE AT A PICNIC.

5 Bake for 10–15 minutes until the roulade is firm and lightly golden on top. Carefully turn it out on to a sheet of greaseproof or non-stick baking paper sprinkled with 30ml/2 tbsp grated Parmesan. Peel away the lining paper. Roll the roulade up, using the paper as a guide, and leave it to cool.

SERVES SIX

INGREDIENTS
40g/1½oz/3 tbsp butter
50g/2oz/½ cup plain flour
300ml/½ pint/1¼ cups milk
4 eggs, separated
3 courgettes, grated
25g/1oz/⅓ cup freshly grated
  Parmesan cheese
salt and freshly ground black pepper
herb and green leaf salad, to serve
For the filling
75g/3oz/⅔ cup soft goat's cheese
60ml/4 tbsp fromage frais
225g/8oz/2 cups cooked rice, such
  as Thai fragrant rice or Japanese
  short grain
15ml/1 tbsp chopped mixed fresh
  herbs
15ml/1 tbsp olive oil
15g/½oz/1 tbsp butter
75g/3oz/generous 1 cup button
  mushrooms, very finely chopped

1 Preheat the oven to 200°C/400°F/ Gas 6. Line a 33 x 23cm/13 x 9in Swiss roll tin with non-stick baking paper.

2 Melt the butter in a saucepan, stir in the flour and cook for 1–2 minutes, stirring all the time. Gradually add the milk, stirring until the mixture forms a smooth sauce. Remove from the heat and cool for a few minutes.

3 Stir the egg yolks into the sauce, one at a time, and then add the grated courgettes and the Parmesan, and check the seasoning.

4 Whisk the egg whites until stiff, fold them into the courgette mixture and scrape into the prepared tin. Spread evenly, smoothing the surface with a palette knife.

6 To make the filling, mix the goat's cheese, fromage frais, rice and herbs in a bowl. Season with salt and pepper. Heat the olive oil and butter in a small pan and fry the mushrooms until soft.

7 Unwrap the roulade, spread with the rice filling and lay the mushrooms along the centre. Roll up again. The roulade can be served warm or chilled. To heat, place on a baking sheet, cover with foil and heat for 15–20 minutes in a moderately hot oven. To eat cold, wrap in clear film and chill in the fridge. Serve with a herb and green leaf salad.

PROVENÇAL RICE

ONE OF THE GLORIOUS THINGS ABOUT FOOD FROM THE SOUTH OF FRANCE IS ITS COLOUR, AND THIS DISH IS NO EXCEPTION. TO SERVE AS A MAIN COURSE, ALLOW 50G/2OZ/¼ CUP RICE PER PERSON.

SERVES FOUR

INGREDIENTS

2 onions
90ml/6 tbsp olive oil
175g/6oz/scant 1 cup brown long
  grain rice
10ml/2 tsp mustard seeds
475ml/16fl oz/2 cups vegetable stock
1 large or 2 small red peppers,
  seeded and cut into chunks
1 small aubergine, cut into cubes
2–3 courgettes, sliced
about 12 cherry tomatoes
5–6 fresh basil leaves, torn into
  pieces
2 garlic cloves, finely chopped
60ml/4 tbsp white wine
60ml/4 tbsp passata or tomato
  juice
2 hard-boiled eggs, cut into wedges
8 stuffed green olives, sliced
15ml/1 tbsp capers
3 drained sun-dried tomatoes in oil,
  sliced (optional)
butter
sea salt and freshly ground black
  pepper

1 Preheat the oven to 200°C/400°F/ Gas 6. Finely chop one onion. Heat 30ml/2 tbsp of the oil in a saucepan and fry the chopped onion over a gentle heat for 5–6 minutes until softened.

2 Add the rice and mustard seeds. Cook, stirring, for 2 minutes, then add the stock and a little salt. Bring to the boil, then lower the heat, cover and simmer for 35 minutes until the rice is tender.

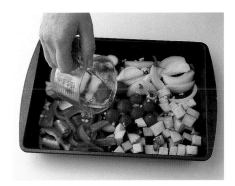

3 Meanwhile, cut the remaining onion into wedges. Put these in a roasting tin with the peppers, aubergine, courgettes and cherry tomatoes. Scatter over the torn basil leaves and chopped garlic. Pour over the remaining olive oil and sprinkle with sea salt and black pepper. Roast for 15–20 minutes until the vegetables begin to char, stirring halfway through cooking. Reduce the oven temperature to 180°C/350°F/Gas 4.

4 Spoon the rice into an earthenware casserole. Put the roasted vegetables on top, together with any vegetable juices from the roasting tin, then pour over the wine and passata.

5 Arrange the egg wedges on top of the vegetables, with the sliced olives, capers and sun-dried tomatoes, if using. Dot with butter, cover and cook for 15–20 minutes until heated through.

VEGETABLE TARTE TATIN

THIS UPSIDE-DOWN TART COMBINES MEDITERRANEAN VEGETABLES WITH A MEDLEY OF RICE, GARLIC, ONIONS AND OLIVES.

SERVES FOUR AS A STARTER

INGREDIENTS
    30ml/2 tbsp sunflower oil
    about 25ml/1½ tbsp olive oil
    1 aubergine, sliced lengthways
    1 large red pepper, seeded and cut
      into long strips
    5 tomatoes
    2 red shallots, finely chopped
    1–2 garlic cloves, crushed
    150ml/¼ pint/⅔ cup white wine
    10ml/2 tsp chopped fresh basil
    225g/8oz/2 cups cooked white or
      brown long grain rice
    40g/1½oz/⅔ cup stoned black olives,
      chopped
    350g/12oz puff pastry, thawed if
      frozen
    freshly ground black pepper

VARIATION
Courgettes and mushrooms could
be used as well, or instead of, the
aubergines and peppers, or use strips
of lightly browned chicken breast and
serve for two as a main meal.

1 Preheat the oven to 190°C/375°F/Gas 5.
Heat the sunflower oil with 15ml/1 tbsp
of the olive oil in a frying pan and fry the
aubergine slices for 4–5 minutes on each
side until golden brown. Lift out and
drain on kitchen paper.

2 Add the pepper strips to the oil
remaining in the pan, turning them to
coat. Cover the pan with a lid or foil and
sweat the peppers over a moderately
high heat for 5–6 minutes, stirring
occasionally, until the pepper strips are
soft and flecked with brown.

3 Slice two of the tomatoes and set
them aside. Plunge the remaining
tomatoes briefly into boiling water,
then peel them, cut them into quarters
and remove the core and seeds. Chop
them roughly.

4 Heat the remaining oil in the frying
pan and fry the shallots and garlic for
3–4 minutes until softened. Add the
chopped tomatoes and cook for a few
minutes until softened. Stir in the wine
and basil, with black pepper to taste.
Bring to the boil, then remove from the
heat and stir in the cooked rice and
black olives.

5 Arrange the tomato slices, aubergine
slices and peppers in a single layer over
the bottom of a heavy, 30cm/12in,
shallow ovenproof dish. Spread the rice
mixture on top.

6 Roll out the pastry to a circle slightly
larger than the diameter of the dish and
place on top of the rice, tucking the
overlap down inside the dish.

7 Bake for 25–30 minutes, until the
pastry is golden and risen. Cool slightly,
then invert the tart on to a large,
warmed serving plate. Serve in slices,
with a leafy green salad or simply
dressed lamb's lettuce.

COOK'S TIP
This tart would make a lovely lunch
or supper dish for two people. Serve
it hot with buttered new potatoes and
a green vegetable, such as mangetouts
or French beans.

SOUFFLEED RICE PUDDING

USING SKIMMED MILK TO MAKE THIS PUDDING IS A HEALTHY OPTION, BUT YOU COULD USE WHOLE MILK IF YOU PREFER A CREAMIER TASTE.

SERVES FOUR

INGREDIENTS
65g/2½oz/⅓ cup short grain pudding rice
45ml/3 tbsp clear honey
750ml/1¼ pints/3 cups skimmed milk
1 vanilla pod or 2.5ml/½ tsp vanilla essence
butter, for greasing
2 egg whites
5ml/1 tsp freshly grated nutmeg
wafer biscuits, to serve (optional)

1 Place the rice, honey and milk in a heavy or non-stick saucepan, and bring the milk to just below boiling point, watching it closely to prevent it from boiling over. Add the vanilla pod, if using.

2 Reduce the heat to the lowest setting and cover the pan. Leave to cook for about 1–1¼ hours, stirring occasionally to prevent sticking, until most of the liquid has been absorbed.

3 Remove the vanilla pod or, if using vanilla essence, add this to the rice mixture now. Preheat the oven to 220°C/425°F/Gas 7. Grease a 1 litre/ 1¾ pint/4 cup baking dish with butter.

4 Place the egg whites in a large grease-free bowl and whisk them until they hold soft peaks. Using either a large metal spoon or a spatula, carefully fold the egg whites evenly into the rice and milk mixture. Tip into the baking dish.

5 Sprinkle with grated nutmeg and bake in the oven for about 15–20 minutes, until the rice pudding has risen well and the surface is golden brown. Serve the pudding hot, with wafer biscuits, if you like.

COOK'S TIP
This pudding is delicious topped with a stewed, dried fruit salad.

PEAR, ALMOND AND GROUND RICE FLAN

GROUND RICE GIVES A DISTINCTIVE, SLIGHTLY GRAINY TEXTURE TO PUDDINGS THAT GOES PARTICULARLY WELL WITH AUTUMN FRUIT. PEARS AND ALMONDS ARE A DIVINE COMBINATION.

2 Cream the butter and caster sugar until light and fluffy, then beat in the eggs and almond essence. Fold in the flour and ground rice.

3 Carefully spoon the almond-flavoured egg and ground rice mixture over the quartered pears and level the surface with a palette knife.

SERVES SIX

INGREDIENTS
 4 ripe pears
 30ml/2 tbsp soft light brown sugar
 115g/4oz/½ cup unsalted butter
 115g/4oz/generous ½ cup caster sugar
 2 eggs
 a few drops of almond essence
 75g/3oz/⅔ cup self-raising flour
 50g/2oz/⅓ cup ground rice
 25g/1oz/¼ cup flaked almonds
 custard or crème fraîche, to serve (optional)

1 Preheat the oven to 180°C/350°F/ Gas 4. Grease a shallow 25cm/10in flan dish. Peel and quarter the pears and arrange them in the flan dish. Sprinkle with the brown sugar.

4 Sprinkle the top with the flaked almonds, then bake the flan for 30–35 minutes until the topping is golden. Serve with custard or crème fraîche.

CAJUN, CREOLE AND SOUTH AMERICA

Rice is grown in all parts of Louisiana, in the south of the United States, and across the border in Central and South America. The rice dishes from these regions make use of a wealth of ingredients, and many have become world classics – jambalayas and gumbos from Cajun country, tortillas from Mexico and a rice casserole from Brazil.

LOUISIANA RICE

AUBERGINE AND PORK COMBINE WITH HERBS AND SPICES TO MAKE A HIGHLY FLAVOURSOME DISH.

SERVES FOUR

INGREDIENTS
   60ml/4 tbsp vegetable oil
   1 onion, chopped
   1 small aubergine, diced
   225g/8oz minced pork
   1 green pepper, seeded and
      chopped
   2 celery sticks, chopped
   1 garlic clove, crushed
   5ml/1 tsp cayenne pepper
   5ml/1 tsp paprika
   5ml/1 tsp freshly ground black
      pepper
   2.5ml/½ tsp salt
   5ml/1 tsp dried thyme
   2.5ml/½ tsp dried oregano
   475ml/16fl oz/2 cups chicken stock
   225g/8oz chicken livers, chopped
   150g/5oz/¾ cup white long grain rice
   1 bay leaf
   45ml/3 tbsp chopped fresh parsley

1 Heat the oil in a frying pan. When it is piping hot, add the onion and aubergine and stir-fry for about 5 minutes.

2 Add the pork and cook for 6–8 minutes until browned, using a wooden spoon to break up any lumps.

3 Stir in the green pepper, celery and garlic, with all the spices and herbs. Cover and cook over a high heat for 5–6 minutes, stirring frequently from the bottom of the pan to scrape up and distribute the crispy brown bits.

4 Pour in the chicken stock and stir to remove any sediment from the bottom of the pan. Cover and cook for 6 minutes over a moderate heat. Stir in the chicken livers and cook for 2 minutes more.

5 Stir in the rice and add the bay leaf. Lower the heat, cover and simmer for 6–7 minutes. Turn off the heat and leave to stand, still covered, for 10–15 minutes more until the rice is tender. Remove the bay leaf and stir in the chopped parsley. Serve the rice hot.

DIRTY RICE

CONTRARY TO POPULAR BELIEF, THIS DISH DOESN'T GET ITS NAME FROM ITS APPEARANCE, BUT FROM ITS ASSOCIATION WITH NEW ORLEANS, THE HOME OF JAZZ, WHICH HAS OFTEN BEEN REFERRED TO AS "DIRTY MUSIC".

SERVES FOUR

INGREDIENTS
    60ml/4 tbsp vegetable oil
    25g/1oz/¼ cup plain flour
    50g/2oz/4 tbsp butter
    1 large onion, chopped
    2 garlic cloves, crushed
    200g/7oz minced pork
    225g/8oz chicken livers, trimmed
      and finely chopped
    dash of Tabasco sauce
    1 green pepper, seeded and sliced
    2 celery sticks, sliced
    300ml/½ pint/1¼ cups chicken stock
    225g/8oz/generous 1 cup cooked
      white long grain rice
    4 spring onions, chopped
    45ml/3 tbsp chopped fresh parsley
    salt and freshly ground black pepper
    celery leaves, to garnish

1 Heat half the oil in a heavy-based saucepan. Stir in the flour and cook over a low heat, stirring constantly, until the roux is smooth and the colour is a rich chestnut-brown. Immediately remove the pan from the heat and place it on a cold surface such as the draining board of a sink.

2 Heat the remaining oil with the butter in a frying pan and stir-fry the onion for 5 minutes.

3 Add the garlic and pork. Cook for 5 minutes, breaking up the pork and stirring until it is evenly browned, then stir in the chicken livers and fry for 2–3 minutes until they have changed colour all over. Season with salt, pepper and Tabasco sauce. Stir in the green pepper and celery.

4 Stir the roux into the stir-fried mixture, then gradually add in the stock. When the mixture begins to bubble, cover and cook for 30 minutes, stirring occasionally. Stir in the rice, spring onions and parsley. Toss over the heat until the rice has heated through. Serve garnished with celery leaves.

LOUISIANA SEAFOOD GUMBO

GUMBO IS A SOUP, BUT IS SERVED OVER RICE AS A MAIN COURSE. IN LOUISIANA, OYSTERS ARE CHEAP AND PROLIFIC, AND WOULD BE USED HERE INSTEAD OF MUSSELS.

SERVES SIX

INGREDIENTS

    450g/1lb fresh mussels
    450g/1lb raw prawns, in the shell
    1 cooked crab, about 1kg/2¼lb
    small bunch of parsley, leaves
      chopped and stalks reserved
    150ml/¼ pint/⅔ cup vegetable oil
    115g/4oz/1 cup plain flour
    1 green pepper, seeded and chopped
    1 large onion, chopped
    2 celery sticks, sliced
    3 garlic cloves, finely chopped
    75g/3oz smoked spiced sausage,
      skinned and sliced
    275g/10oz/1½ cups white long grain
      rice
    6 spring onions, shredded
    cayenne pepper, to taste
    Tabasco sauce, to taste
    salt

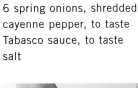

1 Wash the mussels in several changes of cold water, pulling away the black "beards". Discard any mussels that are broken or do not close when you tap them firmly.

2 Bring 250ml/8fl oz/1 cup water to the boil in a deep saucepan. Add the mussels, cover the pan tightly and cook over a high heat, shaking frequently, for 3 minutes. As the mussels open, lift them out with tongs into a sieve set over a bowl. Discard any that fail to open. Shell the mussels, discarding the shells. Return the liquid from the bowl to the pan and make the quantity up to 2 litres/3½ pints/8 cups with water.

3 Peel the prawns and set them aside, reserving a few for the garnish. Put the shells and heads into the saucepan.

4 Remove all the meat from the crab, separating the brown and white meat. Add all the pieces of shell to the saucepan with 5ml/2 tsp salt.

5 Bring the shellfish stock to the boil, skimming it regularly. When there is no more froth on the surface, add the parsley stalks and simmer for 15 minutes. Cool the stock, then strain it into a measuring jug and make up to 2 litres/3½ pints/8 cups with water.

6 Heat the oil in a heavy-based pan and stir in the flour. Stir constantly over a medium heat with a wooden spoon or whisk until the roux reaches a golden-brown colour. Immediately add the pepper, onion, celery and garlic. Continue cooking for about 3 minutes until the onion is soft. Stir in the sausage. Reheat the stock.

7 Stir the brown crab meat into the roux, then ladle in the hot stock a little at a time, stirring constantly until it has all been smoothly incorporated. Bring to a low boil, partially cover the pan, then simmer the gumbo for 30 minutes.

8 Meanwhile, cook the rice in plenty of lightly salted boiling water until the grains are tender.

9 Add the prawns, mussels, white crab meat and spring onions to the gumbo. Return to the boil and season with salt if necessary, cayenne and a dash or two of Tabasco sauce. Simmer for a further minute, then add the chopped parsley leaves. Serve immediately, ladling the soup over the hot rice in soup plates.

COOK'S TIP

It is vital to stir constantly to darken the roux without burning. Should black specks occur at any stage of cooking, discard the roux and start again. Have the onion, green pepper and celery ready to add to the roux the minute it reaches the correct golden-brown stage, as this arrests its darkening.

CHICKEN AND PRAWN JAMBALAYA

*THE MIXTURE OF CHICKEN, SEAFOOD AND RICE SUGGESTS A CLOSE RELATIONSHIP TO THE SPANISH
PAELLA, BUT THE NAME IS MORE LIKELY TO HAVE DERIVED FROM JAMBON (THE FRENCH FOR HAM),
À LA YA (CREOLE FOR RICE). JAMBALAYAS ARE A COLOURFUL MIXTURE OF HIGHLY FLAVOURED
INGREDIENTS, AND ARE ALWAYS MADE IN LARGE QUANTITIES FOR FEASTS AND CELEBRATION MEALS.*

SERVES TEN

INGREDIENTS

    2 chickens, each about 1.5kg/3–3½lb
    450g/1lb piece raw smoked gammon
    50g/2oz/4 tbsp lard or bacon fat
    50g/2oz/½ cup plain flour
    3 medium onions, finely sliced
    2 green peppers, seeded and sliced
    675g/1½lb tomatoes, peeled and
      chopped
    2–3 garlic cloves, crushed
    10ml/2 tsp chopped fresh thyme or
      5ml/1 tsp dried thyme
    24 raw Mediterranean prawns, peeled
      and deveined
    500g/1¼lb/3 cups white long grain rice
    1.2 litres/2 pints/5 cups water
    2–3 dashes Tabasco sauce
    45ml/3 tbsp chopped fresh flat leaf
      parsley, plus tiny fresh parsley
      sprigs, to garnish
    salt and freshly ground black pepper

4 Add the diced gammon, onions, green
peppers, tomatoes, garlic and thyme.
Cook, stirring regularly, for 10 minutes,
then add the prawns and mix lightly.

5 Stir the rice into the pan and pour in
the water. Season with salt, pepper and
Tabasco sauce. Bring to the boil, then
cook gently until the rice is tender and
all the liquid has been absorbed. Add a
little extra boiling water if the rice looks
like drying out before it is cooked.

6 Mix the parsley into the finished
dish, garnish with tiny sprigs of flat leaf
parsley and serve immediately.

1 Cut each chicken into 10 pieces and
season with salt and pepper. Dice the
gammon, discarding the rind and fat.

2 Melt the lard or bacon fat in a large,
heavy-based frying pan. Add the
chicken pieces in batches, brown them
all over, then lift them out with a slotted
spoon and set them aside.

3 Reduce the heat. Sprinkle the flour
into the fat in the pan and stir until the
roux turns golden brown. Return the
chicken pieces to the pan.

BRAZILIAN PORK AND RICE CASSEROLE

WE TEND TO ASSOCIATE BRAZIL WITH BEEF, BUT THERE ARE ALSO SOME EXCELLENT PORK RECIPES, INCLUDING THIS HEARTY DISH OF MARINATED PORK, VEGETABLES AND RICE.

SERVES FOUR TO SIX

INGREDIENTS
500g/1¼lb lean pork, such as fillet, cut into strips
60ml/4 tbsp corn oil
1 onion, chopped
1 garlic clove, crushed
1 green pepper, cut into pieces
about 300ml/½ pint/1¼ cups chicken stock
225g/8oz/generous 1 cup white long grain rice
150ml/¼ pint/⅔ cup double cream
40g/1½oz/½ cup freshly grated Parmesan cheese
salt and freshly ground black pepper
For the marinade
120ml/4fl oz/½ cup dry white wine
30ml/2 tbsp lemon juice
1 onion, chopped
4 juniper berries, lightly crushed
3 cloves
1 fresh red chilli, seeded and finely sliced

1 Mix all the marinade ingredients, add the pork and set aside to marinate for 3–4 hours, turning occasionally. Transfer the pork to a plate and pat dry. Strain the marinade and set aside.

2 Heat the oil in a heavy-based saucepan and fry the pork for a few minutes until evenly brown. Transfer to a plate using a slotted spoon.

3 Add the chopped onion and the garlic to the saucepan and fry for 3–4 minutes. Stir in the pepper, cook for 3–4 minutes more, then return the pork to the pan. Pour in the reserved marinade and the stock. Bring to the boil and season with salt and fresh black pepper, then lower the heat, cover and simmer gently for 10 minutes until the meat is nearly tender.

4 Preheat the oven to 160°C/325°F/Gas 3. Cook the rice in plenty of lightly salted boiling water for 8 minutes or until three-quarters cooked. Drain well. Spread half the rice over the bottom of a buttered, oval baking dish. Using a slotted spoon, make a neat layer of meat and vegetables on top, then spread over the remaining rice.

5 Stir the cream and 30ml/2 tbsp of the Parmesan into the liquid in which the pork was cooked. Tip into a jug. Carefully pour the cream mixture over the rice and sprinkle with the remaining Parmesan cheese. Cover with foil and bake for 20 minutes, then remove the foil and cook for 5 minutes more, until the top is lightly brown.

CHICKEN FAJITAS

FAJITAS ARE WARMED SOFT TORTILLAS, FILLED AND FOLDED LIKE AN ENVELOPE. THEY ARE TRADITIONAL MEXICAN FAST FOOD, DELICIOUS AND EASY TO PREPARE, AND A FAVOURITE FOR SUPPER.

SERVES FOUR

INGREDIENTS

  115g/4oz/generous ½ cup white long
    grain rice
  15g/1oz/3 tbsp wild rice
  15ml/1 tbsp olive oil
  15ml/1 tbsp sunflower oil
  1 onion, cut into thin wedges
  4 skinless, boneless chicken breasts,
    cut into thin strips
  1 red pepper, seeded and finely
    sliced
  5ml/1 tsp ground cumin
  generous pinch of cayenne pepper
  2.5ml/½ tsp ground turmeric
  175ml/6fl oz/¾ cup passata
  120–175ml/4–6fl oz/½–¾ cup
    chicken stock
  12 small or 8 large wheat tortillas,
    warmed
  soured cream, to serve
For the salsa
  1 shallot, roughly chopped
  1 small garlic clove
  ½–1 fresh green chilli, seeded and
    roughly chopped
  small bunch of fresh parsley
  5 tomatoes, peeled, seeded and
    chopped
  10ml/2 tsp olive oil
  15ml/1 tbsp lemon juice
  30ml/2 tbsp tomato juice
  salt and freshly ground black pepper
For the guacamole
  1 large ripe avocado
  2 spring onions, chopped
  15–30ml/1–2 tbsp fresh lime or
    lemon juice
  generous pinch of cayenne pepper
  15ml/1 tbsp chopped fresh coriander

COOK'S TIP

To warm the tortillas, either wrap them in foil and place them in a warm oven for 5 minutes, or wrap 4 or 5 at a time in microwave film and microwave for 20 seconds on 100% Full Power.

1 Cook the long grain and wild rice separately, following the instructions on the packets. Drain and set aside.

2 Make the salsa. Finely chop the shallot, garlic, chilli and parsley in a blender or food processor. Spoon into a bowl. Stir in the chopped tomatoes, olive oil, lemon juice and tomato juice. Season to taste with salt and pepper. Cover with clear film and chill.

3 Make the guacamole. Scoop the avocado flesh into a bowl. Mash it lightly with the spring onions, citrus juice, cayenne, fresh coriander and seasoning, so that small pieces still remain. Cover the surface closely with clear film and chill.

4 Heat the olive and sunflower oils in a frying pan and fry the onion wedges for 4–5 minutes until softened. Add the chicken strips and red pepper slices and fry until evenly browned.

5 Stir in the cumin, cayenne and turmeric. Fry, stirring, for about 1 minute, then stir in the passata and chicken stock. Bring to the boil, then lower the heat and simmer gently for 5–6 minutes until the chicken is cooked through. Season to taste.

6 Stir both types of rice into the chicken and cook for 1–2 minutes until the rice is warmed through.

7 Spoon a little of the chicken and rice mixture on to each warmed tortilla. Top with salsa, guacamole and soured cream and roll up. Alternatively, let everyone assemble their own fajita at the table.

VARIATION

Fajitas are very popular family fare, so don't be surprised if there are demands for this dish time and time again. To ring the changes, use brown long grain and red Camargue rice instead of the white rice and wild rice, and try using pork fillet or beef steak in place of the chicken.

MEXICAN SPICY BEEF TORTILLA

THIS DISH IS NOT UNLIKE A LASAGNE, EXCEPT THAT THE SPICY MEAT IS MIXED WITH RICE AND IS LAYERED BETWEEN MEXICAN TORTILLAS, WITH A HOT SALSA SAUCE FOR AN EXTRA KICK.

SERVES FOUR

INGREDIENTS
1 onion, chopped
2 garlic cloves, crushed
1 fresh red chilli, seeded and sliced
350g/12oz rump steak, cut into
   small cubes
15ml/1 tbsp oil
225g/8oz/2 cups cooked long grain
   rice
beef stock, to moisten
3 large wheat tortillas
For the salsa picante
   2 x 400g/14oz cans chopped tomatoes
   2 garlic cloves, halved
   1 onion, quartered
   1–2 fresh red chillies, seeded and
      roughly chopped
   5ml/1 tsp ground cumin
   2.5–5ml/½–1 tsp cayenne pepper
   5ml/1 tsp fresh oregano or 2.5ml/½
      tsp dried oregano
   tomato juice or water, if required
For the cheese sauce
   50g/2oz/4 tbsp butter
   50g/2oz/½ cup plain flour
   600ml/1 pint/2½ cups milk
   115g/4oz/1 cup grated Cheddar cheese
   salt and freshly ground black pepper

1 Preheat the oven to 180°C/350°F/Gas 4. Make the salsa picante. Place the tomatoes, garlic, onion and chillies in a blender or food processor and process until smooth. Pour into a small saucepan, add the spices and oregano and season with salt. Gradually bring to the boil, stirring occasionally. Boil for 1–2 minutes, then lower the heat, cover and simmer for 15 minutes. The sauce should be thick, but of a pouring consistency. If it is too thick, dilute it with a little tomato juice or water.

2 Make the cheese sauce. Melt the butter in a pan and stir in the flour. Cook for 1 minute. Add the milk, stirring all the time until the sauce boils and thickens. Stir in all but 30ml/2 tbsp of the cheese and season to taste. Cover the pan closely and set aside.

3 Mix the onion, garlic and chilli in a large bowl. Add the steak cubes and mix well. Heat the oil in a frying pan and stir-fry the meat mixture for about 10 minutes, until the meat cubes have browned and the onion is soft. Stir in the rice and enough beef stock to moisten. Season to taste with salt and freshly ground black pepper.

4 Pour about a quarter of the cheese sauce into the bottom of a round ovenproof dish. Add a tortilla and then spread over half the salsa followed by half the meat mixture.

5 Repeat these layers, then add half the remaining cheese sauce and the final tortilla. Pour over the remaining cheese sauce and sprinkle the reserved cheese on top. Bake in the oven for 15–20 minutes until golden on top.

COOK'S TIP
You can use any type of beef for this dish. If braising or stewing steak are used, they should be very finely chopped or even minced and the bake should be cooked for an extra 10–15 minutes.

TOMATO RICE

PROOF POSITIVE THAT YOU DON'T NEED ELABORATE INGREDIENTS OR COMPLICATED COOKING METHODS TO MAKE A DELICIOUS DISH.

SERVES FOUR

INGREDIENTS
   30ml/2 tbsp sunflower oil
   2.5ml/½ tsp onion seeds
   1 onion, sliced
   2 tomatoes, chopped
   1 orange or yellow pepper, seeded
      and sliced
   5ml/1 tsp crushed fresh root ginger
   1 garlic clove, crushed
   5ml/1 tsp chilli powder
   1 potato, diced
   7.5ml/1½ tsp salt
   400g/14oz/2 cups basmati rice,
      soaked
   750ml/1¼ pints/3 cups water
   30–45ml/2–3 tbsp chopped fresh
      coriander

1 Heat the oil and fry the onion seeds for about 30 seconds. Add the sliced onion and fry for about 5 minutes.

2 Stir in the tomatoes, pepper, ginger, garlic, chilli powder, potato and salt. Stir-fry over a medium heat for about 5 minutes more.

3 Drain the rice and add to the pan, then stir for about 1 minute until the grains are well coated.

4 Pour in the water and bring the rice to the boil, then lower the heat, cover the pan and cook the rice for 12–15 minutes. Remove from the heat, without lifting the lid, and leave the rice to stand for 5 minutes. Stir in the chopped coriander and serve.

PERUVIAN DUCK WITH RICE

THIS IS A VERY RICH DISH, BRIGHTLY COLOURED WITH SPANISH TOMATOES AND FRESH HERBS.

SERVES FOUR TO SIX

INGREDIENTS
    4 boned duck breasts
    1 Spanish onion, chopped
    2 garlic cloves, crushed
    10ml/2 tsp grated fresh root ginger
    4 tomatoes (peeled, if liked),
      chopped
    225g/8oz Kabocha or onion squash,
      cut into 1cm/½in cubes
    275g/10oz/1½ cups long grain rice
    750ml/1¼ pints/3 cups chicken
      stock
    15ml/1 tbsp finely chopped fresh
      coriander
    15ml/1 tbsp finely chopped fresh
      mint
    salt and freshly ground black
      pepper

2 Pour all but 15ml/1 tbsp of the fat into a jar or cup, then fry the breasts, meat side down, in the fat remaining in the pan for 3–4 minutes until brown all over. Transfer to a board, slice thickly and set aside in a shallow dish. Deglaze the pan with a little water and pour this liquid over the duck.

4 Add the squash, stir-fry for a few minutes, then cover and allow to steam for about 4 minutes.

5 Stir in the rice and cook, stirring, until the rice is coated in the tomato and onion mixture. Pour in the stock, return the slices of duck to the pan and season with salt and pepper.

6 Bring to the boil, then lower the heat, cover and simmer gently for 30–35 minutes until the rice is tender. Stir in the coriander and mint and serve.

1 Heat a heavy-based frying pan or flameproof casserole. Using a sharp knife, score the fatty side of the duck breasts in a criss-cross pattern, rub the fat with a little salt, then dry-fry the duck, skin side down, for 6–8 minutes to render some of the fat.

3 Fry the onion and garlic in the same pan for 4–5 minutes until the onion is fairly soft, adding a little extra duck fat if necessary. Stir in the ginger, cook for 1–2 minutes more, then add the tomatoes and cook, stirring, for another 2 minutes.

COOK'S TIP
While rice was originally imported to South America, squash was very much an indigenous vegetable. Pumpkin could also be used for this recipe. Kabocha squash has a thick skin and lots of seeds, which need to be removed before the flesh is cubed.

VARIATION
In Peru, these kinds of all-in-one dishes are based around whatever meat is available in the shops, or, in the case of vegetables, what is growing in the garden. Chicken or rabbit can be used instead of duck, and courgettes and carrots would work well when squash is out of season.

PERUVIAN SALAD

THIS REALLY IS A SPECTACULAR-LOOKING SALAD. IT COULD BE SERVED AS A SIDE DISH OR WOULD MAKE A DELICIOUS LIGHT LUNCH. IN PERU, WHITE RICE WOULD BE USED, BUT BROWN RICE ADDS AN INTERESTING TEXTURE AND FLAVOUR.

SERVES FOUR

INGREDIENTS
    225g/8oz/2 cups cooked long grain
      brown or white rice
    15ml/1 tbsp chopped fresh parsley
    1 red pepper
    1 small onion, sliced
    olive oil, for sprinkling
    115g/4oz green beans, halved
    50g/2oz/½ cup baby sweetcorn
    4 quails' eggs, hard-boiled
    25–50g/1–2oz Spanish ham, cut into
      thin slices (optional)
    1 small avocado
    lemon juice, for sprinkling
    75g/3oz mixed salad
    15ml/1 tbsp capers
    about 10 stuffed olives, halved
For the dressing
    1 garlic clove, crushed
    60ml/4 tbsp olive oil
    45ml/3 tbsp sunflower oil
    30ml/2 tbsp lemon juice
    45ml/3 tbsp natural yogurt
    2.5ml/½ tsp mustard
    2.5ml/½ tsp granulated sugar
    salt and freshly ground black pepper

1 Make the dressing by placing all the ingredients in a bowl and whisking with a fork until smooth. Alternatively, shake the ingredients together in a jam jar.

2 Put the cooked rice into a large, glass salad bowl and spoon in half the dressing. Add the chopped parsley, stir well and set aside.

3 Cut the pepper in half, remove the seeds and pith, then place the halves, cut side down, in a small roasting tin. Add the onion rings. Sprinkle the onion with a little olive oil, place the tin under a hot grill and grill for 5–6 minutes until the pepper blackens and blisters and the onion turns golden. You may need to stir the onion once or twice so that it grills evenly.

4 Stir the onion in with the rice. Put the pepper in a plastic bag and knot the bag. When the steam has loosened the skin on the pepper halves and they are cool enough to handle, peel them and cut the flesh into thin strips.

COOK'S TIP
This dish looks particularly attractive if served in a deep, glass salad bowl. Guests can then see the various layers, starting with the white rice, then the green salad leaves, topped by the bright colours of peppers, corn, eggs and olives.

5 Cook the green beans in boiling water for 2 minutes, then add the sweetcorn and cook for 1–2 minutes more, until tender. Drain both vegetables, refresh them under cold water, then drain again. Place in a large mixing bowl and add the red pepper strips, quails' eggs and ham, if using.

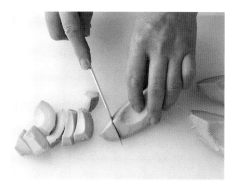

6 Peel the avocado, remove the stone, and cut the flesh into slices or chunks. Sprinkle with the lemon juice. Put the salad in a separate mixing bowl, add the avocado and mix lightly. Arrange the salad on top of the rice.

7 Stir about 45ml/3 tbsp of the remaining dressing into the green bean and pepper mixture. Pile this on top of the salad.

8 Scatter the capers and stuffed olives on top and serve the salad with the remaining dressing.

CALAS

THESE SWEET RICE FRITTERS ARE A CREOLE SPECIALITY, SOLD BY "CALAS" WOMEN ON THE STREETS OF THE FRENCH QUARTER OF NEW ORLEANS TO RESIDENTS AND OFFICE WORKERS, FOR WHOM THEY MAKE A POPULAR AND TASTY BREAKFAST.

MAKES OVER 40

INGREDIENTS
    115g/4oz/generous ½ cup short grain
      pudding rice
    900ml/1½ pints/3¾ cups mixed milk
      and water
    30ml/2 tbsp caster sugar
    50g/2oz/½ cup plain flour
    7.5ml/1½ tsp baking powder
    5ml/1 tsp grated lemon rind
    2.5ml/½ tsp ground cinnamon
    1.5ml/¼ tsp ground ginger
    generous pinch of grated nutmeg
    2 eggs
    oil, for deep frying
    salt
    icing sugar, for dusting
    cherry or strawberry jam and thick
      cream, to serve

1 Put the rice in a saucepan and pour in the milk and water. Add a pinch of salt and bring to the boil. Stir, then cover and simmer over a very gentle heat for 15–20 minutes until the rice is tender.

2 Switch off the heat under the pan, then add the sugar. Stir well, cover and leave until completely cool, by which time the rice should have absorbed all the liquid and become very soft.

3 Put the rice in a food processor or blender and add the flour, baking powder, lemon rind, spices and eggs. Process for about 20–30 seconds so that the mixture is like a thick batter.

4 Heat the oil in a wok or deep-fryer to 160°C/325°F. Scoop up a generous teaspoon of the rice batter and, using a second spoon, push this off carefully into the hot oil. Add four or five more and fry for 3–4 minutes, turning them occasionally, until the calas are a deep golden brown. Drain on kitchen paper and keep warm while cooking successive batches.

5 Dust the calas generously with icing sugar and serve warm with fruit jam and thick cream.

FRUITY RICE PUDDING CUSTARD

THERE ARE MANY DELICIOUS VARIATIONS ON RICE PUDDING IN LATIN AMERICA, THANKS TO SPANISH, PORTUGUESE AND FRENCH SETTLERS WHO ADAPTED FAVOURITE RECIPES FROM THEIR NATIVE COUNTRIES AND ADDED LOCAL INGREDIENTS LIKE RUM, THAT THEY HAD ACQUIRED A LIKING FOR.

SERVES FOUR TO SIX

INGREDIENTS
  60ml/4 tbsp rum or brandy
  75g/3oz/½ cup sultanas
  75g/3oz/scant ½ cup short grain
    pudding rice
  600ml/1 pint/2½ cups creamy milk
  1 strip pared lemon rind
  ½ cinnamon stick
  115g/4oz/scant ½ cup caster sugar
  150ml/¼ pint/⅔ cup single cream
  2 eggs, plus 1 egg yolk
  almond biscuits, to serve (optional)

1 Warm the rum or brandy in a small pan, then pour it over the sultanas. Soak for 3–4 hours or overnight.

2 Cook the rice in boiling water for 10 minutes until slightly softened. Drain well and return to the saucepan.

3 Stir 300ml/½ pint/1¼ cups of milk into the rice in the pan. Add the strip of lemon rind and the cinnamon stick, bring to the boil, then lower the heat and simmer for about 5 minutes. Remove the pan from the heat and stir in half of the sugar. Cover tightly with a damp dish towel held firmly in place with the saucepan lid. Leave the rice to cool for 1–2 hours.

4 Preheat the oven to 180°C/350°F/ Gas 4. Butter a medium-size baking dish and scatter the sultanas (with any remaining rum or brandy) over the bottom. Stir the rice, which should by now be thick and creamy, most of the liquid having been absorbed, and discard the cinnamon stick and lemon rind. Spoon the rice over the sultanas in the baking dish.

5 Heat the remaining milk with the cream until just boiling. Meanwhile, mix the eggs and egg yolk in a jug. Whisk in the remaining sugar, then the hot milk. Pour the mixture over the rice.

6 Stand the dish in a roasting tin, pour in hot water to come halfway up the sides of the dish and bake for 1–1¼ hours until the top is firm. Serve hot, with almond biscuits, if you like.

COOK'S TIP
This makes a light, creamy rice pudding. If you like your pudding to be denser, cook it for longer.

AFRICA AND THE CARIBBEAN

*Rice has been an important crop
in Africa for centuries, and some
of the oldest rice dishes, although
not necessarily the best known, come
from here. Traditional recipes and,
probably, the rice seeds, were brought
from Africa to the Caribbean, and
a new cuisine evolved — a rich and
unforgettable blend of tradition and
exotic produce.*

JOLOFF CHICKEN AND RICE

IN WEST AFRICA, WHERE IT ORIGINATED, THIS DISH IS USUALLY MADE IN LARGE QUANTITIES, USING JOINTED WHOLE CHICKENS. THIS VERSION IS SOMEWHAT MORE SOPHISTICATED, BUT STILL HAS THE TRADITIONAL FLAVOUR.

SERVES FOUR

INGREDIENTS

2 garlic cloves, crushed
5ml/1 tsp dried thyme
4 skinless, boneless chicken breasts
30ml/2 tbsp palm or vegetable oil
400g/14oz can chopped tomatoes
15ml/1 tbsp tomato purée
1 onion, chopped
450ml/¾ pint/scant 2 cups chicken stock
30ml/2 tbsp dried shrimps or crayfish, ground
1 fresh green chilli, seeded and finely chopped
350g/12oz//1¾ cups white long grain rice
750ml/18fl oz/2½ cups water
chopped fresh thyme, to garnish

1 Mix the garlic and thyme in a bowl. Rub the mixture into the chicken breasts. Heat the oil in a frying pan.

2 Add the chicken breasts to the pan to brown in the oil, then remove to a plate. Add the chopped tomatoes, tomato purée and onion to the pan. Cook over a moderately high heat for about 15 minutes until the tomatoes are well reduced, stirring occasionally at first and then more frequently as the tomatoes thicken.

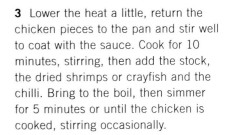

3 Lower the heat a little, return the chicken pieces to the pan and stir well to coat with the sauce. Cook for 10 minutes, stirring, then add the stock, the dried shrimps or crayfish and the chilli. Bring to the boil, then simmer for 5 minutes or until the chicken is cooked, stirring occasionally.

4 Meanwhile, put the rice in a separate saucepan. Pour in 750ml/18 fl oz/ 2½ cups of water, and top up with the sauce from the chicken. Bring to the boil, then lower the heat and cover the pan. Cook over a low heat for 12–15 minutes until the liquid has been absorbed and the rice is tender.

5 Pack the rice in four individual moulds and set aside. Lift out the chicken breasts from the sauce and put them on a board. If the sauce is runny, cook it over a high heat to reduce it a little. Unmould a rice timbale on each of four serving plates. Spoon the sauce around, then quickly slice the chicken breasts and fan them on the sauce. Garnish with fresh thyme sprigs and serve immediately.

TANZANIAN VEGETABLE RICE

SERVE THIS TASTY DISH WITH BAKED CHICKEN OR FISH. ADD THE VEGETABLES NEAR THE END OF COOKING SO THAT THEY REMAIN CRISP.

SERVES FOUR

INGREDIENTS
350g/12oz/1¾ cups basmati rice
45ml/3 tbsp vegetable oil
1 onion, chopped
2 garlic cloves, crushed
750ml/1¼ pints/3 cups vegetable stock or water
115g/4oz/⅔ cup fresh or drained canned sweetcorn kernels
½ red or green pepper, seeded and chopped
1 large carrot, grated
fresh chervil sprigs, to garnish

1 Rinse the rice in a sieve under cold water, then leave to drain thoroughly for about 15 minutes.

2 Heat the oil in a large saucepan and fry the onion for a few minutes over a medium heat until it starts to soften.

3 Add the rice and fry for about 10 minutes, stirring constantly to prevent the rice sticking to the pan. Then stir in the crushed garlic.

4 Pour in the stock or water and stir well. Bring to the boil, then lower the heat, cover and simmer for 10 minutes.

5 Scatter the sweetcorn kernels over the rice, then spread the chopped pepper on top. Sprinkle over the grated carrot. Cover the saucepan tightly. Steam over a low heat until the rice is tender, then mix together with a fork, pile on to a platter and garnish with chervil. Serve immediately.

MOROCCAN PAELLA

PAELLA IS PERENNIALLY POPULAR. THIS VERSION HAS CROSSED THE SEA FROM SPAIN TO MOROCCO, AND ACQUIRED SOME SPICY TOUCHES. UNLIKE SPANISH PAELLA, IT IS MADE WITH LONG GRAIN RICE.

SERVES SIX

INGREDIENTS
    2 large skinless, boneless chicken
      breasts
    about 150g/5oz prepared squid, cut
      into rings
    275g/10oz cod or haddock fillets,
      skinned and cut into bite-size
      chunks
    8–10 raw king prawns, peeled and
      deveined
    8 scallops, trimmed and halved
    350g/12oz fresh mussels
    250g/9oz/1⅓ cups white long grain
      rice
    30ml/2 tbsp sunflower oil
    1 bunch spring onions, cut into strips
    2 small courgettes, cut into strips
    1 red pepper, cored, seeded and cut
      into strips
    400ml/14fl oz/1⅔ cups chicken stock
    250ml/8fl oz/1 cup passata
    salt and freshly ground black pepper
    fresh coriander sprigs and lemon
      wedges, to garnish
For the marinade
    2 fresh red chillies, seeded and
      roughly chopped
    generous handful of fresh coriander
    10–15ml/2–3 tsp ground cumin
    15ml/1 tbsp paprika
    2 garlic cloves
    45ml/3 tbsp olive oil
    60ml/4 tbsp sunflower oil
    juice of 1 lemon

1 Make the marinade. Place all the ingredients in a food processor with 5ml/1 tsp salt and process until thoroughly blended. Cut the chicken into bite-size pieces. Place in a bowl.

2 Place the fish and shellfish (apart from the mussels) in a separate glass bowl. Divide the marinade between the fish and chicken and stir well. Cover with clear film and leave to marinate for at least 2 hours.

3 Scrub the mussels, discarding any that do not close when tapped sharply, and keep in a bowl in the fridge until ready to use. Place the rice in a bowl, cover with boiling water and set aside for about 30 minutes. Drain the chicken and fish, and reserve both lots of the marinade separately. Heat the oil in a wok, balti pan or paella pan and fry the chicken pieces for a few minutes until lightly browned.

4 Add the spring onions to the pan, fry for 1 minute and then add the courgettes and red pepper and fry for 3–4 minutes more until slightly softened. Transfer the chicken and then the vegetables to separate plates.

5 Scrape all the marinade into the pan and cook for 1 minute. Drain the rice, add to the pan and cook for 1 minute. Add the chicken stock, passata and reserved chicken, season with salt and pepper and stir well. Bring the mixture to the boil, then cover the pan with a large lid or foil and simmer very gently for 10–15 minutes until the rice is almost tender.

6 Add the reserved vegetables to the pan and place all the fish and mussels on top. Cover again with a lid or foil and cook over a moderate heat for 10–12 minutes until the fish is cooked and the mussels have opened. Discard any mussels that remain closed. Serve garnished with fresh coriander and lemon wedges.

SAVOURY GROUND RICE

SAVOURY GROUND RICE IS OFTEN SERVED AS AN ACCOMPANIMENT TO SOUPS AND STEWS IN WEST AFRICA.

<u>SERVES FOUR</u>

INGREDIENTS
300ml/½ pint/1¼ cups water
300ml/½ pint/1¼ cups milk
2.5ml/½ tsp salt
15ml/1 tbsp chopped fresh parsley
25g/1oz/2 tbsp butter or margarine
275g/10oz/1⅔ cups ground rice

COOK'S TIP
Ground rice is a creamy white colour, with a slightly grainy texture. Although often used in sweet dishes, it is a tasty grain to serve with savoury dishes too. The addition of milk gives a creamier flavour, but a double quantity of water can be used instead, if preferred.

3 Cover the pan and cook over a low heat for about 15 minutes, beating the mixture every 2 minutes to prevent the formation of lumps.

4 To test if the rice is cooked, rub a pinch of the mixture between your fingers: if it feels smooth and fairly dry, it is ready. Serve hot.

1 Place the water in a saucepan. Pour in the milk, bring to the boil and add the salt and parsley.

2 Add the butter or margarine and the ground rice, stirring with a wooden spoon to prevent the rice from becoming lumpy.

MOROCCAN SPICY MEATBALLS WITH RED RICE

CAMARGUE RED RICE IS NATIVE TO FRANCE, BUT IS RAPIDLY GROWING IN POPULARITY THROUGHOUT THE MEDITERRANEAN. IN THIS MOROCCAN DISH, THE NUTTY FLAVOUR OF THE RICE IS A PERFECT MATCH FOR THE SPICY MEATBALLS.

SERVES FOUR TO SIX

INGREDIENTS

225g/8oz/generous 1 cup Camargue
   red rice
675g/1½lb lamb leg steaks
2 onions
3–4 fresh parsley sprigs
3 fresh coriander sprigs, plus
   30ml/2 tbsp chopped fresh coriander
1–2 fresh mint sprigs
2.5ml/½ tsp ground cumin
2.5ml/½ tsp ground cinnamon
2.5ml/½ tsp ground ginger
5ml/1 tsp paprika
30ml/2 tbsp sunflower oil
1 garlic clove, crushed
300ml/½ pint/1¼ cups tomato juice
450ml/¾ pint/scant 2 cups chicken
   or vegetable stock
salt and freshly ground black pepper
Moroccan flat bread and yogurt
   dressing, to serve (optional)

1 Cook the rice in plenty of lightly salted water or stock for 30 minutes or according to the instructions on the packet. Drain.

2 Meanwhile, prepare the meatballs. Chop the lamb roughly, then place it in a food processor and process until finely chopped. Scrape the meat into a large bowl.

3 Cut 1 onion into quarters and add it to the processor with the parsley, coriander and mint sprigs; process until finely chopped. Return the lamb to the processor, add the spices and seasoning and process again until smooth. Scrape the mixture into a bowl and chill for about 1 hour.

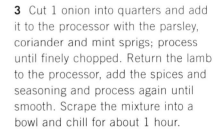

4 Shape the mixture into about 30 small balls. Heat half the oil in a frying pan, add the meatballs, in batches if necessary, and brown them evenly. Transfer to a plate. Chop the remaining onion finely.

5 Drain off the excess fat, leaving around 30ml/2 tbsp in the pan, and fry the chopped onion with the garlic for a few minutes until softened. Stir in the rice. Cook, stirring for 1–2 minutes, then stir in the tomato juice, stock and chopped fresh coriander. Season to taste with salt and pepper.

6 Arrange the meatballs over the rice, cover with a lid or foil and simmer very gently for 15 minutes. Serve solo, or with Moroccan flat bread and a yogurt dressing, if you like.

COOK'S TIP
A yogurt dressing is delicious with these meatballs. Simply stir 10ml/2 tsp finely chopped fresh mint into 90ml/6 tbsp natural yogurt.

AFRICAN LAMB AND VEGETABLE PILAU

SPICY LAMB IS SERVED IN THIS DISH WITH BASMATI RICE AND A COLOURFUL SELECTION OF DIFFERENT VEGETABLES AND CASHEW NUTS. LAMB AND RICE ARE A POPULAR COMBINATION IN AFRICAN COOKING.

SERVES FOUR

INGREDIENTS

   450g/1lb boned shoulder of lamb, cubed
   2.5ml/½ tsp dried thyme
   2.5ml/½ tsp paprika
   5ml/1 tsp garam masala
   1 garlic clove, crushed
   25ml/1½ tbsp vegetable oil
   900ml/1½ pints/3¾ cups lamb stock
   savoy cabbage or crisp lettuce leaves, to serve
For the rice
   25g/1oz/2 tbsp butter
   1 onion, chopped
   1 medium potato, diced
   1 carrot, sliced
   ½ red pepper, seeded and chopped
   1 fresh green chilli, seeded and chopped
   115g/4oz/1 cup sliced green cabbage
   60ml/4 tbsp natural yogurt
   2.5ml/½ tsp ground cumin
   5 green cardamom pods
   2 garlic cloves, crushed
   225g/8oz/generous 1 cup basmati rice, soaked
   about 50g/2oz/½ cup cashew nuts
   salt and freshly ground black pepper

1 Put the lamb cubes in a large bowl and add the thyme, paprika, garam masala and garlic, with plenty of salt and pepper. Stir, cover, and leave in a cool place for 2–3 hours.

2 Heat the oil in a saucepan and fry the lamb, in batches if necessary, over a medium heat for 5–6 minutes, until browned. Stir in the stock, cover the pan and cook for 35–40 minutes. Using a slotted spoon, transfer the lamb to a bowl. Pour the liquid into a measuring jug, topping it up with water if necessary to make 600ml/1 pint/2½ cups.

COOK'S TIP
If the stock looks a bit fatty after cooking the lamb cubes, blot the surface with kitchen paper to remove the excess grease before pouring the stock into the measuring jug.

3 Melt the butter in a separate pan and fry the onion, potato and carrot for 5 minutes. Add the red pepper and chilli and fry for 3 minutes more, then stir in the cabbage, yogurt, spices, garlic and the reserved lamb stock. Stir well, cover, then simmer gently for 5–10 minutes, until the cabbage has wilted.

4 Drain the rice and stir into the stew with the lamb. Cover and simmer over a low heat for 20 minutes or until the rice is cooked. Sprinkle in the cashew nuts and season to taste with salt and pepper. Serve hot, cupped in cabbage or lettuce leaves.

NORTH AFRICAN FISH WITH PUMPKIN RICE

THIS IS A DISH OF CONTRASTS — THE SLIGHTLY SWEET FLAVOUR OF PUMPKIN, THE MILDLY SPICY FISH, AND THE CORIANDER AND GINGER MIXTURE THAT IS STIRRED IN AT THE END — ALL BOUND TOGETHER WITH WELL-FLAVOURED RICE.

SERVES FOUR

INGREDIENTS
    450g/1lb sea bass or other firm fish
      fillets
    30ml/2 tbsp plain flour
    5ml/1 tsp ground coriander
    1.5–2.5ml/¼–½ tsp ground turmeric
    1 wedge of pumpkin, about
      500g/1¼lb
    30–45ml/2–3 tbsp olive oil
    6 spring onions, sliced diagonally
    1 garlic clove, finely chopped
    275g/10oz/1½ cups basmati rice,
      soaked
    550ml/18fl oz/2½ cups fish stock
    salt and freshly ground black pepper
    lime or lemon wedges and fresh
      coriander sprigs, to serve
For the coriander and ginger flavouring
    mixture
    45ml/3 tbsp finely chopped fresh
      coriander
    10ml/2 tsp finely chopped fresh root
      ginger
    ½–1 fresh chilli, seeded and very
      finely chopped
    45ml/3 tbsp lime or lemon juice

1 Remove and discard any skin or stray bones from the fish, and cut into 2cm/¾in chunks. Mix the flour, ground coriander, turmeric and a little salt and pepper in a plastic bag, add the fish and shake for a few seconds so that the fish is evenly coated in the spice mixture. Set aside. Make the coriander and ginger flavouring mixture by mixing all the ingredients in a small bowl.

2 Cut away the skin and scoop out the seeds from the pumpkin. Cut the flesh into 2cm/¾in chunks.

3 Heat 15ml/1 tbsp oil in a flameproof casserole and stir-fry the spring onions and garlic for a few minutes until slightly softened. Add the pumpkin and cook over a fairly low heat, stirring frequently, for 4–5 minutes or until the flesh begins to soften.

4 Drain the rice, add it to the mixture and toss over a brisk heat for 2–3 minutes. Stir in the stock, with a little salt. Bring to simmering point, then lower the heat, cover and cook for 12–15 minutes until both the rice and the pumpkin are tender.

5 About 4 minutes before the rice is ready, heat the remaining oil in a frying pan and fry the spiced fish over a moderately high heat for about 3 minutes until the outside is lightly browned and crisp and the flesh is cooked through but still moist.

6 Stir the coriander and ginger flavouring mixture into the rice and transfer to a warmed serving dish. Lay the fish pieces on top. Serve immediately, garnished with coriander, and offer lemon or lime wedges for squeezing over the fish.

COOK'S TIP
This dish can also be cooked – and served – in a wok, if preferred.

CHICKEN AND VEGETABLE TAGINE

MOROCCAN TAGINES ARE USUALLY SERVED WITH COUSCOUS, BUT RICE MAKES AN EQUALLY DELICIOUS ACCOMPANIMENT. HERE, COUSCOUS IS STIRRED INTO THE RICE TO CREATE AN UNUSUAL AND TASTY DISH, ALTHOUGH YOU COULD USE RICE BY ITSELF.

SERVES FOUR

INGREDIENTS
  30ml/2 tbsp groundnut oil
  4 skinless, boneless chicken breasts,
    cut into large pieces
  1 large onion, chopped
  2 garlic cloves, crushed
  1 small parsnip, cut into 2.5cm/1in
    pieces
  1 small turnip, cut into 2cm/¾in
    pieces
  3 carrots, cut into 4cm/1½in pieces
  4 tomatoes, chopped
  1 cinnamon stick
  4 cloves
  5ml/1 tsp ground ginger
  1 bay leaf
  1.5–2.5ml/¼–½ tsp cayenne pepper
  350ml/12fl oz/1½ cups chicken stock
  400g/14oz can chick-peas, drained
    and skinned
  1 red pepper, seeded and sliced
  150g/5oz green beans, halved
  1 piece of preserved lemon peel,
    thinly sliced
  20–30 stoned brown or green olives
  salt
For the rice and couscous
  750ml/1¼ pints/3 cups chicken stock
  225g/8oz/generous 1 cup long grain
    rice
  115g/4oz/⅔ cup couscous
  45ml/3 tbsp chopped fresh coriander

1 Heat half of the oil in a large, flameproof casserole and fry the chicken pieces for a few minutes until evenly browned. Transfer to a plate. Heat the remaining oil and fry the onion, garlic, parsnip, turnip and carrots together over a medium heat for 4–5 minutes until the vegetables are lightly flecked with brown, stirring frequently. Lower the heat, cover and sweat the vegetables for 5 minutes more, stirring occasionally.

2 Add the tomatoes, cook for a few minutes, then add the cinnamon stick, cloves, ginger, bay leaf and cayenne. Cook for 1–2 minutes.

3 Pour in the chicken stock, add the chick-peas and browned chicken pieces, and season with salt. Cover and simmer for 25 minutes.

4 Meanwhile, cook the rice and couscous mixture. Bring the chicken stock to the boil. Add the rice and simmer for about 5 minutes until almost tender. Remove the pan from the heat, stir in the couscous, cover tightly and leave for about 5 minutes.

5 When the vegetables in the tagine are almost tender, stir in the pepper slices and green beans and simmer for 10 minutes. Add the preserved lemon and olives, stir well and cook for 5 minutes more, or until the vegetables are perfectly tender.

6 Stir the chopped coriander into the rice and couscous mixture and pile it on to a plate. Serve the chicken tagine in the traditional dish, if you have one, or in a casserole.

RICE AND PEAS

THIS IS A POPULAR DISH ON THE ISLANDS OF THE EASTERN CARIBBEAN. THE BEANS MUST BE SOAKED OVERNIGHT, SO ALLOW PLENTY OF TIME FOR THIS RECIPE.

SERVES FOUR TO SIX

INGREDIENTS

175g/6oz/¾ cup red kidney beans
2 fresh thyme sprigs
50g/2oz piece of creamed coconut
2 bay leaves
1 onion, finely chopped
2 garlic cloves, crushed
2.5ml/½ tsp ground allspice
115g/4oz/⅔ cup chopped red pepper
600ml/1 pint/2½ cups water
450g/1lb/2⅓ cups white long grain
   rice
salt and freshly ground black pepper

1 Place the red kidney beans in a large bowl. Cover with water and leave to soak overnight.

2 Drain the beans, place in a large pan and pour in enough water to cover them by 2.5cm/1in. Bring to the boil. Boil over a high heat for 10 minutes, then lower the heat and simmer for 1½ hours or until the beans are tender.

3 Add the thyme, creamed coconut, bay leaves, onion, garlic, allspice and red pepper. Season well and stir in the measured water.

4 Bring to the boil and add the rice. Stir well, lower the heat and cover the pan. Simmer for 25–30 minutes, until all the liquid has been absorbed. Serve as an accompaniment to fish, meat or vegetarian dishes.

COOK'S TIP
To save time, use a 400g/14oz can of red kidney beans. Add them along with the rice.

CARIBBEAN PEANUT CHICKEN

PEANUT BUTTER IS USED A LOT IN MANY CARIBBEAN DISHES. IT ADDS A RICHNESS, AS WELL AS A DELICIOUS DEPTH OF FLAVOUR ALL OF ITS OWN.

SERVES FOUR

INGREDIENTS
    4 skinless, boneless chicken breasts, cut into thin strips
    225g/8oz/generous 1 cup white long grain rice
    30ml/2 tbsp groundnut oil
    15g/½oz/1 tbsp butter, plus extra for greasing
    1 onion, finely chopped
    2 tomatoes, peeled, seeded and chopped
    1 fresh green chilli, seeded and sliced
    60ml/4 tbsp smooth peanut butter
    450ml/¾ pint/scant 2 cups chicken stock
    lemon juice, to taste
    salt and freshly ground black pepper
    lime wedges and sprigs of fresh flat leaf parsley, to garnish
For the marinade
    15ml/1 tbsp sunflower oil
    1–2 garlic cloves, crushed
    5ml/1 tsp chopped fresh thyme
    25ml/1½ tbsp medium curry powder
    juice of half a lemon

1 Mix all the marinade ingredients in a large bowl and stir in the chicken. Cover loosely with clear film and set aside in a cool place for 2–3 hours.

2 Meanwhile, cook the rice in plenty of lightly salted boiling water until tender. Drain well and turn into a generously buttered casserole.

3 Preheat the oven to 180°C/350°F/Gas 4. Heat 15ml/1 tbsp of the oil and butter in a flameproof casserole and fry the chicken pieces for 4–5 minutes until evenly brown. Add more oil if necessary.

4 Transfer the chicken to a plate. Add the onion to the casserole and fry for 5–6 minutes until lightly browned, adding more oil if necessary. Stir in the chopped tomatoes and chilli. Cook over a gentle heat for 3–4 minutes, stirring occasionally. Remove from the heat.

5 Mix the peanut butter with the chicken stock. Stir into the tomato and onion mixture, then add the chicken. Stir in the lemon juice, season to taste, then spoon the mixture over the rice in the casserole.

6 Cover the casserole. Cook in the oven for 15–20 minutes or until piping hot. Use a large spoon to toss the rice with the chicken mixture. Serve at once, garnished with the lime wedges and parsley sprigs.

COOK'S TIP
If the casserole is not large enough to allow you to toss the rice with the chicken mixture before serving, invert a large, deep plate over the casserole, turn both over and toss the mixture on the plate.

SPICY PEANUT BALLS

TASTY RICE BALLS, ROLLED IN CHOPPED PEANUTS AND DEEP-FRIED, MAKE A DELICIOUS SNACK.
SERVE THEM AS THEY ARE, OR WITH A CHILLI SAUCE FOR DIPPING.

MAKES SIXTEEN

INGREDIENTS
  1 garlic clove, crushed
  1cm/½in piece of fresh root ginger,
    peeled and finely chopped
  1.5ml/¼ tsp ground turmeric
  5ml/1 tsp granulated sugar
  2.5ml/½ tsp salt
  5ml/1 tsp chilli sauce
  10ml/2 tsp fish sauce or soy sauce
  30ml/2 tbsp chopped fresh coriander
  juice of ½ lime
  225g/8oz/2 cups cooked white long
    grain rice
  115g/4oz peanuts, chopped
  vegetable oil, for deep-frying
  lime wedges and chilli dipping
    sauce, to serve (optional)

1 Process the garlic, ginger and turmeric in a food processor until the mixture forms a paste. Add the granulated sugar, salt, chilli sauce and fish sauce or soy sauce, with the chopped coriander and lime juice. Process briefly to mix.

2 Add three-quarters of the cooked rice to the paste in the food processor, and process until smooth and sticky. Scrape into a mixing bowl and stir in the remainder of the rice. Wet your hands and shape the mixture into thumb-size balls.

3 Roll the balls in chopped peanuts, making sure they are evenly coated.

4 Heat the oil in a deep-fryer or wok. Deep-fry the peanut balls until crisp. Drain on kitchen paper and then pile on to a platter. Serve hot with lime wedges and a chilli dipping sauce, if you like.

CARIBBEAN CHICKEN WITH PIGEON PEA RICE

GOLDEN, SPICY CARAMELIZED CHICKEN TOPS A RICHLY FLAVOURED VEGETABLE RICE IN THIS HEARTY AND DELICIOUS SUPPER DISH. PIGEON PEAS ARE A COMMON INGREDIENT IN CARIBBEAN COOKING.

SERVES FOUR

INGREDIENTS
  5ml/1 tsp allspice
  2.5ml/½ tsp ground cinnamon
  5ml/1 tsp dried thyme
  pinch of ground cloves
  1.5ml/¼ tsp freshly grated nutmeg
  4 skinless, boneless chicken breasts
  45ml/3 tbsp groundnut or sunflower
    oil
  15g/½oz/1 tbsp butter
  1 onion, chopped
  2 garlic cloves, crushed
  1 carrot, diced
  1 celery stick, chopped
  3 spring onions, chopped
  1 fresh red chilli, seeded and thinly
    sliced
  400g/14oz can pigeon peas
  225g/8oz/generous 1 cup long grain
    rice
  120ml/4fl oz/½ cup coconut milk
  550ml/18fl oz/2½ cups chicken
    stock
  30ml/2 tbsp demerara sugar
  salt and cayenne pepper

1 Mix together the allspice, cinnamon, thyme, cloves and nutmeg. Rub the mixture all over the pieces of chicken. Set aside for 30 minutes.

2 Heat 15ml/1 tbsp of the oil with the butter in a saucepan. Fry the onion and garlic over a medium heat until soft and beginning to brown. Add the carrot, celery, spring onions and chilli. Sauté for a few minutes, then stir in the pigeon peas, rice, coconut milk and chicken stock. Season with salt and cayenne pepper. Bring to simmering point, cover and cook over a low heat for about 25 minutes.

COOK'S TIP
Pigeon peas are sometimes called gungo beans, especially when sold in ethnic markets. If they are not available, use borlotti beans instead.

3 About 10 minutes before the rice mixture is cooked, heat the remaining oil in a heavy-based frying pan, add the sugar and cook, without stirring, until it begins to caramelize.

4 Carefully add the chicken to the pan. Cook for 8–10 minutes until the chicken has a browned, glazed appearance and is cooked through. Transfer the chicken to a board and slice it thickly. Serve the pigeon pea rice in individual bowls, with the chicken on top.

JAMAICAN FISH CURRY

ALTHOUGH THE RICE IS SIMPLY BOILED FOR THIS RECIPE, IT IS AN INTEGRAL PART OF THIS DISH AND IS AN EXCELLENT EXAMPLE OF HOW THE PLAINEST RICE TAKES ON THE FLAVOUR OF THE SAUCE WITH WHICH IT IS SERVED. CURRIES HAVE A DEFINITE PART TO PLAY IN AFRICAN COOKING.

SERVES FOUR

INGREDIENTS
2 halibut steaks, total weight about
    500–675g/1¼–1½lb
30ml/2 tbsp groundnut oil
2 cardamom pods
1 cinnamon stick
6 allspice berries
4 cloves
1 large onion, chopped
3 garlic cloves, crushed
10–15ml/2–3 tsp grated fresh root
    ginger
10ml/2 tsp ground cumin
5ml/1 tsp ground coriander
2.5ml/½ tsp cayenne pepper or to
    taste
4 tomatoes, peeled, seeded and
    chopped
1 sweet potato, about 225g/8oz,
    cut into 2cm/¾in cubes
475ml/16fl oz/2 cups fish stock or
    water
115g/4oz piece of creamed
    coconut
1 bay leaf
225g/8oz/generous 1 cup white long
    grain rice
salt

COOK'S TIPS
Sweet potato discolours very quickly.
If you are preparing the ingredients
in advance, put the cubed potato into
a large bowl and cover with cold water.
Add 30–45ml/2–3 tbsp lemon juice,
and set aside until ready to use.
   This recipe uses some of the most
common spices to appear in dishes from
Africa and the Caribbean, where the
influence of India is clearly visible.
The taste is for pungent flavours rather
than fiery heat. Allspice is widely
used throughout the Caribbean, while
cardamom and cayenne pepper are
essential ingredients in curries.

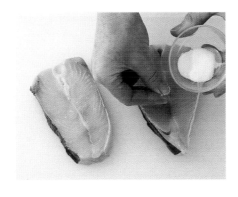

1 Rub the halibut steaks well with salt and set aside.

2 Heat the oil in a flameproof casserole and stir-fry the cardamom pods, cinnamon stick, allspice berries and cloves for about 3 minutes to release the aroma.

3 Add the onion, garlic and ginger. Continue cooking for 4–5 minutes over a gentle heat until the onion is fairly soft, stirring frequently, then add the cumin, coriander and cayenne pepper and cook briefly, stirring all the time.

VARIATION
Pumpkin or onion squash would also work well in this recipe. Pumpkin has a similar sweetness to sweet potato; onion squash on the other hand is more savoury. If you prefer a more authentic sweet flavour, stir in a little sugar or apricot jam to taste before cooking the fish.

4 Stir in the tomatoes, sweet potato, fish stock or water, creamed coconut and bay leaf. Season well with salt. Bring to the boil, then lower the heat, cover and simmer for 15–18 minutes until the sweet potato is tender.

5 Cook the rice according to your preferred method. Meanwhile, add the fish steaks to the pan of sauce and spoon the sauce over to cover them completely. Put a lid on the pan and simmer for about 10 minutes until the fish is just tender and flakes easily.

6 Spoon the rice into a warmed serving dish, spoon over the curry sauce and arrange the halibut steaks on top. Serve immediately.

ORANGE RICE PUDDING

IN MOROCCO, AS IN SPAIN, GREECE AND ITALY, THICK, CREAMY RICE PUDDINGS ARE VERY POPULAR, ESPECIALLY WHEN SWEETENED WITH HONEY AND FLAVOURED WITH ORANGE.

SERVES FOUR

INGREDIENTS

50g/2oz/generous ¼ cup short grain
   pudding rice
600ml/1 pint/2½ cups milk
finely grated rind of ½ small orange
30–45ml/2–3 tbsp clear honey
150ml/¼ pint/⅔ cup double cream
15ml/1 tbsp chopped pistachios,
   toasted (optional)
grated orange rind, to garnish

3 Remove the lid and continue cooking and stirring for 15–20 minutes, until the rice is creamy.

4 Pour in the cream, stirring constantly, then simmer for 5–8 minutes more. Spoon the rice pudding into warmed individual bowls. Sprinkle with the pistachios and orange rind and serve.

1 Mix the rice with the milk and orange rind in a saucepan. Pour in the honey and stir well.

2 Bring to the boil, then lower the heat, cover and simmer very gently for about 1¼ hours, stirring frequently.

VARIATION
Instead of adding double cream, stir in Greek yogurt. Serve immediately (without reheating), topped with toasted pine nuts and fresh orange segments.

CARIBBEAN SPICED RICE PUDDING

CARIBBEAN RECIPES CAN BE EXTREMELY SWEET, AND YOU MAY FIND YOU CAN REDUCE THE SUGAR QUANTITY IN THIS PUDDING BECAUSE OF THE NATURAL SWEETNESS OF THE FRUIT.

SERVES FOUR TO SIX

INGREDIENTS
  25g/1oz/2 tbsp butter
  1 cinnamon stick
  115g/4oz/½ cup soft brown sugar
  115g/4oz/⅔ cup ground rice
  1.2 litres/2 pints/5 cups milk
  2.5ml/½ tsp allspice
  50g/2oz/⅓ cup sultanas
  75g/3oz chopped mandarin oranges
  75g/3oz chopped pineapple

1 Melt the butter in a non-stick pan and then add the cinnamon stick and sugar. Heat over a medium heat until the sugar begins to caramelize: remove from the heat as soon as this happens.

2 Carefully stir in the rice and three-quarters of the milk. Bring to the boil, stirring all the time, without letting the milk burn. Reduce the heat and simmer for 10 minutes until the rice is cooked, stirring constantly.

3 Add the remaining milk, the allspice and the sultanas. Leave to simmer for 5 minutes, stirring occasionally.

4 When the rice is thick and creamy, allow to cool slightly, then stir in the mandarin and pineapple pieces. As an alternative, the fruit can be served separately, with warm or cold rice.

BRITAIN

Rice is a relative newcomer to
Britain. For a surprisingly long
time, the only way to use rice was
to cream it with milk and sugar
in a rice pudding, but the last
twenty years have seen rice earn its
rightful place at the dinner table.
Of today's rice dishes, some have
been adapted from Oriental cuisines;
others are entirely home-grown.

PUMPKIN, RICE AND CHICKEN SOUP

THIS IS A WARM, COMFORTING SOUP WHICH, DESPITE THE SPICE AND BASMATI RICE, IS QUINTESSENTIALLY ENGLISH. FOR AN EVEN MORE SUBSTANTIAL MEAL, ADD A LITTLE MORE RICE AND MAKE SURE YOU USE ALL THE CHICKEN FROM THE STOCK.

SERVES FOUR

INGREDIENTS

  1 wedge of pumpkin, about 450g/1lb
  15ml/1 tbsp sunflower oil
  25g/1oz/2 tbsp butter
  6 green cardamom pods
  2 leeks, chopped
  115g/4oz/generous ½ cup basmati
    rice, soaked
  350ml/12fl oz/1½ cups milk
  salt and freshly ground black pepper
  generous strips of pared orange rind,
    to garnish
For the chicken stock
  2 chicken quarters
  1 onion, quartered
  2 carrots, chopped
  1 celery stalk, chopped
  6–8 peppercorns
  900ml/1½ pints/3¾ cups water

1 First make the chicken stock. Place the chicken quarters, onion, carrots, celery and peppercorns in a large saucepan. Pour in the water and slowly bring to the boil. Skim the surface if necessary, then lower the heat, cover and simmer gently for 1 hour.

2 Strain the chicken stock into a clean, large bowl, discarding the vegetables. Skin and bone one or both chicken pieces and cut the flesh into strips. (If not using both chicken pieces for the soup, reserve the other piece for another recipe.)

3 Skin the pumpkin and remove all the seeds and pith, so that you have about 350g/12oz flesh. Cut the flesh into 2.5cm/1in cubes.

4 Heat the oil and butter in a saucepan and fry the cardamom pods for 2–3 minutes until slightly swollen. Add the leeks and pumpkin. Cook, stirring, for 3–4 minutes over a medium heat, then lower the heat, cover and sweat for 5 minutes more or until the pumpkin is quite soft, stirring once or twice.

5 Measure out 600ml/1 pint/2½ cups of the stock and add to the pumpkin mixture. Bring to the boil, then lower the heat, cover and simmer gently for 10–15 minutes, until the pumpkin is soft.

6 Pour the remaining stock into a measuring jug and make up with water to 300ml/½ pint/1¼ cups. Drain the rice and put it into a saucepan. Pour in the stock, bring to the boil, then simmer for about 10 minutes until the rice is tender. Add seasoning to taste.

7 Remove the cardamom pods, then process the soup in a blender or food processor until smooth. Pour back into a clean saucepan and stir in the milk, chicken and rice (with any stock that has not been absorbed). Heat until simmering. Garnish with the strips of pared orange rind and freshly ground black pepper, and serve with granary or wholemeal bread.

RICE CAKES WITH SMOKED SALMON

These elegant rice cakes are made using a risotto base. You could skip this stage and use leftover Seafood or Mushroom Risotto. Alternatively, use leftover long grain rice and add extra flavour with spring onions.

SERVES FOUR

INGREDIENTS

30ml/2 tbsp olive oil
1 medium onion, chopped
225g/8oz/generous 1 cup risotto rice
about 90ml/6 tbsp white wine
about 750ml/1¼ pints/3 cups fish or
  chicken stock
15g/½oz/2 tbsp dried porcini
  mushrooms, soaked for 10 minutes
  in warm water to cover
15ml/1 tbsp chopped fresh parsley
15ml/1 tbsp snipped fresh chives
5ml/1 tsp chopped fresh dill
1 egg, lightly beaten
about 45ml/3 tbsp ground rice, plus
  extra for dusting
oil, for frying
60ml/4 tbsp soured cream
175g/6oz smoked salmon
salt and freshly ground black pepper
radicchio and oakleaf salad, tossed
  in French dressing, to serve

1 Heat the olive oil in a pan and fry the onion for 3–4 minutes until soft. Add the rice and cook, stirring, until the grains are thoroughly coated in oil. Pour in the wine and stock, a little at a time, stirring constantly over a gentle heat until each quantity of liquid has been absorbed before adding more.

2 Drain the mushrooms and chop them into small pieces. When the rice is tender, and all the liquid has been absorbed, stir in the mushrooms, parsley, chives, dill and seasoning. Remove from the heat and set aside for a few minutes to cool.

COOK'S TIP
For a sophisticated occasion, garnish the rice cakes with roasted baby asparagus spears, lemon slices and dill.

3 Add the beaten egg, then stir in enough ground rice to bind the mixture – it should be soft but manageable. Dust your hands with ground rice and shape the mixture into four patties, about 13cm/5in in diameter and about 2cm/¾in thick.

4 Heat the oil in a shallow pan and fry the rice cakes, in batches if necessary, for 4–5 minutes until evenly browned on both sides. Drain on kitchen paper and cool slightly. Place each rice cake on a plate and top with 15ml/1 tbsp soured cream. Twist two or three thin slices of smoked salmon on top, and serve with a dressed salad garnish.

SALMON IN PUFF PASTRY

THIS IS AN ELEGANT PARTY DISH, MADE WITH RICE, EGGS AND SALMON AND ENCLOSED IN PUFF PASTRY.

SERVES SIX

INGREDIENTS

450g/1lb puff pastry, thawed if
  frozen
1 egg, beaten
3 hard-boiled eggs
90ml/6 tbsp single cream
200g/7oz/1¾ cups cooked long grain
  rice
30ml/2 tbsp finely chopped fresh
  parsley
10ml/2 tsp chopped fresh tarragon
675g/1½lb fresh salmon fillets
40g/1½oz/3 tbsp butter
juice of ½ lemon
salt and freshly ground black pepper

2 In a bowl, mash the hard-boiled eggs
with the cream, then stir in the cooked
rice. Add the parsley and tarragon and
season well. Spoon this mixture on to
the prepared pastry.

5 Roll out the remaining pastry and
cut out a semi-circle piece to cover
the head portion and a tail shape to
cover the tail. Brush both pieces of
pastry with a little beaten egg and place
on top of the fish, pressing down firmly
to secure. Score a criss-cross pattern
on the tail.

1 Preheat the oven to 190°C/375°F/
Gas 5. Roll out two-thirds of the pastry
into a large oval, measuring about
35cm/14in in length. Cut into a
curved fish shape and place on a
lightly greased baking sheet. Use
the trimmings to make narrow strips.
Brush one side of each strip with a
little beaten egg and secure in place
around the rim of the pastry to make
a raised edge. Prick the base all over
with a fork, then bake for 8–10 minutes
until the sides are well risen and the
pastry is lightly golden. Leave to cool.

3 Cut the salmon into 2cm/¾in chunks.
Melt the butter until it starts to sizzle,
then add the salmon. Turn the pieces
over in the butter so that they begin to
colour but do not cook through.

6 Cut the remaining pastry into small
circles and, starting from the tail end,
arrange the circles in overlapping lines
to represent scales. Add an extra one
for an eye. Brush the whole fish shape
with the remaining beaten egg.

7 Bake for 10 minutes, then reduce
the temperature to 160°C/325°F/Gas 3
and cook for a further 15–20 minutes
until the pastry is evenly golden. Slide
the fish on to a serving plate and serve.

COOK'S TIP

If the pastry seems to be browning too
quickly, cover it with foil during cooking
and remove from the oven for the last
5 minutes. It is important that the "fish"
cooks for the recommended time, so that
the salmon is sufficiently cooked through.

4 Remove from the heat and arrange
the salmon pieces on top of the rice,
piled in the centre. Stir the lemon juice
into the butter in the pan, then spoon
the mixture over the salmon pieces.

VARIATION

If time is short you may prefer to use this
simplified version of the recipe. Roll out
the pastry into a rectangle, then make
pastry edges to contain the filling. Part
bake the "fish", top with plain, rolled out
pastry and return it to the oven.

KEDGEREE

A popular Victorian breakfast dish, Kedgeree has its origins in Kitchiri, an Indian rice and lentil dish. Kedgeree can be flavoured with curry powder, but this recipe is mild.

SERVES FOUR

INGREDIENTS

500g/1¼lb smoked haddock
115g/4oz/generous ½ cup basmati
  rice
30ml/2 tbsp lemon juice
150ml/¼ pint/⅔ cup single cream or
  soured cream
pinch of freshly grated nutmeg
pinch of cayenne pepper
2 hard-boiled eggs, peeled and cut
  into wedges
50g/2oz/4 tbsp butter, diced
30ml/2 tbsp chopped fresh parsley
salt and freshly ground black pepper

COOK'S TIP
Taste the kedgeree before you add salt, as the smoked haddock may already be quite salty.

1 Put the haddock in a shallow pan, pour in just enough water to cover and heat to simmering point. Poach the fish for about 10 minutes, until the flesh flakes easily when tested with the tip of a sharp knife. Lift the fish out of the cooking liquid, then remove any skin and bones and flake the flesh. Reserve the cooking liquid,

2 Pour the cooking liquid into a measuring jug and make up the volume with water to 250ml/8fl oz/1 cup.

3 Pour the measured liquid into a pan and bring it to the boil. Add the rice, stir, then lower the heat, cover and simmer for about 10 minutes, until the rice is tender and the liquid has been absorbed. Meanwhile, preheat the oven to 180°C/350°F/Gas 4 and butter a baking dish.

4 When the rice is cooked, remove it from the heat and stir in the lemon juice, cream, flaked haddock, grated nutmeg and cayenne pepper. Add the egg wedges to the rice mixture and stir in gently.

5 Tip the rice mixture into the prepared baking dish. Level the surface and dot with butter. Cover the dish loosely with foil and bake for about 25 minutes.

6 Stir the chopped parsley into the baked kedgeree and add seasoning to taste. Serve immediately.

Chicken and Mango Salad with Orange Rice

Contemporary British cooking draws its inspiration from all over the world.

SERVES FOUR

INGREDIENTS

15ml/1 tbsp sunflower oil
1 onion, chopped
1 garlic clove, crushed
30ml/2 tbsp red curry paste
10ml/2 tsp apricot jam
30ml/2 tbsp chicken stock
about 450g/1lb cooked chicken, cut into small pieces
150ml/¼ pint/⅔ cup natural yogurt
60–75ml/4–5 tbsp mayonnaise
1 large mango, cut into 1cm/½in dice
fresh flat leaf parsley sprigs, to garnish
poppadums, to serve

For the orange rice
175g/6oz/scant 1 cup white long grain rice
225g/8oz carrots, grated (about 1⅓ cups)
1 large orange, cut into segments
40g/1½oz/⅓ cup roasted flaked almonds

For the dressing
45ml/3 tbsp olive oil
60ml/4 tbsp sunflower oil
45ml/3 tbsp lemon juice
1 garlic clove, crushed
15ml/1 tbsp chopped mixed fresh herbs (tarragon, parsley, chives)
salt and freshly ground black pepper

1 Heat the oil in a frying pan and fry the onion and garlic for 3–4 minutes until soft.

2 Stir in the curry paste, cook for about 1 minute, then lower the heat and stir in the apricot jam and stock. Mix well, add the chopped chicken and stir until the chicken is thoroughly coated in the paste. Spoon the mixture into a large bowl and leave to cool.

3 Meanwhile, boil the rice in plenty of lightly salted water until just tender. Drain, rinse under cold water and drain again. When cool, stir into the grated carrots and add the orange segments and flaked almonds.

4 Make the dressing by whisking all the ingredients together in a bowl.

5 When the chicken mixture is cool, stir in the yogurt and mayonnaise, then add the mango, stirring it in carefully so as not to break the flesh. Chill for about 30 minutes.

6 When ready to serve, pour the dressing into the rice salad and mix well. Spoon on to a platter and mound the cold curried chicken on top. Garnish with flat leaf parsley and serve with poppadums.

COOK'S TIP
A simple way of dicing a mango is to take two thick slices from either side of the large flat stone without peeling the fruit. Make criss-cross cuts in the flesh on each slice and then turn inside out. The cubes of flesh will stand proud of the skin and can be easily cut off.

LOIN OF PORK WITH CASHEW AND ORANGE STUFFING

THE ORANGES AND CASHEW NUTS ADD CONTRASTING FLAVOURS AND TEXTURES TO THIS STUFFING,
AND COMBINE WELL WITH THE BROWN RICE. DON'T WORRY IF THE STUFFING DOESN'T BIND — THE
BEST THING ABOUT BROWN RICE IS THAT IT RETAINS ITS OWN TEXTURE.

SERVES SIX

INGREDIENTS

  1.5kg/3–3½lb boned loin of pork
  15ml/1 tbsp plain flour
  300ml/½ pint/1¼ cups dry white
    wine
  salt and freshly ground black pepper
  fresh rosemary sprig and orange
    slices, to garnish
For the stuffing
  25g/1oz/2 tbsp butter
  1 small onion, finely chopped
  75g/3oz/scant ½ cup brown basmati
    rice, soaked and drained
  350ml/12fl oz/scant 1½ cups chicken
    stock
  50g/2oz/½ cup cashew nuts
  1 orange
  50g/2oz/⅓ cup sultanas

1 First cook the rice for the stuffing. Melt the butter in a frying pan and fry the chopped onion for 2–3 minutes until softened but not browned. Add the rice and cook for 1 minute, then pour in the chicken stock and bring to the boil. Stir, then lower the heat, cover and simmer for 35 minutes until the rice is tender and the liquid has been absorbed. Preheat the oven to 220°C/425°F/Gas 7.

2 While the rice is cooking, open out the loin of pork and cut two lengthways slits through the meat, making sure not to cut right through. Turn the meat over. Remove any excess fat, but leave a good layer; this will keep the meat moist during cooking.

3 Spread out the cashew nuts for the stuffing in a roasting tin and roast for 2–4 minutes until golden. Allow to cool, then chop roughly in a food processor or blender. Leave the oven on.

4 Grate 5ml/1 tsp of the orange rind into a bowl, then peel the orange. Working over a bowl to catch the juice, cut the orange into segments. Chop them roughly.

5 Add the chopped orange segments to the cooked rice with the orange rind, roast cashew nuts and sultanas. Season well, then stir in 15–30ml/1–2 tbsp of the reserved orange juice. Don't worry if the rice doesn't bind – it should have a fairly loose consistency.

6 Spread a generous layer of stuffing along the centre of the pork. If you have any stuffing left over, put it in a heatproof bowl and set aside.

7 Roll up the loin and tie securely with kitchen string. Rub a little salt and pepper into the surface of the meat and place it in a roasting tin. Roast for 15 minutes then lower the oven temperature to 180°C/350°F/Gas 4. Roast for 2–2¼ hours more or until the meat juices run clear and without any sign of pinkness. Heat any extra stuffing in the covered bowl alongside the meat for the final 15 minutes.

8 Transfer the meat to a warmed serving plate and keep warm. Stir the flour into the meat juices remaining in the roasting tin, cook for 1 minute, then stir in the white wine. Bring to the boil, stirring until thickened, then strain into a gravy boat.

9 Remove the string from the meat before carving. Stud the pork with the rosemary and garnish with the orange slices. Serve with the gravy and any extra stuffing.

COOK'S TIP
Pork is usually roasted until well done, though cooking times depend on your oven and the size of the joint. As a rule, allow 35–40 minutes at 180°C/350°F/Gas 4 per 450g/1lb for stuffed pork, plus an extra 15–20 minutes. If you like crackling, make sure the skin is completely dry. Just before cooking score it in a diamond pattern and rub generously with salt.

STRAWBERRY SHORTCAKE

GROUND RICE IS WIDELY USED FOR BAKING. IT ADDS A LIGHT, FINE TEXTURE TO THIS SHORTBREAD.

SERVES EIGHT

INGREDIENTS
    350g/12oz/3 cups strawberries
    300ml/½ pint/1¼ cups double cream
    30ml/2 tbsp caster sugar
    15ml/1 tbsp icing sugar (optional)
For the shortbread
    115g/4oz/1 cup plain flour
    50g/2oz/⅓ cup ground rice
    75g/3oz/6 tbsp caster sugar
    115g/4oz/½ cup unsalted butter
    1 egg yolk
    about 15ml/1 tbsp milk

1 Preheat the oven to 180°C/350°F/Gas 4. Make the shortbread. Sift the flour and ground rice into a bowl. Stir in the sugar, then rub in the butter. Stir in the egg yolk and milk, and mix to a dough.

2 Knead the dough lightly, break in half and roll each piece into a 20cm/8in round. Place on a greased baking sheet or in two fluted flan tins. Mark one of the rounds in to eight wedges.

3 Bake the shortbreads for 15–20 minutes until golden. Allow to cool a little on the baking sheet or in the tins. Cut the marked shortbread into wedges, then transfer the whole round and wedges to a wire rack and leave to cool.

4 Reserve the best-looking strawberry for the central decoration, and hull and slice the remainder. Set aside about eight of the strawberry slices to use as decoration. Whip the cream until it is fairly thick and stir in the caster sugar.

5 Spoon about one-third of the cream into a piping bag. Spread the remaining cream mixture over the whole shortbread base, and top with the sliced strawberries.

6 Top with the shortbread wedges, standing them at an angle and piping cream between them. Decorate with the reserved strawberry slices. Slice the whole strawberry almost, but not quite through and fan the slices. Place it in the centre of the shortcake, dust with icing sugar, if you like, and serve.

COOK'S TIP
Ground rice makes a good substitute for wheat flour, and is especially popular with people who cannot tolerate gluten.

TRADITIONAL ENGLISH RICE PUDDING

DON'T BE PUT OFF BY MEMORIES OF SCHOOL-DAYS RICE PUDDING. A PROPER RICE PUDDING IS SMOOTH AND CREAMY WITH JUST A HINT OF FRAGRANT SPICES. SERVE IT WITH A SPOONFUL OF THICK CHERRY JAM, IF LIKED.

SERVES FOUR

INGREDIENTS
    600ml/1 pint/2½ cups creamy milk
    1 vanilla pod
    50g/2oz/generous ¼ cup short grain
      pudding rice
    45ml/3 tbsp caster sugar
    25g/1oz/2 tbsp butter
    freshly grated nutmeg

1 Pour the milk into a pan and add the vanilla pod. Bring to simmering point, then remove from the heat, cover and leave to infuse for 1 hour. Preheat the oven to 150°C/300°F/Gas 2.

2 Put the rice and sugar in an ovenproof dish. Strain the milk over the rice, discarding the vanilla pod. Stir to mix, then dot the surface with the butter.

3 Bake, uncovered, for 2 hours. After about 40 minutes, stir the surface skin into the pudding, and repeat this after a further 40 minutes. At this point, sprinkle the surface of the pudding with grated nutmeg. Allow the pudding to finish cooking without stirring.

COOK'S TIP
If possible, always use a non-stick saucepan when heating milk, otherwise it is likely to stick to the bottom of the pan and burn.

NORTH AMERICA

North America is one of the world's largest rice producing countries. It is no surprise to find here a large number of home-grown rice recipes, as well as a diverse collection of "imports" introduced and adapted over generations by the culturally rich migrant communities, amongst them Italians, Japanese and Chinese.

SEAFOOD CHOWDER

CHOWDER TAKES ITS NAME FROM THE FRENCH WORD FOR CAULDRON — CHAUDIÈRE — THE TYPE OF POT ONCE TRADITIONALLY USED FOR SOUPS AND STEWS. LIKE MOST CHOWDERS, THIS IS A SUBSTANTIAL DISH, WHICH COULD EASILY BE SERVED WITH CRUSTY BREAD FOR A LUNCH OR SUPPER.

SERVES FOUR TO SIX

INGREDIENTS

   200g/7oz/generous 1 cup drained,
     canned sweetcorn kernels
   600ml/1 pint/2½ cups milk
   15g/½oz/1 tbsp butter
   1 small leek, sliced
   1 small garlic clove, crushed
   2 rindless smoked streaky bacon
     rashers, finely chopped
   1 small green pepper, seeded and
     diced
   1 celery stalk, chopped
   115g/4oz/generous ½ cup white long
     grain rice
   5ml/1 tsp plain flour
   about 450ml/¾ pint/scant 2 cups hot
     chicken or vegetable stock
   4 large scallops, preferably with
     corals
   115g/4oz white fish fillet, such as
     monkfish or plaice
   15ml/1 tbsp finely chopped fresh
     parsley
   good pinch of cayenne pepper
   30–45ml/2–3 tbsp single cream
     (optional)
   salt and freshly ground black pepper

1 Place half the sweetcorn kernels in a food processor or blender. Add a little of the milk and process until thick and creamy.

2 Melt the butter in a large saucepan and gently fry the leek, garlic and bacon for 4–5 minutes until the leek has softened but not browned. Add the green pepper and celery and sweat over a very gentle heat for 3–4 minutes more, stirring frequently.

3 Stir in the rice and cook for a few minutes until the grains begin to swell. Sprinkle over the flour. Cook, stirring, for about 1 minute, then gradually stir in the remaining milk and the stock.

4 Bring the mixture to the boil over a medium heat, then lower the heat and stir in the creamed corn mixture, with the whole corn kernels. Season well.

5 Cover the pan and simmer the chowder very gently for 20 minutes or until the rice is tender, stirring occasionally, and adding a little more chicken stock or water if the mixture thickens too quickly or the rice begins to stick to the bottom of the pan.

6 Pull the corals away from the scallops and slice the white flesh into 5mm/¼in pieces. Cut the fish fillet into bite-size chunks.

7 Stir the scallops and fish into the chowder, cook for 4 minutes, then stir in the corals, parsley and cayenne. Cook for a few minutes to heat through, then stir in the cream, if liked. Adjust the seasoning and serve.

THAI-STYLE SEAFOOD PASTIES

THAI-STYLE FOOD IS HUGELY POPULAR IN MANY PARTS OF AMERICA, ESPECIALLY ALONG THE WEST COAST, WHERE RICE IS ONE OF THE MOST IMPORTANT CROPS.

MAKES EIGHTEEN

INGREDIENTS
   500g/1¼lb puff pastry, thawed if
     frozen
   1 egg, beaten with 30ml/2 tbsp water
   fresh coriander leaves and lime
     twists, to garnish
For the filling
   275g/10oz skinned white fish fillets,
     such as cod or haddock
   plain flour seasoned with salt and
     freshly ground black pepper
   8–10 large raw prawns
   15ml/1 tbsp sunflower oil
   about 75g/3oz/6 tbsp butter
   6 spring onions, finely sliced
   1 garlic clove, crushed
   225g/8oz/2 cups cooked Thai
     fragrant rice
   4cm/1½in piece of fresh root ginger,
     grated
   10ml/2 tsp finely chopped fresh
     coriander
   5ml/1 tsp finely grated lime rind

1 Preheat the oven to 190°C/375°F/ Gas 5. Make the filling. Cut the fish into 2cm/¾in cubes and dust with the flour. Peel and devein the prawns and cut each one into four pieces.

2 Heat half of the oil and 15g/½oz/ 1 tbsp of the butter in a frying pan. Add the spring onions and fry them over a gentle heat for 2 minutes. Add the garlic and fry for about 5 minutes more, until the onions are very soft. Transfer to a large bowl.

3 Heat the remaining oil and a further 25g/1oz/2 tbsp of the butter in a clean pan. Fry the fish pieces briefly. As soon as they begin to turn opaque, use a slotted spoon to transfer them to the bowl with the spring onions. Cook the prawns in the fat remaining in the pan. When they begin to change colour, lift them out and add them to the bowl.

4 Add the cooked rice to the bowl, with the ginger, coriander and lime rind. Mix, taking care not to break up the fish.

5 Dust the work surface with a little flour. Roll out the pastry and cut into 10cm/4in rounds. Place spoonfuls of filling just off centre on the pastry rounds. Dot with a little butter. Dampen the edges of the pastry with a little of the egg wash, fold one side of the pastry over the filling and press the edges together firmly.

6 Place these on a lightly greased baking sheet. Decorate the pasties with the pastry trimmings, if you like. Brush them with egg wash and bake for 12–15 minutes or until golden.

7 Transfer to a plate and garnish with fresh coriander leaves and lime twists.

COOK'S TIP
If you prefer, you could make 6 larger pasties to serve as a main course.

CALIFORNIAN CITRUS FRIED RICE

AS WITH ALL FRIED RICE DISHES, THE IMPORTANT THING HERE IS TO MAKE SURE THE RICE IS COLD.
ADD IT AFTER COOKING ALL THE OTHER INGREDIENTS, AND STIR TO HEAT IT THROUGH COMPLETELY.

SERVES FOUR TO SIX

INGREDIENTS
  4 eggs
  10ml/2 tsp Japanese rice vinegar
  30ml/2 tbsp light soy sauce
  about 45ml/3 tbsp groundnut oil
  50g/2oz/½ cup cashew nuts
  2 garlic cloves, crushed
  6 spring onions, diagonally sliced
  2 small carrots, cut into julienne
    strips
  225g/8oz asparagus, each spear cut
    diagonally into 4 pieces
  175g/6oz/2¼ cups button
    mushrooms, halved
  30ml/2 tbsp rice wine
  30ml/2 tbsp water
  450g/1lb/4 cups cooked white long
    grain rice
  about 10ml/2 tsp sesame oil
  1 pink grapefruit or orange,
    segmented
  thin strips of orange rind, to garnish
For the hot dressing
  5ml/1 tsp grated orange rind
  30ml/2 tbsp Japanese rice wine
  45ml/3 tbsp oyster sauce
  30ml/2 tbsp freshly squeezed pink
    grapefruit or orange juice
  5ml/1 tsp medium or hot chilli sauce

3 Heat the remaining oil and add the garlic and spring onions. Cook over a medium heat for 1–2 minutes until the onions begin to soften, then add the carrots and stir-fry for 4 minutes.

4 Add the asparagus and cook for 2–3 minutes, then stir in the mushrooms and stir-fry for a further 1 minute. Stir in the rice wine, the remaining soy sauce and the water. Simmer for a few minutes until the vegetables are just tender but still firm.

5 Mix the ingredients for the dressing, then add to the wok and bring to the boil. Add the rice, scrambled eggs and cashew nuts. Toss over a low heat for 3–4 minutes, until the rice is heated through. Just before serving, stir in the sesame oil and the grapefruit or orange segments. Garnish with strips of orange rind and serve at once.

1 Beat the eggs with the vinegar and 10ml/2 tsp of the soy sauce. Heat 15ml/1 tbsp of the oil in a wok and cook the eggs until lightly scrambled. Transfer to a plate and set aside.

2 Add the cashew nuts to the wok and stir-fry for 1–2 minutes. Set aside.

WALDORF RICE SALAD

WALDORF SALAD TAKES ITS NAME FROM THE WALDORF HOTEL IN NEW YORK, WHERE IT WAS FIRST MADE. THE RICE MAKES THIS SALAD SLIGHTLY MORE SUBSTANTIAL THAN USUAL. IT CAN BE SERVED AS AN ACCOMPANIMENT, OR AS A MAIN MEAL FOR TWO.

SERVES TWO TO FOUR

INGREDIENTS
  115g/4oz/generous ½ cup white long
    grain rice
  1 red apple
  1 green apple
  60ml/4 tbsp lemon juice
  3 celery stalks
  2–3 slices thick cooked ham
  90ml/6 tbsp good quality
    mayonnaise, preferably home-made
  60ml/4 tbsp soured cream
  generous pinch of saffron, dissolved
    in 15ml/1 tbsp hot water
  10ml/2 tsp chopped fresh basil
  15ml/1 tbsp chopped fresh parsley
  several cos or iceberg lettuce leaves
  50g/2oz/½ cup walnuts, roughly
    chopped
  salt and freshly ground black pepper

1 Cook the rice in plenty of boiling salted water until tender. Drain and set aside in a bowl to cool.

2 Cut the apples into quarters, remove the cores and finely slice one red and one green apple quarter. Place the slices in a bowl with half the lemon juice and reserve for the garnish. Peel the remaining apple quarters and cut into julienne strips. Place in a separate bowl and toss with another 15ml/1 tbsp of the lemon juice.

3 Cut the celery into thin strips. Roll up each slice of ham, slice finely and add to the apple sticks, with the celery.

4 Mix together the mayonnaise, soured cream and saffron water, then stir in salt and pepper to taste.

5 Stir the mayonnaise mixture and herbs into the rice. Add the apple and celery, with the remaining lemon juice.

6 Arrange the lettuce leaves around the outside of a salad bowl and pile the rice and apple mixture into the centre. Scatter with the chopped walnuts and garnish with fans of apple slices.

SMOKED SALMON AND RICE SALAD PARCELS

FETA, CUCUMBER AND TOMATOES GIVE A GREEK FLAVOUR TO THE SALAD IN THESE PARCELS, A COMBINATION WHICH GOES WELL WITH THE RICE, ESPECIALLY IF A LITTLE WILD RICE IS ADDED.

SERVES FOUR

INGREDIENTS
  175g/6oz/scant 1 cup mixed wild
    rice and basmati rice
  8 slices smoked salmon, total weight
    about 350g/12oz
  10cm/4in piece of cucumber, finely
    diced
  about 225g/8oz feta cheese, cubed
  8 cherry tomatoes, quartered
  30ml/2 tbsp mayonnaise
  10ml/2 tsp fresh lime juice
  15ml/1 tbsp chopped fresh chervil
  salt and freshly ground black pepper
  lime slices and fresh chervil, to
    garnish

1 Cook the rice according to the instructions on the packet. Drain, tip into a bowl and allow to cool.

2 Line four ramekins with clear film, then line each ramekin with two slices of smoked salmon. Reserve any extra pieces of smoked salmon for the tops of the parcels.

3 Add the cucumber, feta and tomatoes to the rice, and stir in the mayonnaise, lime juice and chervil. Mix together well. Season with salt and pepper to taste.

4 Spoon the rice mixture into the salmon-lined ramekins. (Any leftover mixture can be used to make a rice salad.) Place any extra pieces of smoked salmon on top, then fold over the overlapping pieces of salmon so that the rice mixture is completely encased.

5 Chill the parcels in the fridge for 30–60 minutes, then invert each parcel on to a plate, using the clear film to ease them out of the ramekins. Carefully peel off the clear film, then garnish each parcel with slices of lime and a sprig of fresh chervil and serve.

Stuffed Pancakes with Turkey and Cranberries

This is a wonderful way of using leftover roast turkey. Cranberries add their own bitter-sweet flavour, while the wild rice contributes a nutty flavour and texture.

MAKES SIX TO EIGHT

INGREDIENTS
  50g/2oz/generous ¼ cup wild rice
  stock or water
  15g/½oz/1 tbsp butter
  2.5ml/½ tsp sunflower oil
  1 small onion, finely chopped
  50g/2oz/½ cup small chestnut
    mushrooms, quartered
  75g/3oz/¾ cup cranberries, fresh or
    frozen
  25ml/1½ tbsp granulated sugar
  60–75ml/4–5 tbsp water
  about 275g/10oz cooked turkey
    breast, cut into 2cm/¾in cubes
  150ml/¼ pint/⅔ cup soured cream
  30ml/2 tbsp freshly grated Parmesan
  salt and freshly ground black pepper
For the pancakes
  175g/6oz/1½ cups plain flour
  1 egg
  350ml/12fl oz/1½ cups milk,
    preferably semi-skimmed
  oil, for frying

1 Cook the wild rice in simmering stock or water for 40–50 minutes or according to the instructions on the packet. Drain. Preheat the oven to 190°C/375°F/Gas 5.

2 Meanwhile, make the pancakes. Sift the flour and a pinch of salt into a bowl. Beat in the egg and milk to make a smooth batter. Heat a little oil in a frying pan, pour in about 30ml/ 2 tbsp of the batter and tilt to cover the bottom of the pan. Cook until the underside is a pale brown colour, then flip the pancake over and cook the other side briefly. Carefully slide it out of the pan and cook 5–7 more pancakes in the same way.

3 Heat the butter and sunflower oil in a separate frying pan and fry the chopped onion for 3–4 minutes until soft. Add the chestnut mushrooms and fry for 2–3 minutes, until they are a pale golden colour.

4 Put the cranberries in a small saucepan and add the sugar and measured water. Bring to simmering point and then cover and simmer over a very low heat until the cranberries burst. This will take about 10 minutes if the cranberries are fresh, and about 2–3 minutes if frozen.

5 Transfer the cooked cranberries to a bowl with a slotted spoon, and pour in 45ml/3 tbsp of the cooking liquid. Add the rice, turkey, onion and mushroom mixture and 60ml/4 tbsp of the soured cream. Season with a little salt and pepper and stir to mix, taking care not to break up the cranberries.

6 Fold the pancakes in four and spoon the stuffing into one of the pockets. Arrange in a lightly greased baking dish. Mix the remaining soured cream with the grated Parmesan and spoon over the top of the pancakes. Bake for 10 minutes to heat through, then serve.

FISH PIE WITH SWEET POTATO TOPPING

THIS TASTY DISH IS FULL OF CONTRASTING FLAVOURS — THE SWEET, SLIGHTLY SPICY SWEET POTATO MAKING AN INTERESTING PARTNER FOR THE MILD-FLAVOURED FISH. WITH ITS BRIGHT TOPPING, IT LOOKS ATTRACTIVE, TOO, AND IS DELICIOUS SERVED WITH SUGAR SNAP PEAS.

SERVES FOUR

INGREDIENTS
175g/6oz/scant 1 cup basmati or
    Texmati rice, soaked
450ml/¾ pint/scant 2 cups
    well-flavoured stock
175g/6oz/1½ cups podded broad
    beans
675g/1½lb haddock or cod fillets,
    skinned
about 450ml/¾ pint/scant 2 cups
    milk
For the sauce
40g/1½oz/3 tbsp butter
30–45ml/2–3 tbsp plain flour
15ml/1 tbsp chopped fresh parsley
salt and freshly ground black pepper
For the topping
450g/1lb sweet potatoes, peeled and
    cut in large chunks
450g/1lb floury white potatoes, such
    as King Edwards, peeled and cut in
    large chunks
milk and butter, for mashing
10ml/2 tsp freshly chopped parsley
5ml/1 tsp freshly chopped dill
15ml/1 tbsp single cream (optional)

1 Preheat the oven to 190°C/375°F/ Gas 5. Drain the rice and put it in a saucepan. Pour in the stock, with a little salt and pepper, if needed, and bring to the boil. Cover the pan, lower the heat and simmer for about 10 minutes or until all the liquid has been absorbed.

2 Cook the broad beans in a little lightly salted water until tender. Drain thoroughly. When cool enough to handle, pop the bright green beans out of their skins.

3 To make the potato topping, cook the sweet and white potatoes separately in boiling salted water until tender. Drain them both, then mash them with a little milk and butter. Spoon the mashed potato into separate bowls. Beat parsley and dill into the sweet potatoes, with the single cream, if using.

4 Place the fish in a large frying pan and pour in enough of the milk (about 350ml/12fl oz/1½ cups) to just cover. Dot with 15g/½oz/1 tbsp of the butter and season with salt and pepper. Heat gently and simmer for 5–6 minutes until the fish is just tender. Lift out the fish and break it into large pieces. Pour the cooking liquid into a measuring jug and make up to 450ml/¾ pint/scant 2 cups with the remaining milk.

5 Make a white sauce. Melt the butter in a saucepan, stir in the flour and cook for 1 minute. Gradually add the cooking liquid and milk mixture, stirring, until a fairly thin white sauce is formed. Stir in the parsley, taste and season with a little more salt and pepper, if necessary.

6 Spread out the cooked rice on the bottom of a large oval gratin dish. Add the broad beans and fish and pour over the white sauce. Spoon the mashed potatoes over the top, to make an attractive pattern. Dot with a little extra butter and bake for 15 minutes until lightly browned.

COOK'S TIP
There are several types of sweet potato. The lighter skinned variety, surprisingly, has the redder flesh. If preferred, you could top this pie entirely with sweet potatoes, or you could mash the two types together. Cook them separately, however, as the sweet potato tends to cook more quickly.

WILD RICE PILAFF

WILD RICE ISN'T A RICE AT ALL, BUT IS ACTUALLY A TYPE OF WILD GRASS. CALL IT WHAT YOU WILL, IT HAS A WONDERFUL NUTTY FLAVOUR AND COMBINES WELL WITH LONG GRAIN RICE IN THIS FRUITY MIXTURE. SERVE AS A SIDE DISH.

SERVES SIX

INGREDIENTS
200g/7oz/1 cup wild rice
40g/1½oz/3 tbsp butter
½ onion, finely chopped
200g/7oz/1 cup long grain rice
475ml/16fl oz/2 cups chicken stock
75g/3oz/¾ cup sliced or flaked
  almonds
115g/4oz/⅔ cup sultanas
30ml/2 tbsp chopped fresh parsley
salt and freshly ground black pepper

1 Bring a large saucepan of water to the boil. Add the wild rice and 5ml/1 tsp salt. Lower the heat, cover and simmer gently for 45–60 minutes, until the rice is tender. Drain well.

2 Meanwhile, melt 15g/½oz/1 tbsp of the butter in another saucepan. Add the onion and cook over a medium heat for about 5 minutes until it is just softened. Stir in the long grain rice and cook for 1 minute more.

3 Stir in the stock and bring to the boil. Cover and simmer gently for 30–40 minutes, until the rice is tender and the liquid has been absorbed.

COOK'S TIP
Like all rice dishes, this one must be made with well-flavoured stock. If you haven't time to make your own, use a carton or can of good quality stock.

4 Melt the remaining butter in a small pan. Add the almonds and cook until they are just golden. Set aside.

5 Put the rice mixture in a bowl and add the almonds, sultanas and half the parsley. Stir to mix. Taste and adjust the seasoning if necessary. Transfer to a warmed serving dish, sprinkle with the remaining parsley and serve.

WILD RICE WITH GRILLED VEGETABLES

THE MIXTURE OF WILD RICE — WHICH IS NOT REALLY RICE AT ALL BUT A GRASS — AND LONG GRAIN RICE IN THIS DISH WORKS VERY WELL, AND MAKES AN EXTREMELY TASTY VEGETARIAN MEAL.

SERVES FOUR

INGREDIENTS

225g/8oz/generous 1 cup mixed wild
    and long grain rice
1 large aubergine, thickly sliced
1 red, 1 yellow and 1 green pepper,
    seeded and cut into quarters
2 red onions, sliced
225g/8oz/generous 3 cups brown cap
    or shiitake mushrooms
2 small courgettes, cut in half
    lengthways
olive oil, for brushing
30ml/2 tbsp chopped fresh thyme,
    plus extra to garnish
For the dressing
90ml/6 tbsp extra virgin olive oil
30ml/2 tbsp balsamic vinegar
2 garlic cloves, crushed
salt and freshly ground black pepper

1 Put all the rice in a pan of cold salted water. Bring to the boil, then lower the heat, cover and cook gently for 30–40 minutes (or according to the instructions on the packet) until tender.

2 Make the dressing. Whisk the olive oil, vinegar, garlic and seasoning together in a bowl or shake in a screw-top jar until thoroughly blended. Set aside while you grill the vegetables.

3 Arrange all the vegetables on a grill rack. Brush with olive oil and grill for about 5 minutes.

4 Turn the vegetables over, brush them with more olive oil and grill for 5–8 minutes more, or until tender and charred in places.

5 Drain the rice, tip into a bowl and toss in half the dressing. Spoon on to individual plates and arrange the grilled vegetables on top. Pour over the remaining dressing, scatter over the chopped thyme and serve.

SOUTH-WESTERN RICE PUDDING

COCONUT IS THE SECRET INGREDIENT IN THIS UNUSUAL RICE PUDDING. DO NOT OVERCOOK THE RICE OR IT WILL BECOME STODGY. FRESH FRUITS, SUCH AS STRAWBERRIES, MAKE THE IDEAL PARTNER.

SERVES FOUR

INGREDIENTS

40g/1½oz/¼ cup raisins
about 475ml/16fl oz/2 cups water
200g/7oz/1 cup short grain pudding
  rice
1 cinnamon stick
30ml/2 tbsp granulated sugar
475ml/16fl oz/2 cups milk
250ml/8fl oz/1 cup canned
  sweetened coconut cream
2.5ml/½ tsp vanilla essence
15g/½oz/1 tbsp butter
25g/1oz/⅓ cup shredded coconut
ground cinnamon, for sprinkling

1 Put the raisins in a small bowl and pour over enough water to cover. Leave the raisins to soak.

2 Pour the measured water into a heavy or non-stick pan and bring it to the boil. Add the rice, cinnamon stick and sugar and stir. Return to the boil, then lower the heat, cover, and simmer gently for 15–20 minutes until the liquid has been absorbed.

3 Remove the cinnamon stick from the rice. Drain the raisins and add them to the rice with the milk, coconut cream and vanilla essence. Stir to mix. Replace the lid and cook the mixture for about 20 minutes more, until it is just thick. Do not overcook the rice. Preheat the grill.

4 Transfer the mixture to a serving dish that can safely be used under the grill. Dot with the butter and sprinkle coconut evenly over the surface. Grill about 13cm/5in from the heat until the top is just browned. Sprinkle with cinnamon. Serve the pudding warm or cold.

CARAMEL RICE PUDDING

THIS RICE PUDDING IS DELICIOUS SERVED WITH CRUNCHY FRESH FRUIT.

SERVES FOUR

INGREDIENTS

15g/½oz/1 tbsp butter
50g/2oz/¼ cup short grain pudding
  rice
75ml/5 tbsp demerara sugar
400g/14oz can evaporated milk
  made up to 600ml/1 pint/2½ cups
  with water
2 fresh baby pineapples
2 figs
1 crisp eating apple
10ml/2 tsp lemon juice
salt

1 Preheat the oven to 150°C/300°F/
Gas 2. Grease a soufflé dish lightly with
a little of the butter. Put the rice in a
sieve and wash it thoroughly under cold
water. Drain well and put into the
soufflé dish.

2 Add 30ml/2 tbsp of the sugar to the
dish, with a pinch of salt. Pour on the
diluted evaporated milk and stir gently.

3 Dot the surface of the rice with
butter. Bake for 2 hours, then leave to
cool for 30 minutes.

4 Meanwhile, quarter the pineapple
and the figs. Cut the apple into
segments and toss in the lemon juice.
Preheat the grill.

5 Sprinkle the remaining sugar evenly
over the rice. Grill for 5 minutes or until
the sugar has caramelized. Leave the
rice to stand for 5 minutes to allow the
caramel to harden, then serve with the
fresh fruit.

INDEX

ACKNOWLEDGEMENTS

The photographs in this book are by Dave King and David Jordan except those which appear on the following pages:

page 8 Life File/Emma Lee; *page 9 top* e.t. archive/Free Library Philadelphia; *bottom* e.t. archive/Domenica del Corriere; *page 10 top* e.t. archive/Freer Gallery of Art; *bottom* e.t. archive/ Freer Gallery of Art; *page 11* Life File/Emma Lee; *page 12* Life File/Emma Lee; *page 13 top and bottom* Life File/ Emma Lee.